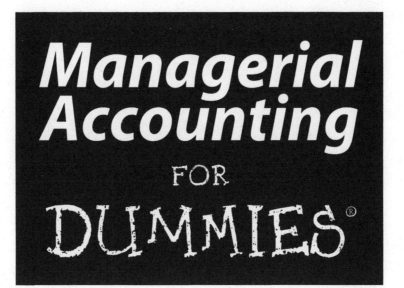

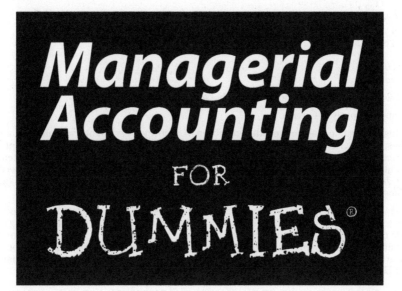

Managerial Accounting FOR DUMMIES®

by Mark P. Holtzman

WILEY

John Wiley & Sons, Inc.

Managerial Accounting For Dummies®

Published by
John Wiley & Sons, Inc.
111 River St.
Hoboken, NJ 07030-5774
www.wiley.com

Copyright © 2013 by John Wiley & Sons, Inc., Hoboken, New Jersey

Published simultaneously in Canada

For general information on our other products and services, please contact our Customer Care Department within the U.S. at 877-762-2974, outside the U.S. at 317-572-3993, or fax 317-572-4002.

For technical support, please visit www.wiley.com/techsupport.

Wiley publishes in a variety of print and electronic formats and by print-on-demand. Some material included with standard print versions of this book may not be included in e-books or in print-on-demand. If this book refers to media such as a CD or DVD that is not included in the version you purchased, you may download this material at http://booksupport.wiley.com. For more information about Wiley products, visit www.wiley.com.

Library of Congress Control Number: 2012955830

ISBN 978-1-118-11642-5 (pbk); ISBN 978-1-118-22442-7 (ebk); ISBN 978-1-118-23764-9 (ebk); ISBN 978-1-118-26255-9 (ebk)

Manufactured in the United States of America

V00348_052518

WILEY

About the Author

Mark Holtzman is chair of the Department of Accounting and Taxation at Seton Hall University in South Orange, New Jersey. After earning his bachelor's degree in Accounting from Hofstra University in Hempstead, Long Island, New York, he joined the New York office of Touche Ross & Co., now part of the accounting firm Deloitte. After attaining certification as a CPA and reaching the level of Senior Auditor, Mark joined the Accounting PhD program at The University of Texas at Austin, where he authored his doctoral dissertation on earnings management in the oil and gas industry. After completing his PhD, Mark joined the accounting faculty at Hofstra University and subsequently moved to Seton Hall, where he teaches financial accounting and managerial accounting courses to both graduate and undergraduate students.

In addition to authoring articles and other research materials in the *CPA Journal, Journal of Accountancy, Accounting Historians Journal, Research in Accounting Regulation, Financial Executive, Strategic Finance,* the *Corporate Controller's Manual,* and *Bank Accounting and Finance,* Mark is coauthor of *Interpreting and Analyzing Financial Statements* with Karen Schoenebeck, now in its 6th edition (Pearson).

Always enthusiastic and eager to share his irreverent and irrelevant opinions, Mark regularly blogs as the accountinator (www.accountinator.com), freaking accountant (www.freakingaccountant.com), and freaking important (www.freakingimportant.com). His Twitter handle is @accountinator.

In his spare time, Mark enjoys spending time with his family, hiking, camping, and studying ancient Hebrew texts.

Dedication

To my family: Rikki, who stoically endures living with a curmudgeon accounting professor, and my astonishing kids, Dovid, Aharon, Levi, and Esther.

Author's Acknowledgments

I would like to thank all of the wonderfully dedicated professionals at Wiley who helped make this book a reality in spite of my best attempts to the contrary. My acquisitions editor, Stacy Kennedy, called me out of the blue, asking if I would be interested in writing this. My project editor, Elizabeth Rea, has been wonderfully tolerant of my fickle approach to meeting deadlines. She was especially patient when I went camping instead of finishing the second quarter, and she didn't complain one bit when I missed the final deadline and then subsequently decided to rearrange the table of contents.

I'd also like to thank my copy editor, Megan Knoll, who somehow managed to translate my resourceful approach to capitalization, italics, commas, hyphenation, quotation marks, and clever profanity into clear English.

Technical editors John Zullo and Steve Markoff painstakingly combed through the manuscripts and offered thoughtful suggestions to make this book clear, accurate, and precise. I am especially grateful to them for identifying certain absent-minded omissions of the word *not*.

Thank you, too, to my colleagues and students at Seton Hall. It is a privilege and joy to learn and work with you.

Publisher's Acknowledgments

We're proud of this book; please send us your comments at http://dummies.custhelp.com. For other comments, please contact our Customer Care Department within the U.S. at 877-762-2974, outside the U.S. at 317-572-3993, or fax 317-572-4002.

Some of the people who helped bring this book to market include the following:

Acquisitions, Editorial, and Vertical Websites

Project Editor: Elizabeth Rea

Acquisitions Editor: Stacy Kennedy

Copy Editor: Megan Knoll

Assistant Editor: David Lutton

Editorial Program Coordinator: Joe Niesen

Technical Editors: Steven R. Markoff, CMA, CPA, CGMA; John J. Zullo, CPA

Editorial Manager: Michelle Hacker

Editorial Assistant: Alexa Koschier

Cover Photos: © iStockphoto.com/ Rob Friedman

Cartoons: Rich Tennant (www.the5thwave.com)

Composition Services

Project Coordinator: Patrick Redmond

Layout and Graphics: Joyce Haughey, Andrea Hornberger, Jennifer Mayberry

Proofreader: Tricia Liebig

Indexer: Sharon Shock

Publishing and Editorial for Consumer Dummies

    Kathleen Nebenhaus, Vice President and Executive Publisher

    David Palmer, Associate Publisher

    Kristin Ferguson-Wagstaffe, Product Development Director

Publishing for Technology Dummies

    Andy Cummings, Vice President and Publisher

Composition Services

    Debbie Stailey, Director of Composition Services

Contents at a Glance

Table of Contents

Introduction

．．．

*I*f accounting is the language of business, then managerial accounting is the language inside a business. Accountants establish very specific definitions for terms such as *revenue, expense, net income, assets,* and *liabilities.* Everyone uses these same definitions when they announce and discuss these attributes, so that when a company reports sales revenue, for example, investors and other businesspeople understand how that figure was calculated. This way, companies, investors, managers, and everyone else in the business community speak the same language, a language for which accountants wrote the dictionary.

Managerial accounting allows a company's managers to understand how their business operates and gives them information needed to make decisions. It helps them plan their business's activities and control its operations. For example, suppose a marketing executive needs to set a price for a new product. To set that price, the executive needs to understand how much the product costs; that's where managerial accounting comes in. Furthermore, the price needs to be set at such a level that at the end of the year, when the company sells all the products it's supposed to sell at whatever prices it sets, it earns the profit and cash flow that it has projected for itself. That, too, is where managerial accounting comes in.

When I teach managerial accounting, I always take care to point out who the users of managerial accounting information usually are. They're the managers, marketing professionals, financial analysts, and information systems professionals working within a company. All have a role not only in developing managerial accounting information but also, more importantly, in using it to make better decisions.

About This Book

If managerial accounting is the language inside a business, then running a business without understanding that topic would be pretty hard. Therefore, I wrote this book for businesspeople — both present and future — who want to better understand how to use managerial accounting to make decisions and how managerial accountants actually develop information.

That said, I have a confession to make: Much to the dismay of my wife and the embarrassment of my children, I really love to do accounting, especially managerial accounting. And better yet, I love to teach it. I believe that contribution margin is the greatest thing since sliced bread (see Chapter 9) and that the theory of constraints can solve most of life's problems (see Chapter 19). And I often think about and admire the legends of managerial accounting that I introduce in Chapter 22.

For all the bad rap that accounting gets for being boring (and for all that financial accountants, of all people, trash their poor managerial brethren for being the most boring of all accountants), I felt a special calling to commit to writing — and share with you — what I believe makes managerial accounting engaging and (yes) exciting, right here in this book.

Therefore, when you start reading this book and soon find that you can't put it down, don't blame me and my lame little puns. Instead, appreciate that after you start discovering accounting, it can be quite difficult to stop.

What You're Not to Read

I tried to write this book so that it spellbinds you, the reader, such that you feel you can't put it down until you read the whole thing. Others may be tempted to peak at the last few pages to see how it ends.

That said, if you're very busy, feel free to focus on the most important stuff that you need to know and skip some of these less important elements:

- ✔ **Technical stuff:** Anything marked with the Technical Stuff icon is especially interesting to managerial accounting geeks like me. However, if you're in a rush, you can skip these paragraphs.
- ✔ **Sidebars:** These fascinating little gray-shaded boxes include factoids and information that I thought you may like, but you can pick up managerial accounting just fine without reading them.

Foolish Assumptions

To write this book, I had to make certain assumptions about you. I assume that you're one of the following people:

- ✔ A college student taking a managerial accounting course who needs some help understanding the topics you're covering in class
- ✔ A businessperson or entrepreneur who wants to know more about how to collect accounting information to make decisions

✔ A recent college graduate interested in pursuing a career in managerial accounting, perhaps as a certified management accountant

✔ A professional accountant or bookkeeper looking for a straightforward refresher in the basics of managerial accounting

How This Book Is Organized

Each of the six parts of this book tackles a different aspect of managerial accounting. The following sections explain how I organized the information so that you can find what you need quickly and easily.

Part I: Introducing Managerial Accounting

Part I gives you a basic taste of what managerial accounting is and why it's important. It also reviews some important aspects of accounting that every businessperson needs to know. I hit profitability, efficiency, productivity, and continuous improvement especially hard.

Part II: Understanding and Managing Costs

At its very crux, managerial accounting is all about costs — be they direct, indirect, overhead, or whatever — and how those costs behave. What drives costs up, down, or sideways? Part II explores the world of costs.

Part III: Using Costing Techniques for Decision-Making

When you understand how costs work, you're ready to make decisions, and that's what Part III deals with. After a brief spiel about my favorite topic — contribution margin — I explain about how to use cost information to make decisions. I cover such areas as whether to buy equipment, which products to make, and how to price.

Part IV: Planning and Budgeting

An important part of managing an organization is planning for the future, and managerial accountants play a critical role in this process by preparing budgets, the topic of Part IV. These budgets integrate information from every part of an organization to develop a plan to meet managers' goals. To make things even more interesting, I explain how managers can *flex* their budgets — prepare budgets that can adapt to changing facts and circumstances.

Part V: Using Managerial Accounting for Evaluation and Control

Accountants have a reputation for being control freaks, but it's part of the job. Managers and managerial accountants not only plan but also need to control. This duty means that they carefully monitor a company's performance and compare that performance to their budgets. That way, managers can quickly identify and address problems before the problems become crises. Part V explains how to evaluate and control the activities throughout an organization, including using responsibility accounting, variance analysis, and two techniques managers utilize to run their companies: the balanced scorecard and the theory of constraints.

Part VI: The Part of Tens

The chapters in this part provide you with a quick reference to the most important formulas in the book. I also share some career options for managerial accountants and profile inspirational role models.

Icons Used in This Book

Throughout the margins of this book, certain symbols emphasize important points, examples, and warnings. Watch for these icons:

This icon highlights facts that are especially important to keep in mind. Tucking these facts away helps you keep key concepts at your fingertips.

This icon pops up alongside examples that show you how to apply an idea to real-life accounting problems.

Like building the Titanic II, not every idea is a good idea. This icon alerts you to situations that require caution. Look out!

This icon marks simple hints that can help you solve problems on tests and in real-life managerial accounting situations.

I couldn't resist sharing these interesting tidbits with you. However, if you're in a hurry, don't panic; just skip them.

Where to Go from Here

All the chapters in this book are modular, so you can study and understand them without reading other chapters. Just go through the table of contents and pick out a topic that you want to know more about. I provide cross-references to topics in other chapters where appropriate, so if you've skipped a foundational concept crucial to what you're reading about, you know where to find what you need.

If you're looking to discover managerial accounting from scratch, or to unlearn some part of managerial accounting that you fear you learned wrong, start with Part I to get the basics. When writing this book, I took special care to explain all the fundamentals that some managerial accounting texts skip. Students with little or no background in accounting should make a point to read Chapter 2.

Managerial accounting itself is built on a few basic principles. In my experience, most students who have trouble learning managerial accounting usually improve their performance after becoming more familiar with these basic principles. Therefore, to better understand these foundations, take a look at Chapter 3 (basic cost principles), Chapter 5 (cost behavior), and Chapter 9 (contribution margin).

If you're studying for a college exam, make sure you know the relevant key formulas in Chapter 20.

Part I

Introducing Managerial Accounting

The 5th Wave   By Rich Tennant

"These numbers don't lie. Bring me some that do."

In this part . . .

Part I gives a brief overview of all topics in managerial accounting. I first explain what managerial accountants do, why they do it, and what you can do to become a managerial accountant. Then I give you some background about business and management to help you understand managerial accounting, including how different kinds of companies operate; how accountants measure profits, efficiency, and productivity; and how managers apply continuous improvement.

Chapter 1

The Role of Managerial Accounting

In This Chapter

▶ Understanding why managerial accounting is important

▶ Costing business activities

▶ Planning for profits and cash flow

▶ Monitoring and evaluating performance

▶ Considering the tasks and accreditation of managerial accountants

After months of work, you find yourself on your long-anticipated road trip, cruising down the highway for a relaxing week at the shore. Your goal is to enjoy a quiet week of sand, surfing, and fun. To reach your goal, you need a strategy, which in this case is loading up your car with luggage, tying the surfboards to the roof, filling the tank with fuel, and hitting the gas.

But you can't forget to attend to important details along the way: Drive carefully, don't speed, follow the directions, and fill up the tank before you run out of gas. Watch for important road signs. Make sure the surfboards stay securely attached to the roof. And out of excitement, try to predict what time you'll reach your destination. Fulfilling your strategy (that is, actually getting to the shore) requires keeping an eye on a wide range of factors, many of which are critical to reaching your goal.

If you set aside the sand, sun, surf, and relaxation, managerial accounting is actually quite similar to going on a long road trip to the shore. Managerial accounting is the collecting and monitoring of information about a venture to make sure that it's on its way to successfully meeting its goals.

This chapter explains what managerial accountants do and why they do it. It also explains what costs are and considers different ways of measuring them. Then you explore the important managerial accounting tasks of planning, budgeting, and monitoring and evaluating operations. You also find out the differences between managerial accounting and financial accounting.

Checking Out What Managerial Accountants Do

Managerial accounting plays a critical role in running a business because it provides valuable information about the business to help managers make educated decisions. The process of gathering information involves

- Analyzing costs to understand how they behave and how they will respond to different activities
- Planning and budgeting for the future
- Evaluating and controlling operations by comparing plans and budgets to actual results

After gathering information, managerial accountants then report the facts and figures to the company's managers, who need this information to run the business. In the following sections, I delve into each aspect of a managerial accountant's job.

Analyzing costs

Managerial accountants carefully collect information about a company's costs in order to understand how costs behave. What causes costs to increase? How can the company decrease them? Managerial accounting offers many useful tools to help understand what drives costs and how different events affect net income.

For example, consider Grux Company, which manufactures grout. Every year, Grux must pay for raw materials, executive salaries, and sales commissions. The cost of raw materials varies with the volume of grout produced — the more grout you want to make, the more raw materials you need to buy. Executive salaries are probably fixed — they don't change at all. Sales commissions vary with the amount of sales — the more sales, the more commissions. Managerial accounting helps Grux understand how different events affect costs and how they affect the company's profits.

Planning and budgeting

After managers set goals and strategies for a company, managerial accountants get to work developing a realistic plan — with numbers, of course — to implement these strategies and ultimately meet their goals. This budgetary process requires coordinating all of a company's functional areas, predicting sales, scheduling production, setting up purchases, planning staff levels, forecasting expenditures, and projecting cash flows.

The end result is a budget that predicts what will happen during the next period, explicitly laid down in dollars and cents.

Evaluating and controlling operations

Planning is one thing, but execution is another. Managerial accountants are responsible for continuously monitoring performance, evaluating it, and comparing it to the budget. This part of the job is a lot like taking an occasional look at the map when you're on a road trip to make sure you're on the right highway and going in the right direction.

Suppose that the Busy Hardware store projects it will sell 75,000 snow shovels next winter. It orders delivery of 25,000 shovels each on December 1, January 1, and February 1. It receives its first shipment on December 1, as planned. That December, the weather is unseasonably warm, and it doesn't snow; no one wants to buy snow shovels. On January 1, Busy Hardware receives its second shipment. But the heat wave continues, and there's no snow.

Carefully watching sales trends and inventory levels, Busy Hardware's managerial accountants notice the drop in snow-shovel sales and the accumulation of 50,000 unsold snow shovels in the back of the store. After checking the weather report, they call the Purchasing department to cancel the February 1 delivery.

Carefully monitoring operations can help a company avert disaster. It can also help a company identify areas for improvement. Managerial accountants typically compare budget to actual results, investigating large differences, or *variances*. Understanding the nature of these variances helps managerial accountants to identify problems that need additional management attention and also can help make future budgets more accurate.

Reporting information needed for decisions

Like other accountants, managerial accountants accumulate, classify, and report information. However, they report this information internally, to the company's own decision-makers, rather than externally, to shareholders.

The information-gathering function focuses on collecting information that is both useful for internal decision-making and also necessary for preparing external financial statements given to investors. Accordingly, managerial accountants classify revenues and costs into many different categories, for many different purposes. They then use this information to prepare reports and other information that helps managers understand how costs behave and how management decisions will impact total costs and profitability. The same accounting information system also provides information for external financial reporting. (I explain more about financial reporting in the later section "Distinguishing Managerial from Financial Accounting.")

Understanding Costs

Managerial accountants are often called *cost accountants* because they focus primarily on costs. They collect information about costs, analyze that information, predict future costs, and use many different techniques to estimate how much different products or processes will cost. A given product may even have several different costs, depending on how managers plan to use the information.

Tom's Taxi service estimates that driving from Tanta Mount to the airport costs $20 in gas plus $10 in wages, a total of $30, so that a round trip costs the company $60. A taxi picks up passenger Pearl, who pays $100 for a ride from Tanta Mount to the airport. Expected profit comes to $40 ($100 – $60).

After dropping Pearl off at the airport, another passenger, Tex, hails the taxi to drive him back to Tanta Mount. However, Tex only has $20 to pay for the taxi ride. Should the driver give Tex an $80 discount and drive him for only $20?

This scenario begs another question: How much will Tex's ride cost? You could say that it doesn't cost anything. After all, Pearl already paid for a round trip, and the taxi needs to be driven back to town anyway. However, you could also say that it costs $30, the cost of gas and wages for driving from the airport back to Tanta Mount. Or, to be fair, you could say that Tex's ride back to town costs $60, just like Pearl's ride to the airport (for which she paid $100). $30? $60?

Or wait, what if driving Tex will prevent the taxi from picking up another passenger on the way back to Tanta Mount? This passenger would pay a $50 fare. Tex is getting to be expensive; in order to drive him back from the airport, you may lose $50 in forgone revenue. Was that part of the cost of driving Tex?

As this example indicates, figuring out how much something costs requires considerable judgment and yet plays a very important role in the decisions you make. In the following sections, I define exactly what a cost is and describe some of the techniques accountants use to understand how costs behave. I briefly explain what to do with overhead costs, which are extremely difficult to assign to products (and which won't go away) and summarize how to cost products made in two different kinds of production environments. Finally, I introduce the idea of relevant and irrelevant costs because for decision-makers, some cost information makes a difference and — quite frankly — some doesn't.

Defining costs

A *cost* is the financial sacrifice a company makes to purchase or produce something. Managers accept this necessary evil with the expectation that costs provide some kind of benefit, such as sales and net income.

Costs can have many components. For example, a can of root beer includes raw material costs — the costs of purchasing water, sweetener, and other flavors. It also includes labor costs because the bottling plant must pay workers to run the machinery. And it includes *overhead,* which is the general expense of running the bottling plant. I describe many different kinds of costs in Chapter 3.

Costs can also be divided into product and period categories:

✔ **Product costs:** The costs of making products, usually inside the factory. These costs include raw materials, labor, and overhead. After a product is made, its cost becomes an asset: inventory.

✔ **Period costs:** The costs of running your business, usually outside the factory — that is, all the business's costs except its product costs. Some examples include office rent, income taxes, and advertising.

Product costs — and any costs that retailers must pay to purchase products — ultimately become part of cost of sales, an expense on the income statement. In Chapter 4, I explain how to compute this figure.

Predicting cost behavior

To make decisions, managers need to understand how certain choices affect costs and profitability. For example, suppose managers are trying to decide whether to pay employees overtime (time-and-a-half) in order to increase factory production. On one hand, more production will increase sales. On the other hand, overtime wages will increase cost rates. Which choice will result in higher profits?

To answer these questions, managerial accountants focus on cost behavior, which can be variable or fixed. *Variable costs* change with volume made or sold: the more you sell, the higher the cost. *Fixed costs* don't change with volume: Regardless of how many items you make or sell, the cost stays the same. Managerial accountants who know which costs are variable and which are fixed can use that information to predict how changes in volume affect total costs.

That said, managerial accountants don't know everything about cost behavior. They develop their understanding from what the company has experienced in the past. Radical changes push managerial accountants out of their comfort zones and make predicting future costs very difficult. For example, if a factory shuts down and then retools to make a new product, then managerial accountants have very little experience from which to make predictions. Similarly, if a factory doubles its production, hiring many more workers, then cost behaviors are also likely to change in unpredictable ways.

I explain the nature of cost behavior in greater detail in Chapter 5.

Driving overhead

Some costs behave very nicely, such that accountants can easily figure out how they relate to finished products. For example, if your factory makes leather wallets, you should have no problem figuring out exactly how much leather is necessary for each wallet. You can also observe and measure how long a single worker takes to sew a wallet together.

However, some costs — namely, overhead — are really hard to handle. These overhead costs include all costs that can't be easily traced to products, such as heat and electricity. How much heat and electricity cost goes into each wallet?

Don't dismiss the importance of this question. A chain is only as strong as its weakest link, and an inaccurate overhead allocation will over- or under-cost your product, causing you to misprice it, too. As factories automate, and as products become more complex to manufacture, companies use less and less labor but more and more overhead, making accurate costs all the more dependent on accurate overhead allocations. (Although I'm sure you've heard managers and other business people disparage overhead, I bet you never imagined it was this big a pain in the neck.)

As I explain in Chapter 6, managerial accountants dedicate much effort to identifying different factors that drive, or bring about, overhead costs. In the old days, when more factories were very labor intensive, overhead seemed to follow the amount of labor worked. Think about the classic sweatshop with underpaid workers operating sewing machines in a hot and crowded room. Overhead included supervisor wages and rent, which are costs of supporting workers. After all, the more workers you have, the more supervisors and rent you need to pay, so direct labor hours or wages drive overhead in this scenario. If Product X requires 30 minutes to make and Product Y requires one hour, a single unit of Product X brings on half the overhead that Product Y does. Note that because the amount of labor that goes into each product is easy to measure, labor itself usually gets excluded from overhead.

These days, with robots running factories, figuring out what drives overhead isn't so simple. Some factories have no direct labor. Therefore, managerial accountants have become more creative when allocating the cost of overhead to units. Many now use a system called activity-based costing to identify a set of overhead cost-drivers for overhead.

Costing jobs and processes

Factories usually use one of two approaches to manufacturing products. Some products are manufactured to meet customer specifications. These products are usually ordered directly by the customer, made especially for that customer, and follow a system called *job order costing*. Other products are mass produced, with the factory making many identical or near-identical units. These mass-production factories follow a system called *process costing*.

Job order costing

When manufacturers make goods to order, they accumulate the cost of each order separately. For example, if an expensive tailor custom-makes shirts, then he computes the cost of materials, labor, and overhead needed to make each shirt. Some shirts require more materials or labor than others and therefore cost more. Chapter 7 explains the fundamentals of job order costing.

Process costing

When manufacturers make many homogeneous products at once, they usually use process costing. Each unit must go through several different manufacturing departments. Therefore, accountants first assign costs to the departments and then assign the costs of the departments to the products made. Chapter 8 explains how to make these allocations.

Distinguishing relevant costs from irrelevant costs

Whether a cost is product or period, fixed or variable, job ordered or process (see the preceding sections for a rundown on all these options), you have to consider one basic rule: Some costs make a difference, and some don't.

When you're faced with a decision, pay attention to the costs that make a difference. Ignore the others. For example, suppose you're trying to decide whether to eat at home or in a restaurant. You want to do whatever is cheapest. Here are some relevant costs:

- The cost of food in the restaurant
- The cost of gasoline to drive to the restaurant
- The extra money you pay if you split the check among friends who order more expensive food or drinks than you
- Any extra groceries you would have to buy in order to eat at home
- The cost of paying a tip to the server

All these costs depend on your decision. However, certain costs are not relevant:

- **Your car's lease payments:** You may think that because you have an expensive lease payment you should justify it by driving your car. However, eating in a restaurant doesn't bring down your lease payments (sorry).
- **The cost of food spoiling in your fridge:** Perhaps you think you should eat at home so that the food in your fridge doesn't spoil. However, you already paid for the food in the fridge, so eating at home won't get you a refund. Choosing to eat in the restaurant doesn't mean you have to pay for the spoiled food twice.
- **Your rent payment:** Perhaps your rent is so high that you feel like it commits you to spending more time in your apartment (and less time in restaurants). However, staying home doesn't lower your rent.

When you're faced with a decision, focus on the costs that actually depend on the outcome of your decision. Ignore all other costs.

Accounting for the Future: Planning and Budgeting

When you understand how costs behave, you can then apply that understanding to develop realistic goals and strategies for the future. Knowing that fixed costs will stay fixed and that variable costs will change with volume, you can accurately predict likely costs, income, and cash flow for coming periods.

Analyzing contribution margin

Analysis of contribution margin provides a simple and powerful approach to planning. A product's *contribution margin* measures how selling that product will impact your overall profits. For example, if a farm stand sells jars of honey for $3 apiece and each jar costs $1 to make, the stand earns a contribution margin of $2 per jar. That is, every jar sold increases the farm stand's profits by $2. Contribution margin also helps you to figure out how many units of a product you need to sell in order for your business to break even. I explain this approach in Chapter 9.

Budgeting capital for assets

Another important planning technique is called *capital budgeting*. When faced with a decision to invest in long-term assets, such as a building or a piece of machinery, capital budgeting analyzes the future cash flows from the investment in order to tell decision-makers whether the investment would deliver sufficient profits for the company. Chapter 10 explains this technique.

Choosing what to sell

Most companies don't have the resources to make or buy every product they want to sell. Therefore, they must carefully choose between different opportunities to determine which ones will yield the highest profits.

For example, suppose a farmer with 100 acres of land must choose between growing corn or barley. The farmer needs to compare the relative profitability of each, selecting whichever yields the highest profits. Chapter 11 provides tools for making this kind of decision.

Pricing goods

Managers must take special care when pricing goods. After all, if you price your product too high, customers won't buy it. If you price it too low, you sacrifice the sales revenue and profits that a higher price would have yielded. Therefore, setting prices requires a measured understanding of how costs behave.

Suppose that your bakery produces fresh cakes costing $10 each. Managers set the retail price for one cake at $14.95 in order to cover the $10 cost with a reasonable profit margin. Furthermore, this price considers that the competing bakery down the block charges $15.95 for its cakes. Your price is neither too high nor too low.

Now suppose it's quitting time and you're preparing to close the store down for the night. Your policy of not selling day-old cakes means that you must throw away the day's merchandise. A customer walks in, offering you $2 for a cake that usually sells for $14.95. Should you accept the offer?

Probably, yes. One way or another, the cake cost you $10, and that money's gone. If you sell the cake for $2, you receive $2. If you choose to throw the cake away, you get nothing. Taking the $2 is the better option.

I explain pricing in greater detail in Chapter 12.

Setting up a master budget

The planning process climaxes with the master budget. To prepare this important document, managerial accountants collaborate with managers throughout the organization to develop a realistic plan, in numbers, for what will happen during the next period. As explained in Chapter 14, the master budget counts on your understanding of cost behavior, the results of capital budgeting, pricing, and other managerial accounting information in order to plan a concrete strategy to meet sales, profit, and cash-flow goals for the coming year.

Budgeting can get frustrating because decision-makers throughout the organization need to agree to a single plan, the master budget. Not only that, but the master budget they agree to must actually *work;* it must result in sustainable cash flows and meet the company's profitability goals.

Suppose Frank in the Sales department expects to sell 1,000 widgets for $20 each. Fran says that the Production department can produce a maximum of 900 widgets, costing $21 each. Sally in Cash Management says the company has $500 in cash. Combining all this information, as shown in Figure 1-1, results in a train wreck.

Projected Cash Flow

Sales revenue (900 widgets selling for $20 each)	$18,000
Cost of units sold (900 widgets costing $21 each)	(18,900)
Net loss	($900)

Projected Cash Flow

Beginning balance	$500
Cash received from sales	$18,000
Cash paid for units produced	(18,900)
Ending cash balance (overdraft)	($400)

Figure 1-1: A budget that doesn't work.

Illustration by Wiley, Composition Services Graphics

First of all, even though the Sales department projects selling 1,000 units, it can only sell as many units as the production department makes: 900 units. Therefore the company will probably not meet customer demand.

Next, the sales price is too low. Because the company spends $21 to make each widget but only sells each one for $20, it loses $1 on every widget, resulting in a projected net loss of $900.

Making matters worse, the company doesn't have enough cash. It has $500 in the bank at the beginning of the year, which will probably turn into a $400 overdraft by the end of the year.

In short, the company doesn't produce enough goods to sell, it sets the sales price too low, its production costs are too high, and it has insufficient cash flow.

Managers and managerial accountants need to work together to develop a budget that works. Suppose that, after some negotiation, the Sales department finds a way to raise its price to $22 per widget. The Production department realizes that it can produce 1,000 units if employees reconfigure their equipment. This equipment change also reduces the cost per unit to $19. Figure 1-2 shows what can happen under these new circumstances.

Projected Cash Flow

Sales revenue (1,000 widgets selling for $22 each)	$22,000
Cost of units sold (1,000 widgets costing $19 each)	(19,000)
Net income	$3,000

Projected Cash Flow

Beginning balance	$500
Cash received from sales	22,000
Cash paid for units produced	(19,000)
Ending cash balance	$3,500

Figure 1-2:
A reworked budget.

Illustration by Wiley, Composition Services Graphics

As a result of close coordination (and perhaps a little arm twisting), the company now projects to fully meet customer demand for 1,000 units. In doing so, it expects (positive) net income of $3,000 and an ending cash balance of $3,500.

What would have happened if management took the departments' plans at face value without preparing a budget? It would have manufactured too few units at too high a cost and sold them at too low a price, incurring a loss. The budgetary process helps avoid this mess; it's a critical step to help a company meet its goals.

Flexing your budget

Unfortunately, things usually don't go as planned. When it comes to buying merchandise, customers get fickle. They may fall in love with your product and buy out all your merchandise. Or they may hate your product and refuse to buy any. How can you budget for such uncertainty?

A flexible budget allows you to plug different scenarios into next year's master budget. For example, if you expect sales to range between 10,000 and 15,000 units, you should prepare a budget that projects what would happen across this entire range. What happens to profits and cash flow if you sell 11,000 units? 12,000 units? And so on. A flexible budget helps prepare your company for a broad range of possibilities. You can read more about flexing the budget in Chapter 15.

Evaluating and Controlling Operations

A budget is a great planning tool for reaching your goals, as long as everyone in the company actually follows it. If everyone does whatever he or she wants, the result is chaos.

So how can managerial accountants ensure that the organization follows its budget? By continuously monitoring actual performance and comparing the budget to what actually happens. Making sure that the company is on course, following its plan, is called *control*.

Allocating responsibility

Companies are usually made up of many parts or departments, each of which takes responsibility for different aspects of operations. Consider some typical departments:

> ✔ **Purchasing department:** Takes responsibility for purchasing raw materials or merchandise to be resold
>
> ✔ **Manufacturing department:** Takes responsibility for different aspects of production
>
> ✔ **Quality control department:** Takes responsibility for ensuring that goods are produced at benchmark quality levels
>
> ✔ **Sales department:** Takes responsibility for selling goods
>
> ✔ **Maintenance department:** Takes responsibility for keeping buildings and equipment clean and in working order
>
> ✔ **Finance department:** Takes responsibility for managing cash activities and keeping records

Responsibility accounting requires attributing performance in different parts of the company to those responsible. For example, suppose you budget to purchase merchandise for $100 per unit. The company actually winds up paying $95 per unit. Credit for this achievement goes to the purchasing department.

Now suppose that even though you budget to sell 105,000 units, the company sells only 99,000. To discover what went wrong, go ask the sales department.

Chapter 16 describes responsibility accounting in greater detail.

Analyzing variances

Responsibility accounting in a factory requires untangling many different causes and effects. *Variance analysis* extricates these different factors to reveal who was responsible for what.

For example, say that a single factory, in a single month, must deal with the following surprises:

> ✔ Raw materials cost an extra 5 percent.
>
> ✔ Four employees unexpectedly quit.
>
> ✔ A shipment of raw materials doesn't arrive on time, delaying production.
>
> ✔ A machine breaks down, requiring unexpected repairs costing $100,000.
>
> ✔ The company can raise prices by 10 percent.

Some of these events increase costs, while others cut costs (employees who quit). And the price increase should boost profits.

When you close your books, you discover that profits are up by 4 percent. Variance analysis reveals how each of these factors impacted profits. By how much did the 5 percent increase in raw materials hurt profitability? As explained in Chapter 17, variance analysis considers a broad range of factors and can reveal who is responsible for each of them.

Producing a cycle of continuous improvement

Managerial accounting runs in cycles of different lengths. Certain sales reports and controls may be repeated every day. Some reports may be prepared every month, or each quarter. Others may be prepared just once a year.

W. Edwards Deming popularized a tool called the PDCA cycle for continuous improvement, as shown in Figure 1-3:

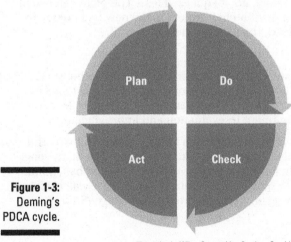

Figure 1-3:
Deming's
PDCA cycle.

Illustration by Wiley, Composition Services Graphics

Deming's PDCA cycle comes from the scientific model of forming hypotheses and then testing them, and it follows these steps:

1. **Plan.**

   Establish your objectives and how you plan to achieve them. In the scientific method, the equivalent step is creating your hypothesis and prediction.

   Ripe OJ's orange juice processing plant experiments with a new technology (the plan) to squeeze more juice out of oranges (the objective).

2. **Do.**

   Implement the plan — you make it happen. In the scientific method, this step is the test of your hypothesis.

   Ripe OJ's processing plant sets up the new technology and tries it out on real oranges.

3. **Check.**

   Measure to determine what happened. The scientific method calls this step the analysis.

   Ripe OJ's managers measure how much orange juice the new technology produced. Did the new technology actually squeeze more juice out of the oranges? Unfortunately, no. It squeezed less. The plant can usually produce 600 gallons in one batch. It expected the new technology to yield 700 gallons. Instead, the process yielded only 550.

4. **Act.**

   Think about root causes that may explain the differences between actual and planned results. To close the cycle of improvement, act on a new plan to implement and test these root causes. This stage reflects the scientific method's commitment to evaluation and improvement.

   Ripe OJ's managers call in the engineers to try to figure out why the plant produced so little orange juice. After much discussion, the engineers and managers believe that the shortfall was caused by a junior engineer's forgetting to plug the big contraption into the wall outlet. They plug it in and try again, returning to the plan stage (Step 1).

Distinguishing Managerial from Financial Accounting

Managerial accounting provides internal reports tailored to the needs of managers and officers inside the company. On the other hand, financial accounting provides external financial statements for general use by stockholders, creditors, and government regulators. Table 1-1 compares the differences between managerial and financial accounting based on the information prepared.

Table 1-1	Contrasting Managerial and Financial Accounting	
Preparing Information	**Managerial Accountants**	**Financial Accountants**
What info?	Internal reports	Financial statements
Who uses info?	Managers who work for the company and officers of the company	Stockholders, creditors, and government regulators
When prepared?	Whenever needed	Quarterly and annually
How detailed?	Very detailed, to address specific decisions to be made by managers	Very general, pertaining to the whole company
How prepared?	In accordance with the needs of managers and officers	In accordance with Generally Accepted Accounting Principles (GAAP)
How verified?	By internal controls among managerial accountants	By external CPAs

Becoming a Certified Professional

In sports, a professional athlete is one who gets paid to play. In accounting, however (as in other professions, such as medicine or law), a professional is someone who demonstrates mastery of a certain field and who agrees to accept personal responsibility to practice his or her work according to established standards. For example, medical doctors take the Hippocratic oath.

Like other professionals, most managerial accountants accept a code of ethics, established by the Institute of Management Accountants (IMA). Agreeing to practice by this code is one of the requirements for becoming a certified managerial accountant.

Following the code of ethics

The IMA Statement of Ethical Professional Practice establishes overarching principles to guide the conduct of managerial accountants relating to honesty, fairness, objectivity, and responsibility.

Furthermore, the statement establishes specific standards. Failure to comply with the following standards can result in disciplinary action by the IMA:

I. COMPETENCE

Each member has a responsibility to:

1. Maintain an appropriate level of professional expertise by continually developing knowledge and skills.

2. Perform professional duties in accordance with relevant laws, regulations, and technical standards.

3. Provide decision support information and recommendations that are accurate, clear, concise, and timely.

4. Recognize and communicate professional limitations or other constraints that would preclude responsible judgment or successful performance of an activity.

II. CONFIDENTIALITY

Each member has a responsibility to:

1. Keep information confidential except when disclosure is authorized or legally required.

2. Inform all relevant parties regarding appropriate use of confidential information. Monitor subordinates' activities to ensure compliance.

3. Refrain from using confidential information for unethical or illegal advantage.

III. INTEGRITY

Each member has a responsibility to:

1. Mitigate actual conflicts of interest, regularly communicate with business associates to avoid apparent conflicts of interest. Advise all parties of any potential conflicts.

2. Refrain from engaging in any conduct that would prejudice carrying out duties ethically.

3. Abstain from engaging in or supporting any activity that might discredit the profession.

IV. CREDIBILITY

Each member has a responsibility to:

1. Communicate information fairly and objectively.

2. Disclose all relevant information that could reasonably be expected to influence an intended user's understanding of the reports, analyses, or recommendations.

3. Disclose delays or deficiencies in information, timeliness, processing, or internal controls in conformance with organization policy and/or applicable law.

Becoming a certified management accountant

The IMA has developed the professional designation of certified management accountant (CMA). According to a 2009 study by the IMA, CMAs earn $22,000 more on average than noncertified accountants. Applicants must meet the following requirements:

✔ Become a member of the IMA.

✔ Pay the entrance fee.

✔ Satisfy the education qualification, which is usually a bachelor's degree in any area from an accredited college or university.

✔ Obtain passing scores on all required CMA examination parts.

✔ Satisfy the experience qualification, which is usually two continuous years of full-time employment working in managerial and/or financial accounting, within seven years of passing the CMA exam.

✔ Comply with the IMA Statement of Ethical Professional Practice.

For more information about CMA certification, see the IMA's website (www. imanet.org).

Becoming a chartered global management accountant

The American Institute of Certified Public Accountants (AICPA) and the U.K. Chartered Institute of Management Accountants (CIMA) recently established a new credential, the chartered global management accountant (CGMA). AICPA voting members can earn this designation by meeting certain experience requirements. CIMA members automatically qualify for this designation, and other managerial accountants can gain it through either the AICPA or the CIMA.

Chapter 2

Using Managerial Accounting in Your Business

*T*here are many ways to build a business fortune. Starting with a single ferry boat, Cornelius Vanderbilt created a railroad empire. The Rockefellers built their fortune on oil and then banking. Steven Spielberg made movies. Mark Zuckerberg developed Facebook.

Now think about a few ways to lose a business fortune. Horace A. Tabor started off alongside Cornelius Vanderbilt, eventually owning millions in silver mines. With uncontrolled spending and a multitude of personal challenges, though, Tabor lost all his holdings and wound up working as a postal clerk. After gambling that the Great Depression would feed greater demand for lavish Broadway musicals, flamboyant Broadway producer Florenz Ziegfeld forfeited his fortune and died penniless. Woolworth heiress Barbara Hutton's fortune disappeared with alcohol, drugs, seven husbands, and out-of-control charitable giving.

In many cases, the difference between maintaining and blowing a fortune has come down to how well the high-roller manages his or her money. In this chapter, I outline some of the basic accounting principles every business should follow and explain how those principles work. Believe it or not, success or failure in ferries, railroads, entertainment, and social media all share a few basic principles.

What Business Are You In? Classifying Companies by Their Output

You can separate businesses into three basic categories:

- ✔ **Service companies:** These companies do things for their customers.
- ✔ **Retailers:** These companies sell products.
- ✔ **Manufacturers:** These companies make products.

Because companies provide many different services and products to their customers, some companies fit more than one of these categories. For example, restaurants are manufacturers and service companies; they prepare meals and serve them. Some retailers are also manufacturers, selling products that they make.

Figure 2-1 illustrates how manufacturers, retailers, and service companies make and sell physical products and provide services for end-user customers.

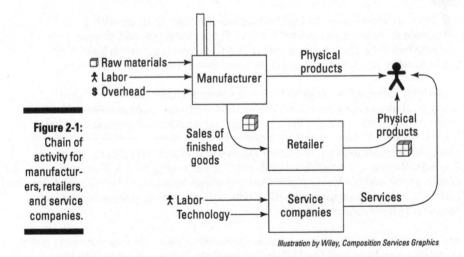

Figure 2-1: Chain of activity for manufacturers, retailers, and service companies.

Illustration by Wiley, Composition Services Graphics

Checking out service companies

Simply put, *service companies* do things for their customers. Here are just a few examples of the wide range of service companies you may encounter:

- ✔ Power utilities
- ✔ Banks and accounting firms

✔ Cellphone, Internet, and TV providers

✔ Medical doctors and hospitals

✔ Universities

✔ Dog walkers

Although I note earlier in the chapter that companies can be part of more than one business category, service companies that sell or give customers physical products incidental to their basic services don't necessarily qualify as retailers. For example, even though a university may sell books and supplies, its main business is a service — to educate. Many dentists give toothbrushes and toothpaste to their patients. Even so, dentists really provide a service — treating patients' teeth. The toiletries are incidental.

Because they earn money by providing services to customers, service companies usually rely on having highly skilled workers or some technology that customers value. Accounting firms, universities, hospitals, and dog-walking services must hire trained and well-qualified professionals. Similarly, power utilities and cellphone providers must offer technologies or other services that competitors can't match.

Perusing retailers

Retail companies buy products with the intention of selling them to customers for a higher price. Some of the businesses that comprise this category include

✔ Department stores

✔ Supermarkets

✔ Convenience stores

✔ Internet retailers

✔ Mail-order catalogs

✔ Auto dealers

Retailers typically create *distribution channels* to get their products to customers. For example, an Internet retailer or a mail-order catalog usually packs and ships products to customers. A supermarket, on the other hand, lets customers physically pick out the products they want to buy and then take them home themselves.

Retailers must know their customers and the types of products their customers want to buy. For example, a clothing retailer must predict which colors and styles their customers will like in order to buy and stock saleable inventories.

Looking at manufacturers

Manufacturers produce goods and then sell them either to retailers or to end-users. Check out a few examples:

- Auto manufacturers
- Soft-drink bottlers
- Oil refineries
- Farms
- Bakeries

Service company, retailer, or manufacturer?

The nearby section "What Business Are You In? Classifying Companies by Their Output" gives you some general examples from each business category, but here are a few real-world names you can associate with each group. First up are service providers:

- The U.S. Postal Service
- Google
- AT&T
- Motel 6
- CNN
- Weight Watchers
- Expedia
- American Express
- United Airlines

Now check out some examples of retailers:

- Wal-Mart
- Best Buy
- Zale's
- Love's Truck Stops
- The Disney Store
- The Gap
- Amazon.com
- Nordstrom
- McDonald's
- Food Lion

Finally, here are some examples of manufacturers and some of the products they make:

- Kraft (various food products)
- Ticonderoga (pencils)
- Poland Spring (water)
- Conoco (gasoline)
- 3M (Scotch tape and Post-it notes)
- Johnson & Johnson (pharmaceuticals and health-care products)
- Ford Motor Company (automobiles)
- Hewlett-Packard (computers, printers, and printer ink)
- Intel (computer chips)
- Vincent van Gogh (paintings)

To make products, manufacturers need long-lived assets, such as a factory loaded up with equipment, and raw materials — inputs into the production process. For example, an auto manufacturer needs steel; a farm needs seeds. Manufacturers also need labor (that is, employees who work to produce the products), and they have to pay *overhead*, the miscellaneous costs of running their factories. (Head to Chapter 3 for more on overhead.)

Many companies manufacture and retail the same goods. For example, mom and pop bakeries usually bake and then sell their own pies. Some oil and gas companies own both refineries (which produce gasoline) and gas stations (which sell that gas). Other manufacturers choose to wholesale their goods to retailers. For example, a soft-drink bottler may produce and bottle fizzy drinks it sells to convenience stores and supermarkets. The soft-drink bottler's customer — the convenience store or supermarket — retails the drinks directly to end-users.

Measuring Profits

To earn money and succeed, a business — whether it's a service company, a retailer, or a manufacturer — needs to create profits. To generate profits, companies must make sales to customers that exceed however much those sales cost. In the following sections, I describe three key components of profits: revenues, the cost of revenues, and other types expenses. Then I explain how companies use this information to compute net income.

Earning revenues

Revenues are inflows from customers. They're the actual amounts that your customers give you or, in some cases, promise to give you. The term *sales* is a synonym for *revenues*.

For example, an airline's revenues come from selling tickets (and charging baggage fees, handling fees, boarding fees, carry-on fees, and late-arrival fees). A clothing retailer's revenues come from peddling clothing to customers. A bakery's revenues come from getting tasty treats to hungry customers.

Companies record revenues when they earn the money and not necessarily when they receive the order or get paid. Suppose an art gallery purchases and takes delivery of a painting in 2012 and pays the artist in 2013. In 2014, a customer agrees to buy the painting from the art gallery, paying a small deposit. In 2015, the art gallery delivers the painting to the customer, who agrees to pay the balance in 2016. The sale gets recorded in 2015 because that's when the art gallery earns its revenue by delivering the painting to the customer.

One caveat: A company obviously can't record revenue until it knows the actual price and feels assured that the customer will pay. For example, if Michelangelo's contract requires a team of evaluators to judge a completed work in order to set its price, he can't record revenue until the actual price is set.

Revenues come only when you sell whatever you usually sell to your customers. If you sell a product you normally don't sell (say, your delivery truck or the naming rights to your building), you record the inflow as a gain or loss rather than as a revenue.

Computing cost of sales

Cost of sales is the cost of buying or making the products that you sell. For example, suppose that a soft-drink bottler sells a can of cola for $0.50. Consider what goes into that can of cola:

- ✓ Water
- ✓ Caramel color
- ✓ Carbonation
- ✓ Sweeteners
- ✓ Natural flavors
- ✓ Caffeine
- ✓ Various preservatives
- ✓ Aluminum
- ✓ Labor
- ✓ Overhead

Now, given all these (inexpensive) ingredients and costs, consider how much it probably costs to produce a can of cola. Would you say $0.15 per can?

Because they don't manufacture the goods themselves, when retailers measure cost of sales, they base it on the amount of money they paid to purchase the goods from a supplier.

Many manufacturers and retailers use the term *cost of goods sold* instead of cost of sales. That's why I use that wording in Chapter 4, which discusses only retailers and manufacturers. This chapter, however, covers all kinds of companies, so I use both the more-specific cost of goods sold and the more-inclusive cost of sales terminology here as appropriate. This point often confuses students, so don't be alarmed if your head is spinning a little. Just know that regardless of the name, these two concepts are largely the same thing.

Don't confuse the accounting treatment for cost of goods sold with the cost of unsold goods. When buying or making goods, companies record the cost of unsold goods on the balance as inventory — an asset. Then, when the goods are sold, their cost is taken out of inventory and put into cost of sales, which is subtracted from revenue on the income statement.

Say you own a convenience store that sold 1,000 bags of chips last year. The chips cost you $0.50 per bag, for a total cost of $500, but you sold them for $0.95 per bag, for total revenues of $950. Use this information to construct the beginning of an income statement (where all revenue and expenses are reported), as shown in Figure 2-2.

Figure 2-2:	**Your Convenience Store, Inc.**	
How rev-	**Income Statement (for Potato Chips)**	
enues and	**For The Year Ended Decemeber 31, 2013**	
cost of		
goods sold	Sales	$950,000	(1,000 bags selling for $0.95 each)
fit into an	Cost of goods sold	500,000	(1,000 bags selling for $0.50 each)
income	Gross profit	$450,000	
statement.		

Illustration by Wiley, Composition Services Graphics

Chapter 4 provides more information on calculating cost of sales, including a handy equation.

Plugging in the cost of sales formula

You can use the formula you use for calculating cost of sales (Beginning + Inputs − Ending = Outputs; see Chapter 4) to compute the quantity of ending inventory units or the value of ending inventory. For example, suppose the Red Corporation started the year with 10 gizmos. During the year, Red purchased 12 gizmos and sold 8 gizmos. To compute the number of gizmos in stock at year-end, just plug these numbers into the formula, placing the number of units sold into the outputs variable:

$$\text{Beginning} + \text{Inputs} - \text{Ending} = \text{Outputs}$$
$$10 \text{ gizmos} + 12 \text{ gizmos} - \text{Ending} = 8 \text{ gizmos}$$
$$\text{Ending} = 14 \text{ gizmos}$$

You can also figure out the value of ending inventory by assigning values to all the units. Suppose that Red paid $100 for each gizmo:

$$\text{Beginning} + \text{Inputs} - \text{Ending} = \text{Outputs}$$
$$10 \text{ gizmos} + 12 \text{ gizmos} - \text{Ending} = 8 \text{ gizmos}$$
$$\$1,000 + \$1,200 - \text{Ending} = \$800$$
$$\text{Ending} = \$1,400$$

Incurring operating expenses

Sales don't just materialize by themselves. To bring in sales, you must pay employees, advertisers, and other marketers, and that's just the beginning. Typical expenses for a company include the following:

- **Selling, general, and administrative expenses:** Costs such as sales commissions and managerial salaries needed to generate sales and run the company

- **Research and development expense:** Costs of finding and advancing innovative technologies needed to create new products

- **Interest expense:** Costs of borrowing money, which companies must pay to their creditors

- **Income tax expense (also known as *provision for income taxes*):** The portion of profits companies are usually required to pay to government authorities

Although cost of sales is always an expense, not every expense qualifies as cost of sales. Cost of sales is the actual cost of producing or buying the item you sell. However, your company may need to pay additional expenses, such as sales commissions and advertising, to sell this item.

The distinction between cost of sales and other expenses is important for determining *gross profit,* the difference between revenues and cost of sales. When calculating gross profit, you deduct cost of sales but not operating or other expenses.

Measuring net income

Net income (also known as *profit*) is the difference between revenues and all expenses, including cost of sales. Investors and managers often refer to net income because it provides a single bottom-line number to measure a company's performance. (Of course, that figure is only considered profit when it's a positive number; a negative net income is called *net loss.*)

You can use this formula to describe net income:

Net income = Revenues – Expenses

Suppose Al's Used Cars earns $1 million in revenue and has $600,000 in cost of goods sold and $300,000 in other expenses. To compute the net income, start with revenue and subtract all expenses, including cost of goods sold:

Net income = Revenues − Expenses

Net income = $1,000,000 − $600,000 − $300,000

Net income = $100,000

This net income formula sets the structure for the income statement, where you start with revenues and then subtract from it cost of sales and all other expenses.

Having positive net income doesn't necessarily guarantee positive cash flow. Even a profitable company may have to pay cash for additional costs not recorded as expenses, such as for new equipment or increased stores of inventory (assets, not expenses). These payments require valuable cash flow but don't affect net income. Similarly, companies don't always collect sales immediately. Such a sale made on credit creates sales revenues, which help net income but not cash flows.

Scoring return on sales

Return on sales asks how much profit your company can squeeze out of its sales. Some companies, such as retailer Costco or the paper manufacturer Weyerhaeuser Company, benefit from a low-price, high-volume strategy. They keep profit margins very low so that they can charge customers the lowest prices possible. Because these companies usually yield relatively little profit from their sales, they usually have to make it up in volume to earn a healthy income.

Other companies, such as leather goods maker Coach or semiconductor manufacturer Intel, develop a high-price, low-volume strategy. These companies differentiate their products so that they can charge customers premium prices that yield rich profit margins and fairly high profits from their sales.

So how do you measure return on sales? Here's the formula:

$$\text{Return on sales} = \frac{\text{Net income}}{\text{Sales}}$$

Two companies that make and sell blue jeans each earned $1 million in profits last year. The Plain Jeans Company makes jeans costing $20 per pair, which it sells to retailers for $25 per pair. The Designer Jeans Company makes jeans costing $40 per pair, which it sells to retailers for $80 per pair.

Plain Jeans earned $1 million on $20 million in sales revenue. Designer Jeans earned $1 million on $2.5 million in sales revenue.

$$\text{Plain Jeans' Return on sales} = \frac{\text{Net income}}{\text{Sales}} = \frac{\$1,000,000}{\$20,000,000} = 5\%$$

$$\text{Designer Jeans' Return on sales} = \frac{\text{Net income}}{\text{Sales}} = \frac{\$1,000,000}{\$2,500,000} = 40\%$$

Even though both companies earned the same amount of net income, Plain Jeans' low return on sales reflects its low-profit-margin/high-volume strategy. Designer Jeans' high return on sales results from its high-profit-margin/low-volume strategy.

People also refer to return on sales as profit margin or net profit margin.

Considering Efficiency and Productivity

Two important concepts in any business are efficiency and productivity, which people sometimes (incorrectly) use interchangeably. But they're two distinct attributes, and businesses — at least good ones — should strive to achieve both. The following sections help you distinguish between the two and then show you how to measure each.

Distinguishing between efficiency and productivity

Efficiency measures how little waste is created when producing and selling a product. In an episode of the TV show *Seinfeld,* Elaine starts a business selling muffin tops. The tastiest part of a muffin is the top, which always seems moister and sweeter than the base. Her muffin tops take off, with just one problem: what to do with the bottoms. Slowly, the discarded muffin bottoms take over the store, leaving little room for anything else.

You see, selling only the top of the muffin isn't efficient. The whole muffin bottom — which requires as much of the ingredients, labor, and overhead as the top does — goes to waste. And then the cost of disposing of the bottoms creates more waste and added costs.

Productivity, on the other hand, considers how to maximize sales and profits while using as few assets as possible. Do you know the legend of the goose that lays golden eggs? As the story goes, a farmer buys an ordinary goose, only to discover that his new purchase lays a solid, 24-karat gold egg every morning. Before long, his golden eggs make him rich.

A goose that lays golden eggs would be a paragon of productivity. Normally, to produce gold you need to find and buy a gold mine, hire miners, and then refine whatever ore the miners find. That setup requires large investments of capital and a lot of work; that's a lot more assets than a small animal that can reliably produce the same output.

Businesses prize productivity because assets, which are necessary to make and sell goods, don't come free. Companies must pay for them, either by borrowing money or by raising money from stockholders. Accordingly, although companies must push to increase revenues and decrease expenses, they also need to minimize their assets so they can produce and sell more while using as few assets as possible.

This fact is one reason why bricks-and-mortar businesses have so much trouble competing against Internet retailers. Bricks-and-mortar businesses must buy and maintain stores, investing in inventory and paying many employees. They can hardly compete against an Internet start-up run by some kid in his garage who has almost no assets to maintain or pay for.

The difference between efficiency and productivity? Efficiency tries to reduce waste, while productivity tries to use assets to generate more revenues and net income.

Understanding cost of capital

No one would need to worry about productivity if money grew on trees. Companies could buy as many assets as they wanted, without worrying about how best to use them. Productivity wouldn't matter. However, money doesn't grow on trees. In fact, it can be quite expensive. That's right: Using money costs money.

If you purchase a factory and you can't pay for it by picking free money from trees, you either have to borrow the money or sell stock in your venture. That's where things get expensive. If you borrow the money, you need to pay interest — that's the money you have to pay to use the money. If you sell stock, you may need to pay dividends. Your money still costs money, this time in the form of returns that you must pay stockholders.

Therefore, managers must take special care to spend valuable capital on those assets that will probably yield the highest productivity. To estimate the cost of money, companies compute a percentage called the *cost of capital.* Cost of capital is based on a weighted average of interest rates and other stock activity; it typically ranges between 6 percent and 15 percent.

All new investments should earn at least enough money to cover their cost of capital. Suppose you need to buy a delivery truck costing $20,000. You borrow the money from the bank at 8-percent interest — the cost of capital. Before you even gas up your truck and drive it away, interest sets you back $1,600 every year. Your truck must earn at least $1,600 in profits a year just to cover interest payments.

Measuring asset turnover

Asset turnover measures a company's productivity. To calculate asset turnover, divide sales revenue by average assets:

$$\text{Asset turnover} = \frac{\text{Sales revenue}}{\text{Average assets}}$$

Suppose a company earned $100,000 in sales. Average assets during the same year equaled $50,000. To compute asset turnover, just divide sales by average assets:

$$\text{Asset turnover} = \frac{\text{Sales revenue}}{\text{Average assets}}$$

$$\text{Asset turnover} = \frac{\$100,000}{\$50,000} = 2$$

To interpret this result, just say that for every $1 worth of assets the company owns, it earns $2 in revenue.

The higher the asset turnover, the more productive the company. Many companies improve turnover by taking care to utilize their scarce assets very carefully. Here are a few ways to do that:

✔ **Use all assets continuously.** Don't let assets sit around doing nothing. Rather, keep your store's shelves fully stocked with saleable merchandise. If you run a factory, make sure your machines manufacture products continuously.

✔ **Don't buy inventory until you need it.** Maintain just enough inventory in stock to keep your customers happy. Unnecessary inventory increases your assets and lowers your turnover.

✔ **Increase your sales without increasing assets.** Expand your hours. Some big-box retailers stay open 24 hours to utilize assets around the clock.

✔ **Reduce your assets.** Consider ways to cut assets without proportionately reducing sales. For example, the U.S. Postal Service closed many of its post offices and mailboxes in response to declining business. Even though this decision reduced the Postal Service's asset base, it probably had a negligible effect on the service's sales revenue.

Putting Profitability and Productivity Together: Return on Assets

Investors have a veritable candy store of different places to invest their money. Thousands of publicly traded companies and other investment vehicles raise money from investors. How do investors choose among all these options?

Return on assets provides a simple measure of investment performance that can be applied to many different types of financial investments and even to companies' own investments in factories, equipment, and other income-producing assets. The formula is

$$\text{Return on assets} = \frac{\text{Net income}}{\text{Average assets}}$$

Both profitability and productivity contribute to return on assets, explaining how some companies can take a low-profit-margin/high-volume approach to creating income while others take advantage of a high-profit-margin/low-volume method of generating income. The following formula explains how profit margin and asset turnover feed off of each other to deliver return on assets:

$$\text{Return on sales} \times \text{Asset turnover} = \text{Return on assets}$$

$$\frac{\text{Net income}}{\text{Sales revenue}} \times \frac{\text{Sales revenue}}{\text{Average assets}} = \text{Return on assets}$$

$$\frac{\text{Net income}}{\text{Average assets}} = \text{Return on assets}$$

Suppose that both the Plain Jeans Company and the Designer Jeans Company each earned $1 million in profits last year and that both companies have $5 million in average assets. For each company, the return on assets then equals 20 percent ($1 million ÷ $5 million).

Because Plain Jeans has a low-profit-margin/high-volume strategy, its return on sales is only 5 percent. However, Designer Jeans' high-profit-margin/low-volume strategy delivers return on sales of 40 percent. (Head to the earlier section "Scoring return on sales" for details on this measurement.)

Both companies have $5 million in assets, such that Plain Jeans has asset turnover of 4.0, indicating that it runs a high-volume business. Designer Jeans has asset turnover of just 0.5, suggesting a low-volume business. Figure 2-3 shows how both companies' strategies combine so that they provide similar return on assets in the end.

Figure 2-3:
A tale of two
companies'
return on
assets.

	Return on Sales	Asset Turnover	Return on Assets
Plain Jeans	5%	4.0	20%
Designer Jeans	40%	0.5	20%

Illustration by Wiley, Composition Services Graphics

Here the numbers tell a fascinating story. Plain Jeans' low prices result in lower return on sales. The company's high volume management style, however, gives the company a high asset turnover. On the other hand, Designer Jeans' high return on sales reflects its high profit margin approach. Its low asset turnover reflects its low volume strategy.

Part II
Understanding and Managing Costs

The 5th Wave   By Rich Tennant

"This is what we call an indirect manufacturing cost."

In this part . . .

In Part II, I discuss everything you need to know about costs. I start by defining different kinds of costs, including the costs needed to make products, costs not needed to make products, costs that affect decision-making, and costs that don't affect decision-making. Then I explain how to compute cost of goods manufactured and cost of goods sold. You also find out how to distinguish variable costs from fixed costs and get a taste for overhead allocation techniques. Finally, I describe how to apply these techniques to job order and process costing.

Chapter 3

Classifying Costs

*H*ow much is that doggie in the window? Well, the list price of $99 includes the dog itself and a "free" collar, but it doesn't include sales tax ($8), dog tag fee ($45), and the pet store's mandatory veterinarian examination fee ($149).

Lest you think you can get a dog for so little money, consider how much that doggie in the window *really* costs. You'll need to pay for food for the rest of its life, plus treats and bones. Visits to the vet, including shots. Local license. Grooming. A dog bed (after all, the doggie needs a place to sleep). A travel container (nice name for cage). Carpet cleaning.

Wait! There's more. Because of your dog, you need to move to a more expensive apartment building — one that allows pets. Don't forget the cost of dog sitting.

Just as Fido presents you with a variety of expenses, many different types of manufacturing costs hit companies: direct materials, direct labor, overhead, and even nonmanufacturing costs. And those costs can quickly spiral out of control. Managerial accounting concerns itself with classifying and keeping track of costs so that you can predict their amounts and stay profitable; consider this chapter your guide to putting every cost in its place.

Distinguishing Direct from Indirect Manufacturing Costs

When manufacturing a product, you can easily trace certain costs to individual products that you make. Call these expenses *direct costs*. On the other hand, certain costs don't easily trace to an individual product; these costs are called *indirect costs*.

For example, consider a good-old-fashioned paper book. To make it, the publisher needs a certain amount of paper and ink, some glue for the binding, and an employee to put the physical book together. These items are all direct costs.

On the other hand, the publisher needs to pay a royalty advance to the author, not to mention salaries to the myriad editors who pore over the manuscript. And don't forget about overhead costs (electricity, telephone, and so on) so that the editors can work in well-lit, air-conditioned offices. These overhead costs are just as important to the finished product as the costs of making the physical book. If the publisher decides not to pay them, the book won't exist. However, trying to figure out exactly how much money in royalties, editor salaries, electricity, and telephone costs went into your single book is an impossible task, so you can't pinpoint them as direct costs. The following sections further break down the differences between direct and indirect costs.

Costing direct materials and direct labor

Direct costs fall into two categories: direct materials and direct labor. *Direct materials* are raw materials that you can directly trace to the manufactured product. To compute the cost of direct materials for any product, just add up the cost of all the individual components or ingredients needed to make the product. Doing so requires understanding how your products are made and exactly what goes into each product.

For example, suppose your bakery manufactures a triple-layer chocolate cake based on this recipe:

> 2 cups sugar
>
> 2 cups flour
>
> ¾ cup cocoa powder
>
> 2 eggs
>
> 1 cup milk
>
> ½ cup vegetable oil

A single cup of sugar costs $0.50. Flour costs $1 a cup and cocoa powder costs $3 a cup. Eggs cost $0.25 each and milk costs $0.90 per cup. Vegetable oil costs $3 per cup.

Figure 3-1 shows you how to calculate the total cost of direct materials needed for one cake, adding together the cost of all the individual ingredients used to make it.

Ingredient	Quantity Used	Cost	Total Cost
Sugar	2 cups	$0.50/cup	$1.00
Flour	2 cups	1.00/cup	2.00
Cocoa powder	¾ cup	3.00/cup	2.25
Eggs	2 eggs	0.25/each	0.50
Milk	1 cup	0.90/cup	0.90
Vegetable oil	½ cup	3.00/cup	1.50
Total cost			**$8.15**

Figure 3-1:
Costing direct materials for a cake.

Illustration by Wiley, Composition Services Graphics

Direct labor is the cost of paying employees to make your products. Companies carefully estimate how much direct labor goes into each product made — that is, how long each kind of worker takes to do the job. Then, to find the total direct labor cost of the product, they multiply this time period by the hourly cost of paying each worker. Just multiply the time needed to make the product by the cost of paying the worker. Say one worker takes two hours to make a product; if that worker earns $12 per hour, then the direct labor cost of the product equals $24.

For example, suppose that brain surgery in a certain hospital requires two hours from a neurological surgeon (billing at $500 per hour) and four hours of nurse time (that is, two nurses working two hours each, costing $100 per hour). Figure 3-2 demonstrates how to estimate the cost of direct labor for this procedure.

Employee Type	Hours	Cost	Total Cost
Neurological surgeon	2	$500/hour	$1,000
Nurse	4	100/hour	400
Total cost			**$1,400**

Figure 3-2: Costing direct labor for brain surgery.

Illustration by Wiley, Composition Services Graphics

Direct labor represents just one component of the total cost of manufacturing goods. Other costs may also be necessary for this brain surgery procedure, such as direct materials (say, blood for a transfusion) and overhead (the cost of lighting and heating the operating room; see the following section for more on overhead).

Understanding indirect costs and overhead

Not all costs are direct. You still need to keep track of indirect costs, even though you can't easily trace them to individual manufactured products. Keep track of these indirect costs and include them in *overhead,* the miscellaneous costs of doing business. (Accountants sometimes refer to overhead in a factory as *manufacturing overhead.*)

Overhead consists of the following:

- **Indirect materials:** The cost of raw materials needed to make products that you can't easily trace to the finished products. Such indirect materials are usually inexpensive, may be used in small quantities, or are difficult to measure. For example, if you bake cakes, you can easily trace the amount of flour or sugar that goes into each cake. However, measuring exactly how much cooking spray you use to grease each cake pan would be an absurd waste of your time. Therefore, you classify the cost of the cooking spray as an indirect cost.

- **Indirect labor:** The cost of labor that you need to make products but that you can't easily trace to the finished products. For example, suppose your factory requires maintenance workers to mop the floors. You can't really tie a specific amount of floor cleaning to every individual product you make, so you label the cleaning cost as indirect.

- **Other costs needed for operations:** The cost of items such as electricity, property and other taxes, insurance, and depreciation of factories and equipment.

If the shoe fits . . .

So how do you distinguish between direct materials, direct labor, and overhead? Think about a factory that makes athletic shoes. Direct materials include the cost of the leather, rubber, cotton, paper, and plastic used to make and package the athletic shoes. Direct labor includes the cost of employing workers who actually assemble the shoes. Overhead includes all other costs, such as electricity, heat, insurance, security, depreciation, maintenance, and even the cost of supervisory managers who run the factory.

Think about overhead costs as "other costs." That is, if a cost isn't direct labor or direct materials, then it goes into overhead.

As factories automate, they in essence replace human workers with machines. Therefore, as they implement new manufacturing technologies, factories rely less on direct labor and more on overhead. In a modern factory, direct labor can account for 5 percent or less of total manufacturing cost. A completely automated factory doesn't need any direct labor at all.

Assessing Conversion Costs

Conversion costs do the magic. They "convert" direct materials into finished goods. To determine conversion costs, you add direct labor costs and overhead.

The distinction between direct materials and conversion costs is important to understand because direct materials are usually added at the beginning of production, while conversion costs are added evenly throughout production.

Suppose you hire a craftsperson to make a piece of furniture with provided materials. To begin making the furniture, you first set up all the raw materials — wood, hardware, and finishing supplies. Then the craftsperson works for a period of time and requires overhead (heat, electricity, and soft drinks). As such, direct materials (the wood, hardware, and finishing supplies) are added at the beginning of production while the conversion costs (cost of paying the craftsperson plus cost of heat, electricity, and soft drinks) are incurred evenly as the furniture is produced.

Telling the Difference between Product and Period Costs

Accountants split all costs into two categories — product costs and period costs — depending on whether these costs go toward making products. *Product costs* include all the costs of making products:

- ✔ Direct materials
- ✔ Direct labor
- ✔ Overhead

You classify product costs as inventory, an asset on the balance sheet, until you actually sell the product. (Flip to the earlier section "Distinguishing Direct from Indirect Manufacturing Costs" for more on the listed costs.)

Suppose your company spends $10,000 on direct materials, $3,000 on direct labor, and $6,000 on overhead to make 100 gadgets during the year. Total product costs in this scenario equal $19,000. Classify the costs of making these gadgets as inventory on the balance sheet until you sell them.

All other costs are considered *period costs*. This category includes selling and administrative expenses. Subtract these costs from revenues on the income statement when you get the benefit from them. For example, suppose you pay salespeople $10 in commission for every whatchamacallit they sell. If they sell 30 whatchamcallits, then they must subtract $300 in sales commission expense on the period's income statement.

Figure 3-3 illustrates the separation of product and period costs.

Think hard before classifying certain costs as product or period. Classification depends on the purpose of the cost: If you need it for manufacturing, it's a product cost. Otherwise, treat it as a period cost. For example, classify depreciation on a factory as a product cost. However, depreciation on the headquarters' office building is a period cost. Similarly, paying employees working in the factory is a product cost (they're usually direct labor); however, the cost of employees working in a sales office is a period cost.

Splitting up overlapping costs

Some costs overlap, so you need to allocate these costs between the product and period categories. For example, suppose that your doughnut bakery dedicates one-third of the building's square footage to baking and two-thirds of it to selling. If your monthly rent is $3,000, you classify one-third of that amount ($1,000) as a product cost (overhead) because you need this floor space to make products. This product cost gets recorded as inventory on the balance sheet because it comprises part of the cost of the doughnut inventory. Two-thirds of the rent ($2,000) goes down as a period cost (selling expense) because you use this floor space to sell products. Like all period costs, these costs get recorded as expenses on the income statement. Treat all occupancy costs (such as rent, heat, and maintenance) in this way for any business that both manufactures and sells goods on the same premises.

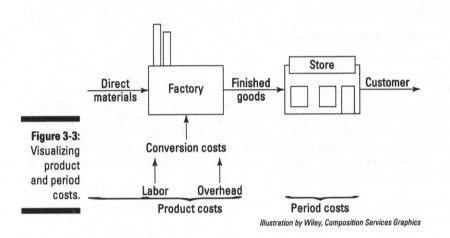

Figure 3-3: Visualizing product and period costs.

Illustration by Wiley, Composition Services Graphics

Searching for Incremental Costs

When you need to choose between two alternatives, *incremental costs* change depending on which alternative you choose. Accountants sometimes refer to incremental costs as *relevant costs*. Other costs don't change — you can just treat these expenses as irrelevant.

For example, suppose you're deciding whether to travel to Cancun, Mexico, for vacation. Some incremental costs of making the trip include the following:

- ✔ Airfare
- ✔ Hotel
- ✔ Ground transportation to and from the airport
- ✔ A new swimsuit
- ✔ A souvenir T-shirt that says "My sister went to Cancun, and all I got was this lousy T-shirt"

You have to pay these incremental costs if you go to Cancun but not if you stay home. On the other hand, some costs remain the same, and you ignore them for the purposes of making your vacation decision:

- ✔ Rent on your apartment
- ✔ Auto insurance premiums
- ✔ Interest on student loans

Additionally, if you go to Cancun, certain everyday costs may change. For example, you normally pay $100 a week for food and drink at home, but in Cancun, your food and drink may cost you $175 for the week. These incremental costs of your vacation — the amount that varies because you decide to make the trip — come to $75. On the other hand, if you decide to stay home, you incur the incremental cost of running your air conditioner during the time you would've been away.

As a manager, incremental costs come up as you encounter some of these decisions:

- ✔ **Accepting special orders:** You own a hotel with empty rooms for tonight. At 11 p.m., a mysterious stranger approaches the counter, offering to pay just $20 for a room. Your rooms normally go for $100 a night and up. Should you take the money?

  Consider some of the incremental costs:

  - Electricity to power the air conditioning, TV, and any light bulbs
  - Gas to heat water for the shower and to power the laundry to clean the linens
  - Chocolate mints for the pillows

Forget housekeeping expenses because you pay your housekeepers the same wage every day, regardless of how many rooms they clean. Because the electricity, gas, and chocolate mints certainly cost less than $20 for the night, you should take the money and direct your guest to his room.

✔ **Choosing whether to make a product or buy it from another manufacturer:** You run a restaurant and must decide whether to grow your own tomatoes or buy them from a local market. Carefully think about the additional costs necessary to grow your own tomatoes — such as seeds, fertilizer, soil, growing space, and the labor required to tend the plants — to determine whether these incremental costs outweigh the cost of buying the tomatoes from the market.

✔ **Considering whether to repair or replace old or broken equipment:** Your old delivery truck is on its last leg. You paid $20,000 for it, but now it's worth only about $2,000. You're thinking about selling it and using the $2,000 to buy something more reliable. Incremental costs of changing vehicles include

- Difference in gas mileage

- Difference in cost of auto insurance

- Difference in cost of repairs and maintenance

Don't even think about the original cost of your current truck because you'll never see that money again. It's irrelevant.

✔ **Eliminating an unprofitable product or segment of your business:** You run a martial arts studio with three different divisions: kids (in the afternoon), adults (in the evenings), and senior citizens (in the morning). You're considering closing down the senior citizen division that meets each morning because it's the least profitable of the three divisions.

Consider some of the incremental costs:

- Paying instructors to lead classes

- Heat and other utilities needed to keep the studio open during the day

- Additional insurance (charges are based on number of lessons given)

Don't get confused by the costs that won't change. For example, even if you cancel the senior citizen division, your rent will stay the same. So, too, will the salary you pay the studio manager.

As you analyze decisions, take special care to consider only incremental costs and to ignore all other costs.

Accounting for Opportunity Costs

Sometimes choosing one alternative means losing money because you turned down another alternative. These costs are called *opportunity costs.*

For example, suppose you can either visit your mother in Peoria or work on an internship. Choosing to go to Peoria means you lose the internship income. You don't actually have to pay for this choice because you never got the internship income in the first place. However, you miss out on money you could've received if you hadn't gone to visit your mother. Your opportunity costs result from income *not* earned because you decided to do something else.

(*Relevant costs,* on the other hand, are costs that you actually incur and pay because you chose the alternative that brought them on. Here's the difference: If Mom's the jealous type, choosing the internship over visiting her may, in the long run, may bring on relevant costs far worse than the opportunity cost of missing the internship.)

In business, opportunity costs commonly arise from the reality that businesses have limited resources. Say an arcade decides to replace an old pinball machine with a new video game. The income lost from the old pinball machine represents the opportunity cost arising from this decision.

Thinking about opportunity costs

When you make decisions, consider the opportunity costs that you sacrifice. For example, by going to college for four years after high school, a student chooses not to work full-time during this period, losing four years of income. By choosing to rent a home instead of buying one, a person loses the opportunity costs that come with owning real estate that may appreciate in value.

Ignoring Sunk Costs

Sometimes you wish you hadn't incurred certain costs in the past. For example, you may have purchased an office building that is too large to suit your needs or made repairs to a piece of equipment that later needed to be replaced anyway due to obsolescence. Such costs incurred in the past are called *sunk costs*. When making decisions, you can ignore sunk costs because they can't be changed.

One of the most significant sunk costs is the original cost of your factory and equipment. Because you already purchased your factory and equipment and can't sell them, you can completely ignore these sunk costs and any depreciation on them.

Suppose you spend $5,000 to repair a piece of equipment. A week later, your suppliers introduce a more powerful model that allows you to produce more units at a lower cost. When deciding whether to replace the machine with the new model, you should completely ignore the $5,000 sunk cost from the repair.

Chapter 4

Figuring Cost of Goods Manufactured and Sold

In This Chapter

▶ Understanding how inventory flows through a business

▶ Applying the outputs formula to discover the amount of direct materials used, the cost of goods manufactured, and the cost of goods sold

▶ Creating a cost of goods manufactured schedule

*T*o earn money, manufacturers must make products for less money than they can sell them for. Similarly, retailers must buy products for less money than they can sell them for. Therefore, measuring the cost of products manufactured or purchased is critically important to understanding a business's profitability.

This concept explains why *cost of goods sold* usually appears as the first and largest expense on a manufacturer or retailer's income statement. How well a company can make or buy goods and then sell them at a profit is fundamentally important to the company's profitability and success. This fact applies to businesses across the spectrum, from mass-market retailers to elite, high-end retailers to manufacturers.

In this chapter, I show you how a simple formula explains how goods and their costs flow through a business. You can then use the same formula to understand how to calculate cost of goods manufactured and cost of goods sold. Finally, I explain how to prepare the statement of cost of goods manufactured. All this information gives you a crucial understanding of your business.

Tracking Inventory Flow

Retailers purchase products from other companies and then sell those products in stores, online, or through catalogs to their customers. For example, Wal-Mart and almost every mall store are considered retailers.

Products flow through a retailer in the following order, shown in Figure 4-1:

1. The supplier ships purchased products to the retailer.

2. The retailer displays the products so that customers can see them.

3. The customer buys and takes the product home.

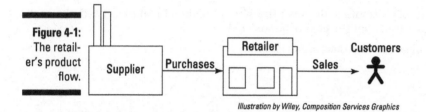

Figure 4-1:
The retailer's product flow.

Illustration by Wiley, Composition Services Graphics

Product costs flow through a retailer's books just as the products themselves flow through the retailer's operations. When the retailer purchases products, it owes the cost of those products to the supplier. Then when the retailer sells the products to its customers, it records both sales and cost of goods sold. Cost of goods sold then appears on the income statement as an expense.

Manufacturers go through basically the same process as retailers, except with a few more-involved steps necessary to actually make the products (see Figure 4-2).

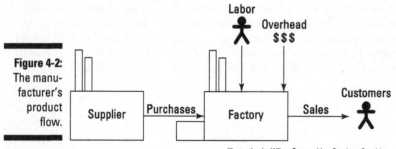

Figure 4-2:
The manufacturer's product flow.

Illustration by Wiley, Composition Services Graphics

Note how manufacturers make goods:

1. Manufacturers purchase raw materials.

2. Manufacturers pay for labor and overhead to work on those raw materials. After they go into production, raw materials become work-in-process inventory, which I discuss later in this section.

3. When completed, work-in-process inventory becomes finished goods.

4. Just as with a retailer, when the goods are sold, they go to the customer.

At the same time as the goods themselves flow through a manufacturer's operations, the cost of those goods flows through to the manufacturer's books.

The following sections explain how to keep track of costs as you manufacture goods.

Dealing with direct materials

Direct materials are the physical materials needed to make products. They're "direct" in the sense that you can easily trace direct materials to individual products. For example, suppose your factory produces doodads. Each doodad requires assembling one widget with one gizmo and one doohickey. Each of these parts, which you purchase from outside suppliers, is a direct material.

The terms *direct materials* and *raw materials* aren't exactly interchangeable. As I explain in Chapter 3, direct materials are the cost of raw materials that can be easily traced directly to the actual products made. Raw materials, therefore, may include both direct materials and *indirect materials,* materials that you can't easily trace directly to individual products. Indirect materials are included in overhead.

The company and its supplier usually negotiate and set the price of buying direct materials. However, the overall cost of direct materials may also include charges for shipping direct materials to your place of business (if, say, your gizmo supplier is in China and your plant is in the United States) and any costs of storing and maintaining the direct materials.

Investigating work-in-process inventory

Work-in-process inventory involves materials that have gone into production but haven't yet been finished. The assembly process for doodads described in Figure 4-3 usually takes a single employee eight hours to complete. The work-in-process inventory for this process is the stock of incomplete doo-dads — items the employee has started assembling but hasn't yet finished.

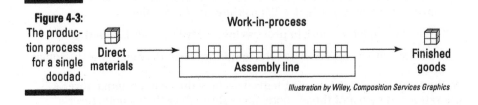

Figure 4-3:
The production process for a single doodad.

Illustration by Wiley, Composition Services Graphics

Getting a handle on finished goods

After factory workers complete the work-in-process, it graduates to become *finished goods inventory. Finished goods* are completed products that are ready for sale. The cost of all completed factory output, known as *cost of goods manufactured,* includes all the costs associated with the products: direct materials, direct labor, and overhead.

Cracking cost of goods sold

When a retailer or manufacturer sells goods, those goods become an expense called *cost of goods sold.* Cost of goods sold includes all the direct materials, direct labor, and overhead associated with the items sold during the year; it's usually the largest expense on a manufacturer's or retailer's income statement.

Just-in-time

Many companies use a system called *just-in-time,* which is designed to minimize inventory levels of direct materials, work-in-process inventory, and finished goods. Just-in-time requires the manufacturer to time purchasing and production to meet customer demand.

When a customer orders goods, the just-in-time manufacturer immediately orders and takes delivery of direct materials, rushes them through the assembly line production process, and then ships them to the customer.

Don't confuse cost of goods sold with cost of goods manufactured. Cost of goods sold is measured as the cost of goods that were actually sold during the period regardless of when they were completed. It goes onto the income statement. Cost of goods manufactured is measured as the cost of goods that were actually completed during a period regardless of whether they were sold.

Calculating Inventory Flow

You can use a single powerful formula to compute both the flow and cost of inventory as the inventory is manufactured and sold:

Beginning + Inputs – Ending = Outputs

Depending on what specific cost you want to calculate — such as cost of goods manufactured, cost of goods sold, and so on — you can substitute various values into this one formula. The following sections show you how to determine which values to plug into this formula in order to calculate

1. The volume of goods at different stages in the production process

2. Total costs needed to prepare statements and internal reports

3. Individual costs per unit

Computing direct materials put into production

Although some purchased direct materials are put into production, some are stored for future use. Therefore, the amount of direct materials purchased is probably different from the amount of direct materials actually put into production.

Your simple outputs formula helps explain this relationship:

Beginning + Inputs – Ending = Outputs

| Cost of beginning direct materials inventory | + | Cost of direct materials purchased | – | Cost of ending direct materials inventory | = | Cost of direct materials put into production |

In this case, Beginning equals beginning inventory on the first day of the time period. Inputs refers to purchases or transfers from other parts of the company. Ending is ending inventory at the end of the last day of the time period. Finally, the Outputs value indicates what completed the production process — the stuff that's ready for the next stage of production (or for sale to customers). You can apply this formula to the quantity of units in inventory and put into production, and also to the costs of those same units.

For example, suppose that a convenience store started the year with ten cans of coffee. During the year, it bought another 200 cans of coffee. At the end of the year, it counted seven cans of coffee in stock. How many cans did the store sell?

$$\text{Beginning} + \text{Inputs} - \text{Ending} = \text{Outputs}$$
$$10 \text{ cans} + 200 \text{ cans purchased} - 7 \text{ cans} = 203 \text{ cans sold}$$

You can think of direct material storage in the same way: A factory keeps direct materials (or cans of coffee) on hand so that they're ready to be put into production (or be sold to customers).

Units of direct materials put into production

For direct materials, you can use the outputs formula in the preceding section; just set your Beginning value as the number of units of beginning inventory, Inputs as the number of new units purchased, Ending as the number of units of ending inventory, and Outputs as the number of units put into production.

Suppose your factory makes chocolate milk. You started with 500 gallons of chocolate syrup and then purchased another 2,000 gallons during the year. At the end of the year, you counted 400 gallons of chocolate syrup in stock. This formula computes the number of gallons of chocolate syrup put into production:

$$\text{Beginning} + \text{Inputs} - \text{Ending} = \text{Outputs}$$
$$500 \text{ gallons} + 2,000 \text{ gallons} - 400 \text{ gallons} = 2,100 \text{ gallons}$$

During the year, 2,100 gallons were moved out of storage and put into production (to blend chocolate milk).

Cost of direct materials put into production

Naturally, factories need to keep track of both the quantity and the total costs of different items at each stage of the production process. To figure out total costs, you can apply the outputs formula to the total cost of direct materials.

Suppose that your chocolate milk factory pays $2 for each gallon of chocolate syrup. To compute the cost of direct materials put into production, just multiply the quantities for Beginning, Inputs, and Ending by the $2 cost per unit:

$$\text{Beginning} + \text{Inputs} - \text{Ending} = \text{Outputs}$$
$$500 \text{ gallons} + 2,000 \text{ gallons} - 400 \text{ gallons} = 2,100 \text{ gallons}$$
$$\$1,000 + \$4,000 - \$800 = \$4,200$$

Your calculation reveals that you put 2,100 gallons into production, for a total cost of $4,200.

You have to do similar computations for every type of direct material needed to make products. For example, you also need to compute the milk input for your chocolate milk factory.

Determining cost of goods manufactured

Cost of goods manufactured is based on the amount of work-in-process completed. This work-in-process includes costs of direct materials put into production, plus direct labor and overhead.

To determine work-in-process, you enter the number of units or costs into the same outputs formula that you use to calculate direct materials put into production earlier in this chapter:

$$\text{Beginning} + \text{Inputs} - \text{Ending} = \text{Outputs}$$

| Cost of beginning work-in-process | + | Production costs | − | Cost of ending work-in-process | = | Cost of goods manufactured |

The following sections give you insight into calculating the cost of goods manufactured.

Number of units manufactured

Knowing how many units of direct materials each finished product requires helps you figure out how many units you manufacture and how much those units cost. For example, to make one gallon of chocolate milk, you need 0.950 gallons of whole milk and 0.05 gallons of chocolate syrup.

To compute the number of units manufactured, start with the number of units of work-in-process in beginning inventory (Beginning). Add the number of units of direct materials put into production (Inputs) and then subtract the number of units of work-in-process in ending inventory (Outputs).

Suppose that your chocolate milk factory started the year with 200 gallons of unmixed ingredients in the blenders. During the year, another 4,000 gallons of ingredients were taken out of storage and poured into the blenders. At the end of the year, 300 gallons of unmixed ingredients were still in the blenders (planned for production next year). Plug these numbers into the outputs formula:

$$\text{Beginning} + \text{Inputs} - \text{Ending} = \text{Outputs}$$
$$200 \text{ gallons} + 4{,}000 \text{ gallons} - 300 \text{ gallons} = 3{,}900 \text{ gallons}$$

The factory completed 3,900 gallons of chocolate milk during the period. From here, you're ready to figure out the total cost of chocolate milk manufactured and its cost per unit.

Cost of goods manufactured

Direct materials, direct labor, and overhead all get input into the production process. Therefore, to compute the cost of goods manufactured, think about all product costs, including not only direct materials but also direct labor and overhead.

Consider the cost of goods manufactured for the chocolate milk factory. Your beginning inventory cost $2,000. The factory put $10,000 worth of direct materials into production and spent $5,000 on direct labor and another $4,000 on overhead. At the end of the year, you counted $3,000 worth of ending inventory. Feeling overwhelmed? Hang in there! To compute cost of goods manufactured, just apply the outputs formula:

$$\text{Beginning} + \text{Inputs} - \text{Ending} = \text{Outputs}$$

$$\$2{,}000 + \begin{bmatrix} \$10{,}000 & \$5{,}000 & \\ \text{Direct} & + \text{Direct} & + \$4{,}000 \\ \text{Materials} & \text{Labor} & \text{Overhead} \end{bmatrix} - \$3{,}000 = \$18{,}000$$

This result tells you that the factory's output of chocolate milk during the year cost $18,000.

Congratulations! You now have enough information to calculate the cost of chocolate milk per gallon. The preceding section tells you that the factory produced 3,900 gallons. Therefore, total cost of $18,000 divided by 3,900 gallons equals $4.62. Your chocolate milk cost $4.62 per gallon. Per-unit costs like these help managers to make decisions about pricing (Chapter 12), transfer pricing (Chapter 13), and budget planning (Chapters 14 and 15).

Computing cost of goods sold

After you know the cost of goods manufactured for a product (see the preceding section), the next phase for the product is to store it as finished goods until your customers buy it — at which point you can figure out cost of goods sold. As I note in this chapter's introduction, cost of goods sold is a key figure on the income statement. It's most companies' largest expense and an important determinant of net income.

As with other phases of production (direct materials that go into production, work-in-process, and finished goods), you need to compute both the number of units sold and the cost of goods sold. The number of units sold helps you keep track of inventory as it flows through operations. Cost information is critical to computing income and managerial decision-making. Furthermore, dividing cost of goods sold by the number of units sold yields the cost per unit, an important value when accounting for inventory.

The following formula, explained earlier in this chapter, computes the flow of inventory through any manufacturer or retailer:

$$\text{Beginning + Inputs} - \text{Ending} = \text{Outputs}$$

| Cost of beginning finished goods inventory | + | Purchases or cost of goods manufactured | – | Cost of ending finished goods inventory | = | Cost of goods sold |

Number of units sold

Companies need to know the actual number of units sold. To compute this amount, simply start with the number of units in beginning inventory of finished goods. Add the number of units manufactured (flip to the earlier section "Number of units manufactured"), and subtract the number of units in ending inventory of finished goods.

In your chocolate milk factory, suppose that you started the year with 400 gallons of finished goods. Another 3,900 gallons were completed during the year. By the end of the year, you counted 100 gallons of finished goods:

$$\text{Beginning} + \text{Inputs} - \text{Ending} = \text{Outputs}$$
$$400 \text{ gallons} + 3,900 \text{ gallons} - 100 \text{ gallons} = 4,200 \text{ gallons}$$

Therefore, you must have sold 4,200 gallons of chocolate milk.

Cost of goods sold

To compute cost of goods sold, start with the cost of beginning inventory of finished goods, add the cost of goods manufactured (which I cover in the earlier section "Cost of goods manufactured"), and then subtract the cost of ending inventory of finished goods.

Suppose your chocolate milk factory started out with $2,000 worth of beginning inventory of finished goods. Your cost of goods manufactured was $18,000, and your ending inventory of finished goods was $500:

$$\text{Beginning} + \text{Inputs} - \text{Ending} = \text{Outputs}$$
$$\$2,000 + \$18,000 - \$500 = \$19,500$$

You have $19,500 in cost of goods sold, an amount that goes right to the income statement. To figure out the cost per unit, divide the total cost by the 4,200 units sold: $3.64 ($19,500 ÷ 4,200 gallons).

As you may know from your financial accounting course, retailers use this same formula. Their inputs are purchases of merchandise. Furthermore, retailers have only one class of inventory rather than three (direct materials, work-in-process, and finished goods) because retailers usually purchase goods that are ready for sale.

Preparing a Schedule of Cost of Goods Manufactured

The *schedule of cost of goods manufactured* shows the calculation of cost of goods manufactured, which follows the outputs formula I use throughout the chapter:

$$\text{Beginning} + \text{Inputs} - \text{Ending} = \text{Outputs}$$

The schedule of cost of goods manufactured splits this formula into two parts:

Beginning + Inputs = Available

Available − Ending = Outputs

First, you calculate the direct materials available for production by adding Inputs to the beginning balance. Then you subtract the ending inventory from that number to find the direct materials put into production (read: Outputs).

Similarly, first calculate work-in-process available, and then subtract ending inventory of work-in-process to compute cost of goods manufactured. Figure 4-4 shows a cost of goods manufactured schedule for the fictional chocolate milk company I mention throughout much of the chapter. From here, cost of goods manufactured can be used as the Inputs component of finished goods to compute cost of goods sold.

Delicious Chocolate Milk, Inc.
Cost of Goods Manufactured Schedule
For the Year Ended December 31, 2014

Work-in-process, January 1			**$2,000**
Direct materials:			
Direct materials inventory, January 1	$2,000		
Direct materials purchased	9,000		
Direct materials available	11,000		
Less: Direct materials inventory, December 31	1,000		
Direct materials put into production		$10,000	
Direct labor		5,000	
Overhead		4,000	
Total manufacturing costs			19,000
Work-in-process available			21,000
Less: Work-in-process, December 31			3,000
Cost of goods manufactured			$18,000

Figure 4-4:
Cost of goods manufactured schedule.

Illustration by Wiley, Composition Services Graphics

Chapter 5

Teaching Costs to Behave: Variable and Fixed Costs

. . . .

In This Chapter

▶ Looking at fixed and variable costs in terms of cost drivers

▶ Breaking down mixed costs into variable and fixed components

▶ Keeping within your relevant range

. . . .

Training your dog involves teaching him to react to different stimuli. When you say "Sit!", the little guy sits on his hind legs. When you hold your hand up in the air, he tries to stand on his hind legs. When you whisper "Quiet," he stops barking. Unfortunately, dogs have trouble learning certain things. No matter how hard you try to train the dog, he'll always sit and watch you eat, waiting for delicious human food to fall on the floor.

Like pet dogs, costs react to some stimuli but not to others. For example, manufacturing twice as many goods will most likely double your costs, but no matter how many goods your factory produces, rent will remain the same. In this chapter, I explain how to tell the difference between variable costs, which change in response to the number of goods you make, and fixed costs, which remain the same. These distinctions help you predict how costs react to different stimuli within your business.

Predicting How Costs Behave

Some costs are *variable* — they change in response to certain stimuli — while other costs are *fixed* — they remain the same. Determining whether a cost is variable or fixed requires considering the nature of the cost. The following sections explain the nature of variable and fixed costs, and the importance of understanding how certain factors drive variable costs.

Recognizing how cost drivers affect variable costs

Variable costs change in response to certain stimuli, called *cost drivers.* Get it? Cost drivers drive up the cost.

For example, a common cost driver is the number of units produced. Units produced is the cost driver for total direct materials; the more units that you produce, the more direct materials you need. (You can read about direct materials in Chapter 4.) Suppose that your factory manufactures baseball caps and that every baseball cap requires two square feet of fabric, which costs $1 per square foot. Manufacturing 100 baseball caps requires 200 square feet of fabric (100 caps × 2 square feet per hat). Therefore, you can determine that this batch of hats costs $200 (200 square feet × $1).

In this chapter, I focus on number of units produced as a cost driver. However, as I explain in Chapter 6, managers often identify several different cost drivers.

You can graphically represent costs by charting total cost (on the left axis) against the cost driver (on the bottom axis). In Figure 5-1, you can see how producing 100 caps drives total variable costs of $200.

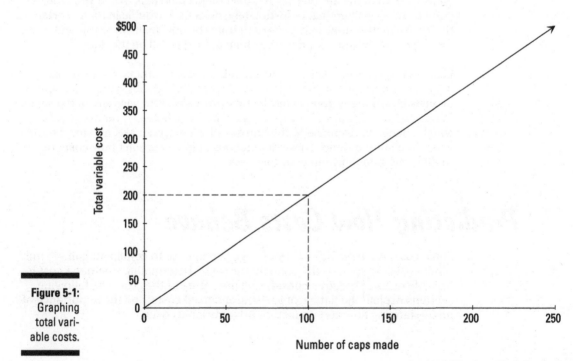

Figure 5-1:
Graphing total variable costs.

Number of caps made

A change in a cost driver always results in a corresponding change to the total cost. For example, increasing the cost driver by 50 percent causes total variable costs to increase by 50 percent.

When it comes to manufacturing your caps, then, increasing the number of caps produced by 50 percent (to 150; $100 + [0.5 × $100]) costs 50 percent more, or $300 ($200 + [0.5 × $200]).

Figure 5-2 shows how a 50 percent increase in the number of caps made affects total variable costs. Producing 50 more units (a 50-percent bump) increases total variable costs by $100 (a 50-percent rise in total variable costs).

Most direct costs are variable with respect to the number of units produced. *Direct labor* (the cost of employee wages that can be directly traced to the products those employees make) is another common variable cost. (Head to Chapter 3 for more on direct labor.) Take a shoe factory as an example: The more shoes the factory makes, the higher the direct labor cost.

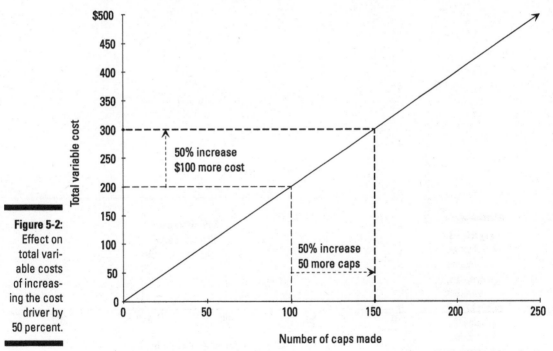

Figure 5-2:
Effect on total variable costs of increasing the cost driver by 50 percent.

Illustration by Wiley, Composition Services Graphics

Variable cost per unit describes the relationship between the cost driver (say, the number of units produced) and total cost (direct materials or direct labor). Just multiply the variable cost per unit by the cost driver to get total cost. Suppose a shoe factory's variable cost per unit of direct labor is $30. To make 1,000 shoes, the factory must pay a total of $30,000 for direct labor.

To compute variable cost per unit, divide total variable cost by the number of units produced:

$$\text{Variable cost per unit} = \frac{\text{Total variable cost}}{\text{Number of units produced}}$$

Variable cost per unit usually does *not* change with volume. To graph the relationship between the cost driver and variable cost per unit, draw a horizontal line as shown in Figure 5-3. Here, the variable cost per unit of direct materials needed to make baseball caps is $2 per unit. Even when the company ratchets up production from 100 caps to 150, the variable cost per unit remains steady at $2.

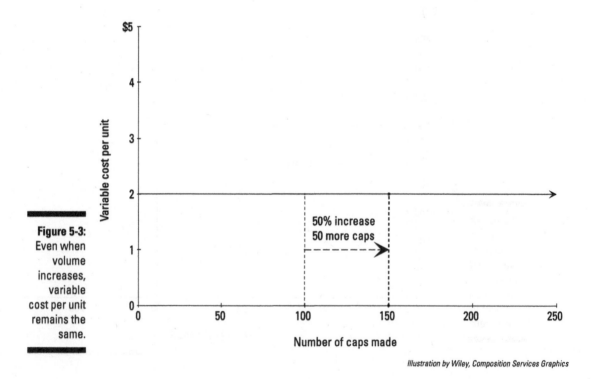

Figure 5-3: Even when volume increases, variable cost per unit remains the same.

50% increase
50 more caps

Variable cost per unit

Number of caps made

Illustration by Wiley, Composition Services Graphics

As the activity level changes, don't confuse total variable costs with variable costs per unit. Total variable costs change in proportion to the change in activity level (diagonal line pointing upward), while variable costs per unit remain the same (horizontal line).

Remembering that fixed costs don't change

Unlike total variable costs, total fixed costs remain the same regardless of changes in activity. For example, a factory may need to pay a fixed amount of property taxes and supervisor salaries regardless of how many units it actually produces. You don't connect any cost driver with fixed costs because these costs don't change.

When you graph costs on activity level, sketch fixed costs as a straight horizontal line as shown in Figure 5-4. Here you can see an entertainment company that produces and sells music videos online. No matter what the activity level — 80,000 or 120,000 downloads — the company must still pay the same amount for salaries and utilities: $100,000.

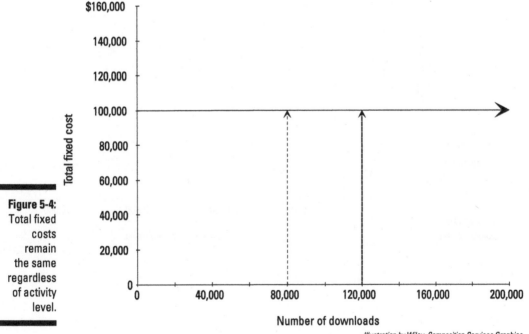

Figure 5-4:
Total fixed costs remain the same regardless of activity level.

Number of downloads

Illustration by Wiley, Composition Services Graphics

On the other hand, fixed cost per unit does decrease with volume. The more units you make, the lower the fixed cost per unit. Figure 5-5 illustrates this relationship. If your music video download company sells only 20,000 downloads, the fixed costs of one download equal $5 ($100,000 total fixed cost ÷ 20,000 units). However, if the company sells 200,000 units, the fixed cost per unit drops to $0.50 ($100,000 total fixed cost ÷ 200,000 units). If the company sells only one download, the fixed costs for that one download equal $100,000!

High fixed costs require significant activity to produce sales to offset those costs. In other words, if your company must pay $100,000 in fixed costs, it needs to sell enough products to cover this cost. I explain this concept further in Chapter 9.

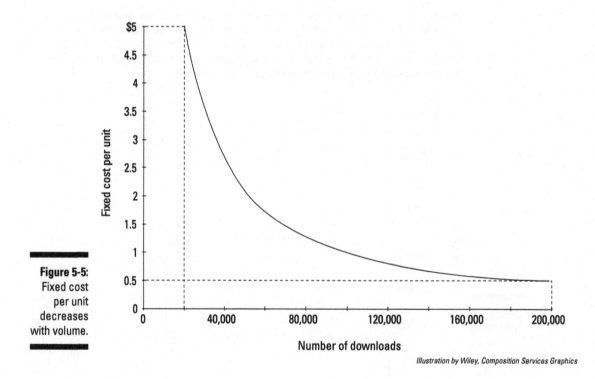

Figure 5-5:
Fixed cost
per unit
decreases
with volume.

Separating Mixed Costs into Variable and Fixed Components

Factories and other companies typically must pay costs that include variable and fixed components, challenging accountants to figure out which camp these costs belong in. These *mixed costs* typically change with the level of activity, but not proportionately. Therefore, in order to predict cost behavior, you need to split mixed costs into variable and fixed components with one of four techniques:

- ✔ Analyzing accounts
- ✔ Scattergraphing
- ✔ Using the high-low method
- ✔ Fitting a regression

The following sections break down these techniques, using the example of the fictional Xeon Company, which incurred $120,000 in costs to produce 1,200 units. Notice that even though the data used for each method is the same, each method yields a different answer. Because these methods are designed to estimate and predict future costs, their results typically vary.

When estimating fixed and variable costs with any method, try the eyeball test. That is, eyeball your numbers to make sure that they make sense. Does your regression indicate that variable costs are negative (for example, the greater the volume, the lower the cost)? If so, your numbers just flunked the eyeball test. Check everything and try again. Does your high-low test indicate that variable costs come to $0.00000000001 per unit? That's probably not accurate. Try again.

Analyzing accounts

Call this technique the common sense method. It requires four steps:

1. **Break out total costs into individual categories or accounts, such as direct materials, direct labor, and utilities.**

   When checking out the trial balance for Xeon Company, you notice the breakdown of costs specified in Figure 5-6.

Account	Total
Direct materials	$20,000
Direct labor	45,000
Depreciation	5,000
Fixed utilities	6,000
Variable utilities	5,000
Supervisor salaries	25,000
Other variable overhead	14,000
Total	**$120,000**

Figure 5-6: Xeon Company's product costs.

Illustration by Wiley, Composition Services Graphics

2. **Use your knowledge of operations and your common sense to classify each account as variable or fixed.**

   Flip to the earlier section "Predicting How Costs Behave" for details on distinguishing variable and fixed costs.

   As I note earlier in the chapter, variable costs change with the cost driver, but fixed costs don't. Figure 5-7 shows the categorized Xeon Company costs.

   If appropriate, you can classify some accounts as mixed and then assign percentages of each that are variable and fixed. For example, an account may be 50 percent variable and 50 percent fixed.

3. **Place variable costs and fixed costs in separate columns and add them up.**

   According to the classifications that you set up in the preceding section, fully separate and add up the variable and fixed costs as shown in Figure 5-8.

Account	Total	Variable or Fixed?
Direct materials	$20,000	Variable
Direct labor	45,000	Variable
Depreciation	5,000	Fixed
Fixed utilities	6,000	Fixed
Variable utilities	5,000	Variable
Supervisor salaries	25,000	Fixed
Other variable overhead	14,000	Variable
Total	$120,000	

Figure 5-7:
Classifying fixed and variable costs.

Illustration by Wiley, Composition Services Graphics

Account	Total	Fixed Costs	Variable Costs
Direct materials	$20,000		20,000
Direct labor	45,000		45,000
Depreciation	5,000	5,000	
Fixed utilities	6,000	6,000	
Variable utilities	5,000		5,000
Supervisor salaries	25,000	25,000	
Other variable overhead	14,000		14,000
Total	$120,000	$36,000	$84,000

Figure 5-8:
Xeon Company's fixed and variable cost.

Illustration by Wiley, Composition Services Graphics

4. **Compute variable cost per unit by dividing total variable costs by the number of units produced.**

   To compute variable cost per unit, divide total variable cost by the number of units produced:

   $$\text{Variable cost per unit} = \frac{\text{Total variable cost}}{\text{Number of units produced}}$$

   $$\text{Variable cost per unit} = \frac{\$84,000}{1,200 \text{ units}} = \$70 \text{ per unit}$$

   You can read more about variable cost per unit in the earlier section "Recognizing how cost drivers affect variable costs."

After completing the four steps for the Xeon Company example, you know that total fixed costs come to $36,000, and variable costs amount to $70 per unit. Figuring out the total variable costs and adding in fixed costs allows you to predict total cost:

$$\text{Total cost} = (\text{Variable cost per unit} \times \text{Units produced}) + \text{Total fixed cost}$$

Using this formula lets you determine that making 1,000 units would cost $70,000 (1,000 units × $70 per unit). Total fixed costs always equal $36,000; therefore, total costs equal $106,000:

$$\text{Total cost} = (\text{Variable cost per unit} \times \text{Units produced}) + \text{Total fixed cost}$$

$$\text{Total cost} = (\$70 \times 1,000 \text{ units}) + \$36,000 = \$106,000$$

Figure 5-9 shows how to graph this information. Note that while the total fixed cost line is horizontal, the slope of the total cost line equals variable cost per unit. The graph shows that when producing no units (a situation known as *zero production*), the company incurs only total fixed costs.

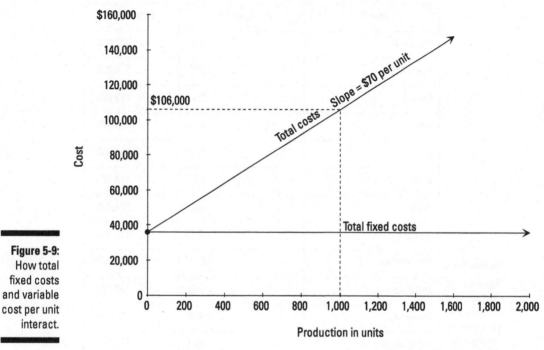

Illustration by Wiley, Composition Services Graphics

Figure 5-9:
How total
fixed costs
and variable
cost per unit
interact.

Scattergraphing

A *scattergraph* helps you visualize the relationship between activity level and total cost. To scattergraph, just follow three steps (with explanations for creating the scattergraph in Microsoft Excel):

1. **Set up a table that shows production level and total cost by time period.**

   To prepare a scattergraph, you need basic data about the number of units produced and the total costs per time period. Arrange this data by month, week, or some other time period as Figure 5-10 demonstrates.

Month	Production	Total Cost
January	800	$93,000
February	1,100	114,000
March	1,200	119,000
April	950	103,000
May	1,300	126,000
June	1,250	124,000
July	1,000	107,000
August	1,050	110,000
September	1,000	105,000
October	900	100,000
November	1,050	110,000
December	1,200	119,500

Figure 5-10:
Production
level and
total cost by
time period.

Illustration by Wiley, Composition Services Graphics

2. **Set up a graph with units produced at the bottom axis and total cost in the left axis.**

   Your graph should have the total cost (which includes fixed and variable costs) on the *y*-axis and the number of units produced along the *x*-axis as shown in Figure 5-11.

3. **On this graph, plot each point from the table.**

   Plot each data point on your graph. You can do so manually by using graph paper or electronically by using Excel's Chart Wizard:

   A. Enter the data from Step 1 (see Figure 5-10) into the Excel spreadsheet.

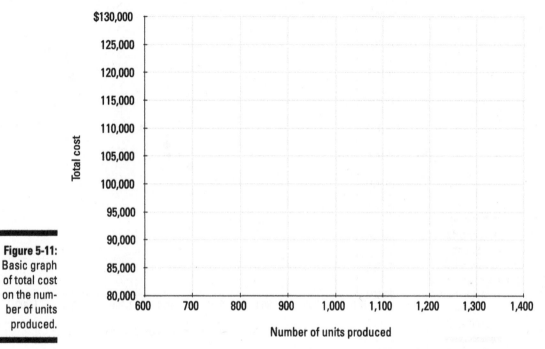

Figure 5-11:
Basic graph
of total cost
on the num-
ber of units
produced.

Illustration by Wiley, Composition Services Graphics

B. Select only the two columns of data ("Production" and "Total Cost").

C. In the "Insert" menu, click on "Scatter" and then "Scatter with only Markers."

A scattergraph should appear. Figure 5-12 shows the resulting scattergraph for Xeon Company.

4. **Label the axes appropriately.**

If you're trying to predict total costs for a future month, select the anticipated activity level for that month along the *x*-axis. Then use data points from previous months to estimate the total cost.

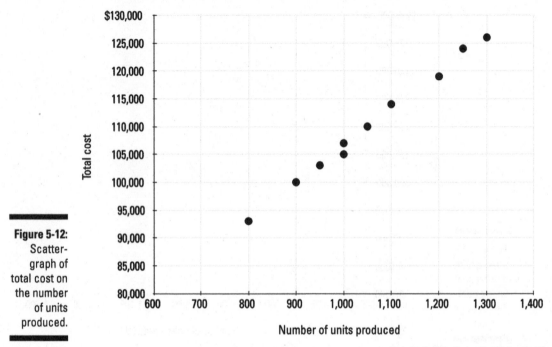

Illustration by Wiley, Composition Services Graphics

Figure 5-12:
Scatter-
graph of
total cost on
the number
of units
produced.

Using the high-low method

The high-low method estimates variable and fixed costs based on the highest and lowest levels of activity during the period. Just follow three steps:

1. **Based on a table of total costs and activity levels, determine the high and low activity levels.**

   Look at the production level and total costs to identify the high and low activity levels. Figure 5-10 indicates that Xeon Company's highest production level occurred in May, when the company produced 1,300 units at a total cost of $126,000. The lowest production level occurred in January, when the company produced just 800 units costing $93,000.

2. **Use the high and low activity levels to compute the variable cost per unit.**

To figure out the variable cost per unit, divide the change in total cost by the change in activity:

$$\text{Variable cost per unit} = \frac{\text{Total cost}_{\text{high activity}} - \text{Total cost}_{\text{low activity}}}{\text{Units produced}_{\text{high activity}} - \text{Units produced}_{\text{low activity}}}$$

$$= \frac{\$126,000 - \$93,000}{1,300 - 800} = \frac{\$33,000}{500} = \$66$$

3. **Figure out the total fixed cost.**

   To compute the total cost, pick either the high or the low cost information (either one works); for this example, I've picked the high production level — making 1,300 units for $126,000. Plug this information, along with the variable cost per unit from the preceding section, into the total cost formula:

   $$\text{Total cost} = (\text{Variable cost per unit} \times \text{Units produced}) + \text{Total fixed cost}$$

   $$\$126,000 = (\$66 \times 1,300) + \text{Total fixed cost}$$

   $$\$126,000 = \$85,800 + \text{Total fixed cost}$$

   $$\$40,200 = \text{Total fixed cost}$$

   Based on your answer, you can determine that making 1,000 units would mean total variable costs of $66,000 (1,000 units × $66 per unit). Total fixed costs equal $40,200. Therefore, total costs would equal $106,200:

   $$\text{Total cost} = (\text{Variable cost per unit} \times \text{Units produced}) + \text{Total fixed cost}$$

   $$\text{Total cost} = (\$66 \times 1,000 \text{ units}) + \$40,200 = \$106,200$$

The high-low method focuses only on two points: the highest and lowest activity levels. When using this method, don't get confused by activity levels between these two points, even if their costs are out of the bounds of the costs of the highest and lowest activity levels.

Fitting a regression

Statistical regression allows you to apply basic statistical techniques to estimate cost behavior. Don't panic! Excel (or a statistical analysis package) can quickly figure this information out for you; the following sections show you how.

Before starting, make sure you've installed the Microsoft Office Excel Analysis ToolPak. To confirm whether you already have it, click on "Data" and look for an item in the drop-down menu that says "Data Analysis." If you don't see this item, you need to install the ToolPak. Go to "Excel Options" and click on "Add-Ins." From here, go to the "Manage" box and click on "Excel Add-ins" and then "Go." From the "Add-Ins Available" box, click on the "Analysis ToolPak" check box and then click on "OK."

1. **Enter the data into Excel.**

    Create a table of data in Excel, listing each month's production activity level and total cost, similar to what appears in Figure 5-10 earlier in the chapter.

2. **Run a regression analysis in Excel.**

    Run a regression on the data in Excel by following these steps:

    A. Click on "Data."

    B. Click on "Data Analysis" and then "Regression;" then click on "OK."

    C. Under "Input Y Range," enter the range for the total cost data, including the heading, as shown in Figure 5-13.

    D. Under "Input X Range," enter the production data, including the heading, as shown in Figure 5-13.

    E. Click on the box for "Labels."

    F. Select an output range on your spreadsheet.

    G. Click on "OK."

When regressing total cost on a cost driver, the total cost data always goes into the "Input Y Range," and the cost driver data always goes into the "Input X Range."

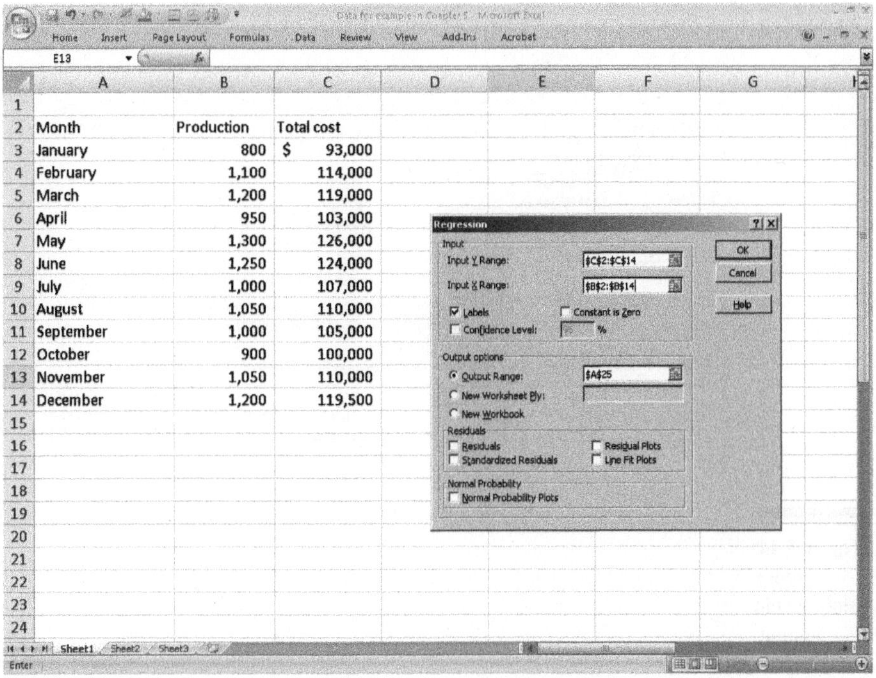

Figure 5-13: Input into Excel's Regression menu.

Illustration by Wiley, Composition Services Graphics

From all the information shown in the output (see Figure 5-14), you really only need two numbers. In the bottom table, look at the column marked "Coefficients." The number labeled "Intercept" ($39,739) is a statistical estimate of the fixed cost. The number labeled "Production" ($66.69) gives you a statistical estimate of the variable cost per unit.

		Data for example in Chapter 5 - Microsoft Excel								

Home Insert Page Layout Formulas Data Review View Add-Ins Acrobat

E31

	A	B	C	D	E	F	G	H	I	J
23										
24										
25	SUMMARY OUTPUT									
26										
27	*Regression Statistics*									
28	Multiple R	0.997717425								
29	R Square	0.995440061								
30	Adjusted R Square	0.994984067								
31	Standard Error	708.8961728								
32	Observations	12								
33										
34	ANOVA									
35		*df*	*SS*	*MS*	*F*	*Significance F*				
36	Regression	1	1097037162	1097037162	2183.011765	4.86097E-13				
37	Residual	10	5025337.838	502533.7838						
38	Total	11	1102062500							
39										
40		*Coefficients*	*Standard Error*	*t Stat*	*P-value*	*Lower 95%*	*Upper 95%*	*Lower 95.0%*	*Upper 95.0%*	
41	Intercept	39739.86486	1536.187921	25.86915302	1.71298E-10	36317.02623	43162.7035	36317.02623	43162.7035	
42	Production	66.68918919	1.427339877	46.72271144	4.86097E-13	63.50887777	69.86950061	63.50887777	69.86950061	
43										
44										
45										
46										
47										
48										
49										
50										
51										
52										
53										

H ◀ ▶ H   Sheet1 Sheet2 Sheet3

Ready

Figure 5-14:
Excel's
Regression
output.

Illustration by Wiley, Composition Services Graphics

Based on these regression results, you can determine that making 1,000 units would create total variable costs of $66,690 (1,000 units × $66.69 per unit). Total fixed costs would equal $39,739, so total costs would be $106,429:

$$\text{Total cost} = (\text{Variable cost per unit} \times \text{Units produced}) + \text{Total fixed cost}$$

$$\text{Total cost} = (\$66,690 \times 1,000 \text{ units}) + \$39,739 = \$106,429$$

Statistical regression analysis provides useful information to judge the reliability of your estimates. An "Adjusted R-square" close to 1 (the one in Figure 5-14 is approximately 0.99498) indicates that the model fits the data. Low P-values of the coefficients (here, 1.713×10^{-10} and 4.861×10^{-13}) indicate that the model has high statistical significance. In other words, this model looks pretty accurate.

Sticking to the Relevant Range

When predicting costs, take care to stay within the *relevant range* of activity, where you can expect to make reasonably accurate predictions and estimates based on experience. Outside the relevant range, such as when a plant exceeds its normal capacity or undergoes a shut-down period, the normal patterns of behavior change. Production may go so high that you have to pay workers overtime (thereby increasing direct labor rates and variable costs) or add a shift (increasing fixed overhead costs). Similarly, as production drops, your factory may begin to release workers and turn off the air conditioning. Outside the relevant range, the normal cost patterns change.

This limitation means that you can only make cost predictions within a certain range of activity. Consider Figure 5-15, which shows how wildly costs and production can change outside the relevant range.

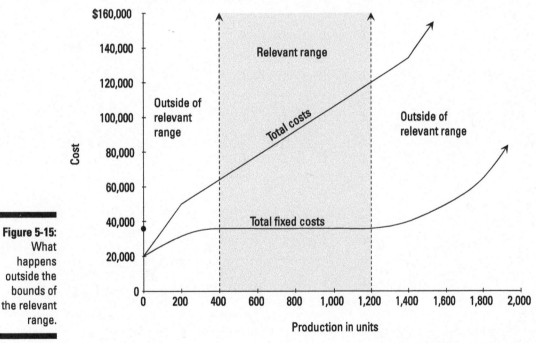

Figure 5-15:
What happens outside the bounds of the relevant range.

Chapter 6

Allocating Overhead

. . . .

In This Chapter

▶ Using direct labor to apply overhead

▶ Identifying cost pools and drivers

▶ Assigning overhead with activity-based costing

. . . .

After the Olympians claimed victory in the War of the Titans, Zeus sentenced Atlas to support all the celestial spheres on his shoulders, an event that many mythologist accountants consider the ultimate allocation of overhead. I know many managers who probably feel a lot like Atlas because they, too must bear unreasonably disproportionate shares of overhead.

Overhead costs include all the miscellaneous costs of doing business: utilities, supervision, security, and any other costs that don't fit neatly into *direct materials* and *direct labor* — the materials and labor you can directly trace to a product. (You can read more about identifying direct and indirect/overhead costs in Chapter 3.) That said, you can't ignore overhead just because it's difficult to allocate. Ignoring overhead causes you to underestimate costs of products and processes, which can spell disaster if you underprice based on those figures and lose money.

As factories and processes automate (and people get replaced by robots), the direct labor needed to manually produce goods tends to decrease, and the overhead necessary to operate, maintain, and repair the machines tends to increase. Accordingly, as the overall importance of overhead increases, managers and accountants must pay careful attention to how they allocate overhead to the different products their companies make.

In this chapter, I explain how and why you need to allocate the cost of overhead to individual products. I describe a traditional system for allocating overhead, based on direct labor, as well as a more innovative allocation system known as activity-based costing. For both systems, I explain what to do when you allocate too much or too little overhead to products.

Distributing Overhead through Direct Labor Costing

Overhead costs are the miscellaneous costs of making goods. They include the following:

- ✔ Indirect materials
- ✔ Indirect labor
- ✔ All other fixed and variable costs

Figure 6-1 shows how all these costs, plus costs of direct materials and direct labor, flow into the cost of products that you make and sell.

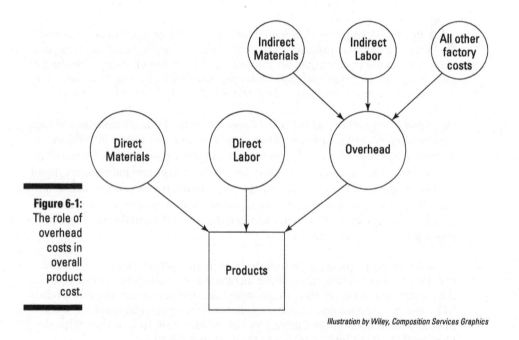

Figure 6-1:
The role of overhead costs in overall product cost.

Illustration by Wiley, Composition Services Graphics

When measuring the cost of products, you need to determine exactly how much direct labor/materials and overhead go into each item you make. You can often measure exactly how much of the direct costs go into each product. For example, a pencil may contain 300 grams of wood and 100 grams of graphite, so you apply the costs of those specific amounts of materials to that individual pencil. Similarly, if each worker takes an average of one hour to assemble a gadget, the cost of direct labor equals the cost of paying that worker for one hour.

Allocating overhead is another story. By definition, overhead is indirect, so understanding how it benefits individual products is difficult. How much electricity cost should be applied to each widget on your assembly line?

One way to allocate overhead costs is to use direct labor cost as a guide: the more direct labor cost that goes into a product, the more overhead that goes with it. This approach makes sense because direct labor cost itself seems to cause overhead to increase. The more hours worked, the more direct labor cost and the more money you need to pay for electricity, maintenance, and other overhead costs. The following sections give you the lowdown on the direct labor costing method of allocating overhead.

Rather than allocating overhead based on direct labor costs, managerial accountants may choose to use direct labor hours worked or even machine hours.

Calculating overhead allocation

Suppose a simple factory makes two products — call them Product A and Product B. The factory needs no direct materials (yes, that means it makes products out of thin air; please suspend your disbelief). It paid $1,600 in direct labor to its workers and $400 for overhead, knowing that each product required half of the direct labor costs — $800 each — as shown in Figure 6-2. The $400 in overhead also gets divided equally — $200 to each product. As shown in this figure, the total cost you need to apply (in this case, $2,000) equals the total cost that you apply to your products (again, $2,000).

This example is relatively simple because each product gets an equal amount of overhead. But not all companies manufacture products that require the same amount of overhead, and in those cases, the calculations aren't quite as simple.

For example, suppose a similar company plans to make two products, Product J and Product K. It plans to pay $1,600 in direct labor to its workers. Product J requires 120 hours of that direct labor, while Product K requires 40 hours. The company also expects to pay $200 for rent, $150 for maintenance, and $50 for coffee. Figure 6-3 illustrates how much overhead goes to each product line in this scenario.

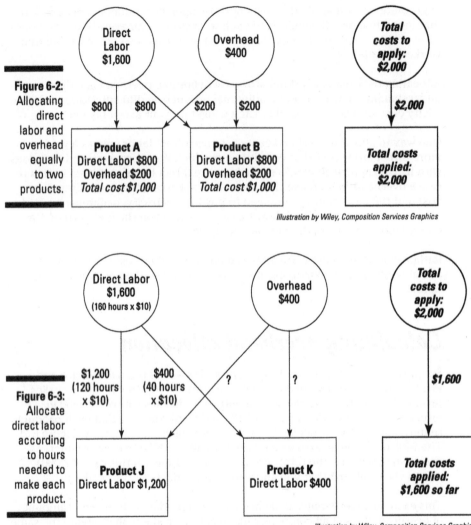

Figure 6-2: Allocating direct labor and overhead equally to two products.

Direct Labor $1,600

Overhead $400

$800 $800 $200 $200

Total costs to apply: $2,000

$2,000

Product A
Direct Labor $800
Overhead $200
Total cost $1,000

Product B
Direct Labor $800
Overhead $200
Total cost $1,000

Total costs applied: $2,000

Illustration by Wiley, Composition Services Graphics

Figure 6-3: Allocate direct labor according to hours needed to make each product.

Direct Labor $1,600 (160 hours x $10)

Overhead $400

$1,200 (120 hours x $10) $400 (40 hours x $10)   ?   ?

Total costs to apply: $2,000

$1,600

Product J
Direct Labor $1,200

Product K
Direct Labor $400

Total costs applied: $1,600 so far

Illustration by Wiley, Composition Services Graphics

To help you keep uneven allocations straight, remember that overhead allocation entails three steps:

1. **Add up total overhead.**

   This step requires adding indirect materials, indirect labor, and all other product costs not included in direct materials and direct labor. Here, overhead is estimated to include indirect materials ($50 worth of coffee), indirect labor ($150 worth of maintenance), and other product costs ($200 worth of rent), for a total of $400.

2. **Compute the *overhead allocation rate* by dividing total overhead by the number of direct labor hours.**

   You know that total overhead is expected to come to $400. Add up the direct labor hours associated with each product (120 hours for Product J + 40 hours for Product K = 160 total hours). Now plug these numbers into the following equation:

   $$\text{Overhead allocation rate} = \frac{\text{Total overhead}}{\text{Total direct labor hours}}$$
   $$= \frac{\$400}{160 \text{ hours}} = \$2.50$$

   For every hour needed to make a product, you need to apply $2.50 worth of overhead to that product.

   Some accountants and managers refer to the overhead allocation rate as the *predetermined overhead allocation rate* because it needs to be estimated at the beginning of a period.

3. **Apply overhead by multiplying the overhead allocation rate by the number of direct labor hours needed to make each product.**

   Because Product J requires 120 hours, apply $300 worth of overhead ($120 hours × $2.50) to this product. Product K requires 40 hours, so apply $100 to that product.

Figure 6-4 illustrates how this process allocates all direct labor and overhead costs to the products made.

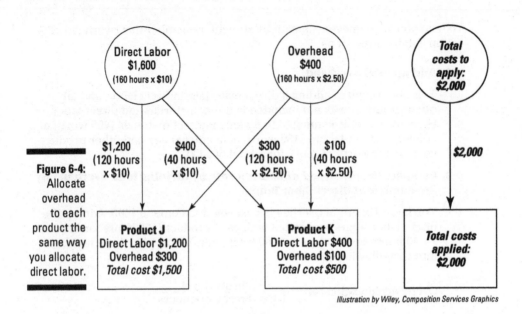

Illustration by Wiley, Composition Services Graphics

Figure 6-4: Allocate overhead to each product the same way you allocate direct labor.

Experimenting with direct labor costing

Now try an example of how to apply overhead costs, alongside direct materials and direct labor costs, to units produced. The Jackson Company, which makes gadgets, spent the following over a specific time period:

- ✔ $5,000 on direct materials to purchase 1,000 pounds of raw material
- ✔ $8,000 on direct labor
- ✔ $3,000 on indirect materials
- ✔ $2,000 on other overhead

During this time period, employees worked for a total of 1,000 hours. Jackson allocates overhead based on the number of direct labor hours worked.

Jackson Company built a specialty widget, model GO. This widget requires 200 pounds of raw (direct) material and 100 hours of direct labor. How much does making widget model GO cost Jackson Company?

Direct materials

First, figure out the cost of the direct materials. Because Jackson bought 1,000 pounds of raw material for $5,000, the raw material must cost $5 per pound ($5,000 ÷ 1,000 pounds).

Now use this overall rate to figure out the cost of direct materials for widget model GO. Widget model GO requires 200 pounds of raw material at $5 per pound, so the total cost of direct materials is 200 pounds × $5 per pound, or $1,000.

Direct labor

Because Jackson paid $8,000 for 1,000 hours of direct labor, the overall direct labor cost comes to $8 per hour ($8,000 ÷ 1,000 hours). Widget model GO required 100 hours of direct labor, which cost $800 (100 hours × $8 per hour).

Overhead

To find the allocated overhead for widget model GO, follow the steps in the earlier section "Calculating overhead allocation":

1. **Add up total overhead.**

   Jackson spent $3,000 on indirect materials and $2,000 on other overhead costs, bringing total overhead to $5,000.

2. **Compute the overhead allocation rate.**

   Jackson allocates overhead based on direct labor hours (not the direct labor cost). Therefore, divide total overhead by total direct labor hours.

   $$\text{Overhead allocation rate} = \frac{\text{Total overhead}}{\text{Total direct labor hours}}$$
   $$= \frac{\$5,000}{1,000 \text{ hours}} = \$5$$

   According to this overhead allocation, every hour spent laboring on a product results in $5 worth of overhead.

3. **Apply overhead.**

   Widget model GO required 100 hours of direct labor. Multiply these hours by the overhead allocation rate of $5 to arrive at total overhead applied, $500.

Adding it all up

To better see how allocating overhead fits into the bigger financial picture for widget model GO, figure out the widget's total cost by adding up direct materials, direct labor, and overhead, as shown in Figure 6-5.

Figure 6-5:
Total cost of product includes direct materials, direct labor, and overhead.

Direct materials	$1,000
Direct labor	800
Overhead	500
Total cost of widget model GO	**$2,300**

Illustration by Wiley, Composition Services Graphics

Figure 6-6 provides a more graphical explanation for the example, showing how direct materials, direct labor, and overhead all flow into the cost of the product. You can see that of the $18,000 in total costs to apply, you have so far applied only $2,300 to a single product. The company will eventually apply all remaining product costs to other products.

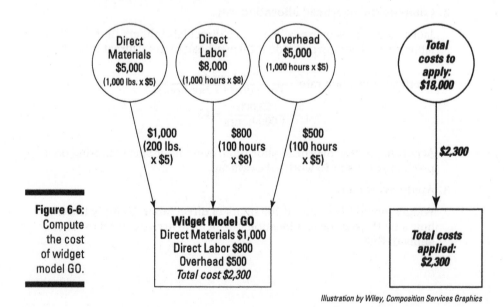

Figure 6-6:
Compute the cost of widget model GO.

Illustration by Wiley, Composition Services Graphics

Applying over- and underestimated overhead to cost of goods sold

The system of costing merchandise requires you to apply all direct materials, direct labor, and overhead costs to products made. The record-keeping for both direct materials and direct labor should mirror whatever happens in the factory. For example, as the factory uses direct materials, their costs should be transferred over to the cost of the products made. Similarly, as employees work, the cost of their direct labor should go to the products that they work on.

However, allocating overhead can get messy. Because the overhead allocation rate needs to be estimated at the beginning of the period based on predictions of total overhead costs and its base (such as direct labor cost, direct labor hours, or machine hours), this rate may turn out to be inaccurate. In this situation, companies apply more overhead to products than the products actually require or apply too little overhead, such that a portion of overhead gets left over and not applied to any products.

If a company applies too little overhead to products manufactured, the unapplied overhead increases cost of goods sold because that category is most likely where the overhead costs would've ended up anyway; the cost of manufactured goods, as they are sold, go to cost of goods sold. On the other hand, if the company applies too much overhead to products manufactured, the difference reduces cost of goods sold.

If you use debits and credits to compute product costs, don't panic. Debits go to the left, and credits go to the right. All costs are debits and go to the left. Any reductions of costs are credits, and they go to the right. Figure 6-7 shows you how this setup works. Financial accounting covers other types of accounts, such as liabilities and revenues — so-called "credit" accounts, which work in the opposite direction.

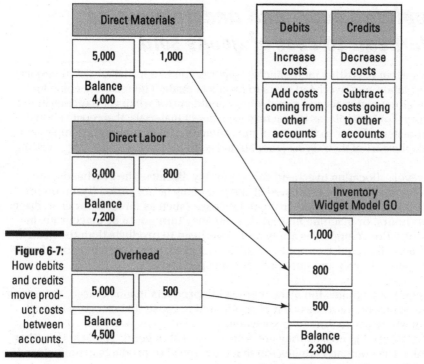

Figure 6-7:
How debits
and credits
move prod-
uct costs
between
accounts.

Taking Advantage of Activity-Based Costing for Overhead Allocation

The direct labor-based costing method covered in the earlier section
"Distributing Overhead through Direct Labor Costing" is based on the idea
that the more direct labor your employees work, the more overhead your
company incurs. This assumption made sense in the days before automation,
but today completely automated factories operate with little or no direct
labor; in these situations, a wide variety of factors can cause overhead to
increase. To gain a better understanding of these factors, managerial accountants use activity-based costing.

Under *activity-based costing* (ABC), you set up different cost pools, identifying different activities that you believe increase these cost pools. These activities, each of which are thought to vary with the total costs of each cost pool, are called *cost drivers*. They drive the costs in each cost pool.

For example, instead of using direct labor to allocate overhead, you may split overhead into three different categories: Logistics, Supervision, and Manufacturing. After some research, you identify a cost driver for each. For Logistics, you set the cost driver as the number of parts in each product. For Supervision, you may use the total number of employees who worked on a product. For Manufacturing, you can use the number of machine hours needed.

Activity-based costing gets around the problem of automated factories that use very little direct labor. It also provides you with valuable insights into how costs behave and can help you reduce the costs and get the manufacturing process to flow more smoothly. (For more on cost drivers and cost behavior, check out Chapter 5.) In this section, I take you through the following steps of activity-based costing:

1. **Add up total overhead.**

   Total overhead includes indirect materials, indirect labor, and other manufacturing costs.

2. **Identify one or more cost drivers.**

   Scrutinize the nature of your overhead to identify different pools of overhead costs and specific measures that affect them. For example, one overhead pool may be storage costs. This pool would be affected by the number of square feet assigned to each department. Ideally, try to identify a single measure that actually causes each overhead pool to increase.

3. **Compute the overhead allocation rate.**

   Divide total overhead in each cost pool by its cost driver:

   $$\text{Overhead allocation rate} = \frac{\text{Estimated overhead}}{\text{Cost driver activity level}}$$

4. **Apply overhead.**

   Multiply the overhead allocation rate for each cost pool by the individual product's cost driver activity level.

Applying the four steps of activity-based costing

Sal Company manufactures gold jewelry. Here's the background information you have to work with:

- ✔ Sal pays $1,000 per ounce for its raw material, 14-karat gold. It purchased 900 ounces this year.

- ✔ Sal pays $10 per hour for direct labor. The company has budgeted 5,000 hours of direct labor this year.

- ✔ Sal has established three cost pools: Purchasing, Quality Control, and Utilities.

  - • The Purchasing cost pool is expected to total $100,000 this year. Sal has established this pool's cost driver as number of parts and plans to use 10,000 parts during the year.

  - • Sal has budgeted $80,000 for Quality Control to inspect 4,000 individual units. The cost driver for this pool is the number of units produced.

  - • Sal must pay $200,000 for Utilities this year. The cost driver for Utilities is direct labor hours.

Using this information, figure out the overhead cost assigned to producing the following jewelry item, model number A340:

- ✔ A340 uses 0.200 ounces of 14-karat gold.

- ✔ It requires two hours of direct labor.

- ✔ It's made up of six different parts.

Step 1: Add up total overhead

Add up indirect materials, indirect labor, and all other product costs not included in direct materials and direct labor.

As shown in Figure 6-8, Sal budgeted $380,000 worth of overhead.

Activity Cost Pool	Estimated Overhead
Purchasing	$100,000
Quality control	80,000
Utilities	200,000
Total overhead	**$380,000**

Figure 6-8: Adding up total overhead.

Illustration by Wiley, Composition Services Graphics

Step 2: Identify one or more cost drivers

Research the nature of your overhead to try to find measurable factors that affect overhead costs. Ideally, try to find a measure that actually causes the total overhead pool to increase. Here are some typical examples of measures that drive different kinds of overhead:

- ✔ Square footage drives storage costs.
- ✔ Machine hours drive the cost of depreciation.
- ✔ Direct labor hours or direct labor cost drives the cost of supervision or human resources.
- ✔ Number of employees drives the cost of supervision or human resources.
- ✔ Number of purchase orders drives the cost of purchasing raw materials.
- ✔ Number of setups drives the cost of operating machinery.
- ✔ Number of parts drives the cost of assembling goods.
- ✔ Number of quality tests drives the cost quality inspection.
- ✔ Weight of units drives the cost of transportation.

Activity-based costing doesn't prohibit using direct labor hours to allocate overhead. If managers decide direct labor hours are a cost driver, that measure can function as part of the activity-based costing system.

This process eventually results in breaking total overhead down into several different cost pools and identifying a single cost driver for each.

Sal established the three cost drivers listed in Figure 6-9.

	Activity Cost Pool	Estimated Overhead	Cost Driver
Figure 6-9: Identifying the cost drivers.	Purchasing	$100,000	Number of parts
	Quality control	80,000	Number of units inspected
	Utilities	200,000	Direct labor hours

Illustration by Wiley, Composition Services Graphics

Step 3: Compute the overhead allocation rate for each cost pool

Divide total overhead in each cost pool by its cost driver:

$$\text{Overhead allocation rate} = \frac{\text{Estimated overhead}}{\text{Cost driver activity level}}$$

$$\text{Overhead allocation rate}_{\text{Purchasing}} = \frac{\$100,000}{10,000 \text{ parts}} = \$10 \text{ per part}$$

$$\text{Overhead allocation rate}_{\text{Quality control}} = \frac{\$80,000}{4,000 \text{ units}} = \$20 \text{ per unit}$$

$$\text{Overhead allocation rate}_{\text{Utilities}} = \frac{\$200,000}{5,000 \text{ hours}} = \$40 \text{ per hour}$$

Figure 6-10 shows how to document these computations in a straightforward table.

	Activity Cost Pool	Estimated Overhead	Cost Driver Activity Level	Overhead Application Rate
Figure 6-10: Computing overhead allocation rates under activity-based costing.	Purchasing	$100,000	10,000 parts	$10/part
	Quality control	80,000	4,000 units	$20/unit
	Utilities	200,000	5,000 hours	$40/hour

Illustration by Wiley, Composition Services Graphics

Step 4: Apply overhead

Multiply the overhead allocation rate for each cost pool by the individual product's cost driver activity level, as shown in Figure 6-11.

Figure 6-11:
Using
activity-
based
costing to
allocate
overhead.

Activity Cost Pool	Activity Level	Overhead Allocation Rate	Cost Assigned
Purchasing	6 parts	$10/part	$60
Quality control	1 unit	20/unit	20
Utilities	2 hours	40/hour	80
Total overhead			**$160**

Finishing up the ABC example

You're not done yet! Don't forget to include the costs of direct materials and direct labor. Remember that Model A340 uses 0.200 ounces of 14-karat gold costing $1,000 per ounce, so that the total cost of direct materials equals $200. Furthermore, Model A340 requires two hours of direct labor, costing $10 per hour. Therefore, total cost of direct labor equals $20.

Now add together all the costs of making one unit of A340, as shown in Figure 6-12.

Figure 6-12:
Adding up
the total
cost of mak-
ing A340.

Direct materials	$200
Direct labor	20
Overhead	160
Total	**$380**

Figure 6-13 visually describes how costs flow from direct materials, direct labor, and the overhead pools to the finished product.

Activity-based costing provides useful information to help managers understand cost behavior and find new ways to keep costs down. This example demonstrates that, although direct labor costs $10 per hour, utilities cost $40 per hour of direct labor. This information may lead managers to examine utility costs to reduce inefficiencies.

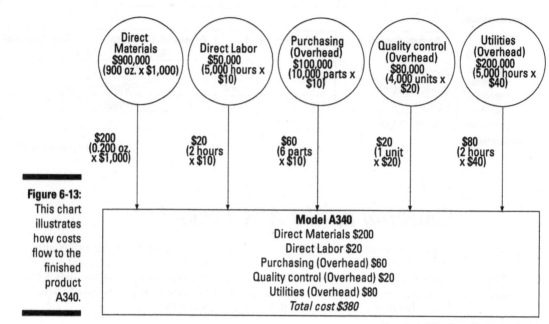

Illustration by Wiley, Composition Services Graphics

Figure 6-13:
This chart
illustrates
how costs
flow to the
finished
product
A340.

Chapter 7

Job Order Costing: Having It Your Way

. . . .

In This Chapter

▶ Organizing the documentation for a job order cost system

▶ Applying direct materials and direct labor to jobs by using the debit-credit system

▶ Accounting for overhead in a job order cost system

. . . .

*L*ooking for a teddy bear? Most people would go no farther than their local drugstore or big-box discount store. There, they can usually choose from a few different colors and sizes in order to find the bear they like. Drugstore bears are usually manufactured on assembly lines, often in batches of thousands of identical bears. To measure the cost of the products made, companies use process costing, which I cover in Chapter 8.

More-discriminating bear aficionados, however, have their teddy bears made to order. This way, they can choose their bears' size, fur color, eye color, paw pads, and even tattoos. They can also choose from a wide selection of clothing or have clothing made to order in any theme they can imagine. When craftspeople sew and assemble these custom bears, they use a system called job order costing to track the exact cost of each bear.

Information about product cost helps managers to set and adjust prices and to decide how to best utilize limited production capacity. In this chapter, I explain how companies accumulate costs in a job order costing system and how they apply overhead to the individual products made.

Keeping Records in a Job Order Cost System

A manufacturer who makes unique goods — or batches of goods — to order usually uses a *job order cost system* to determine how much each job costs to make. Such goods may include custom teddy bears, made-to-order suits or aircraft, catered affairs, or new feature films; the individual units or batches are called *jobs*.

In job order costing, an information system traces the exact value of raw materials put into process and the value of direct labor and overhead used to transform those raw materials into finished goods. This information system ensures that the company accounts for all direct materials, direct labor, and overhead costs and accumulates the cost of each job. The following sections walk you through the record-keeping documents and process.

Getting the records in order

Job order costing uses a few specific forms to keep track of the resources that go into an individual job: a job order cost sheet, materials requisition forms, and time tickets.

Job order cost sheet

To keep track of jobs, companies typically use a form called a *job order cost sheet*. As Figure 7-1 shows, the job order cost sheet accumulates all the direct materials, direct labor, and overhead costs applied to that job. This form is usually kept with the job itself, so that any additional costs incurred can be documented quickly.

Don't let my references to "sheets" and "forms" confuse you into thinking that, in the real world, companies must keep these records on paper. Some do, but most businesses actually store their records electronically.

Job. No._____			
Item_____			
Customer_____			
Quantity_____			
Date requested_____			
Date	Direct Materials	Direct Labor	Overhead
Totals			
Total cost			
Cost per unit			

Figure 7-1:
A blank job order cost sheet.

Materials requisition form

When factory personnel need raw materials, they complete a *materials requisition slip*. This form, illustrated in Figure 7-2, kick-starts the manufacturing process so that the factory can begin to work on the raw materials needed to make the goods. In this case, storage personnel issued ten cases of plastic pellets, stock number AA45, to the Assembly Department. These cases cost $300 each, totaling $3,000.

Figure 7-2:
The materials requisition slip authorizes personnel to issue raw materials.

Date _____ *July 16, 2013* _____				
Job No. _____ *1245* _____				
Deliver goods to Department: _____ *Assembly* _____				
Quantity	Description	Stock No.	Cost per Unit	Total Cost
10 cases	*Plastic Pellets*	*AA45*	*$300*	*$3,000*
Requested by _____ *Steven Kevins* _____				
Approved by _____ *Alysha MacRae* _____				
Received by _____ *Scott King* _____				

After they put the goods into production, factory workers copy the cost of the materials listed on the materials requisition slip on to the job order cost sheet. They keep the two forms together, usually with the job itself.

Time tickets

As employees work, they complete time tickets to indicate how much time they spend working on each job, as shown in Figure 7-3. This time ticket indicates that Jon Garfunkel worked on Job 1245 for two hours. This direct labor adds $40 to the cost of this job.

Figure 7-3:
Employees use a time ticket to keep track of the jobs they work on.

Date	*July 17, 2013*			
Employee name	*Jon Garfunkel*			
Department:	*Assembly*			
Job No.	*1245*			
Start	**Stop**	**Hours**	**Hourly Rate**	**Total Cost**
9:00 a.m.	*11:00 a.m.*	*2.0*	*$20*	*$40*
Employee	*Jon Garfunkel*			
Approved by	*Mary Pat Kinzler*			

Illustration by Wiley, Composition Services Graphics

Allocating overhead

Along with direct materials and direct labor, employees add the cost of overhead to the job order cost sheet. As I note in Chapter 6, the process for allocating overhead under activity-based costing has four steps:

1. **Add up total overhead.**

   At the beginning of the period, add up projections of indirect materials, indirect labor, and all product costs not included in direct materials and direct labor. For purposes of Job 1245, assume that the company incurred $10,000 worth of overhead overall.

2. **Identify one or more cost drivers.**

   Find measures that drive your overhead. Many companies assume that direct labor drives all overhead. Here, assume that the company uses a single overhead cost pool, with direct labor hours as the cost driver.

3. **Compute the overhead allocation rate for each cost pool.**

To compute the overhead allocation rates, divide total overhead in each cost pool by its cost driver. Note that, in this case, employees in the company are projected to work 5,000 direct labor hours this year.

$$\text{Overhead allocation rate} = \frac{\text{Estimated overhead}}{\text{Cost driver activity level}} = \frac{\$10,000}{5,000 \text{ hours}}$$

$$= \$2.00 \text{ per hour}$$

4. **Apply overhead.**

   Multiply the cost pool's overhead allocation rate by each job's cost driver. So far, employees worked two hours on Job 1245. Therefore, this job would absorb $4 worth of overhead (2.0 hours × $2 per hour).

Completing the job order cost sheet

The materials-requisition, time-ticket, and overhead-allocation information all goes on the job order cost sheet. To determine the total cost of the completed job, employees simply add up the job order cost sheet. Figure 7-4 tallies the cost of Job 1245.

Figure 7-4:
Enter information from materials requisition slips and time tickets onto the job order cost sheet.

Job. No _____ **1245** _____

Item _____ **Specialty Gadgets** _____

Customer _____ **SenyoCo** _____

Quantity _____ **1,000 units** _____

Date requested _____ **August 1, 2013** _____

Date	Direct Materials	Direct Labor	Overhead
July 16	$3,000.00		
July 17		$40.00	$4.00
Totals	3,000.00	40.00	4.00
Total cost			$3,044.00
Cost per unit			$3.044

Illustration by Wiley, Composition Services Graphics

Understanding the Accounting for Job Order Costing

Recording journal entries and posting them to general ledger accounts in a managerial cost accounting system isn't difficult. Because almost all accounts in managerial accounting are either assets or expenses, debits increase most balances and credits decrease balances. (There are a few exceptions, which I elaborate on later in this section.) Accordingly, a *T-account* — illustrated in Figure 7-5 — lists increases in the debit column to the left and decreases in the credit column to the right.

Figure 7-5:
Debits (to the left) increase, while credits (to the right) decrease.

Debits	Credits
Increase costs	Decrease costs
Add costs coming from other accounts	Subtract costs going to other accounts

Illustration by Wiley, Composition Services Graphics

Accountants use journal entries to record any changes to these T-accounts. Journal entries record transactions — namely, transfers between different accounts. Therefore, each journal entry affects at least two accounts, and total debits (increases to the left) must equal total credits (decreases to the right). For example, to purchase $1,000 worth of raw materials, debit the account Raw materials inventory (an increase to the left) and credit the account Cash (a decrease in cash to the right), as shown in Figure 7-6.

Figure 7-6:
Journal entries record transactions between different accounts.

Date	Accounts	Debit	Credit
July 20, 2013	*Raw materials inventory*	*1,000*	
	Cash		*1,000*

Illustration by Wiley, Composition Services Graphics

Assume the company started with $10,000 worth of cash. As shown in Figure 7-7, post this journal entry to the accounts, debiting the Raw materials inventory account for $1,000 (increasing to the left) and crediting the Cash account for $1,000 (decreasing to the right). This entry reduces Cash by $1,000 while increasing Raw materials inventory by $1,000.

Figure 7-7:
How the journal entry in Figure 7-6 affects the accounts.

Raw materials inventory			Cash		
Balance			Balance		
	-0-			10,000	
	1,000				*1,000*
Balance			*Balance*		
	1,000			*9,000*	

Illustration by Wiley, Composition Services Graphics

As taught in financial accounting courses, the debit-credit system actually features two different kinds of accounts — so-called *debit accounts* and *credit accounts*. So far in this section, you use debits (to the left side) to increase debit accounts and use credits (to the right side) to decrease debit accounts. However, credit accounts, which include Liabilities, Stockholders' equity, and Revenue accounts, work in the opposite direction. To increase these accounts, credit them (to the right side). To decrease them, you debit them (to the left side).

This book primarily deals with debit accounts, in which debits increase to the left and credits decrease to the right. Here I use only two credit accounts: Accounts payable (which are moneys owed to suppliers), and Wages payable (moneys owed to employees). To increase one of these credit accounts, credit it to the right. To decrease it, debit it to the left.

The following sections take you through an example of accounting for the job order costing system. Here's the premise: fictional National Snow Globe Corp. manufactures custom souvenir snow globes for tourist gift shops. The company makes snow globes in large batches. Each globe features a unique three-dimensional image inside, a custom logo, and one of four different grades of snow.

Purchasing raw materials

On January 3, National Snow Globe purchased $50,000 worth of raw materials on account. As illustrated in Figure 7-8, you debit Raw materials inventory for $50,000 and credit Accounts payable for $50,000.

Figure 7-8:
Journal
entries
to record
purchase of
materials.

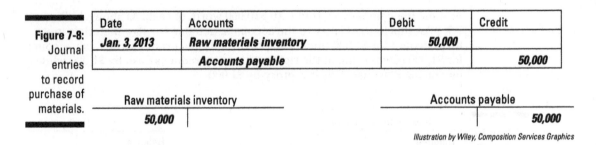

Date	Accounts	Debit	Credit
Jan. 3, 2013	Raw materials inventory	50,000	
	Accounts payable		50,000

Raw materials inventory	Accounts payable
50,000			50,000

Illustration by Wiley, Composition Services Graphics

The debit to Raw materials inventory (a debit account) increases that account's balance; the credit to Accounts payable (a credit account) increases that account's balance.

Paying for direct labor

On January 31, National Snow Globe recorded payroll for direct labor amounting to $20,000. Over this time period, employees worked 2,000 hours. As shown in Figure 7-9, you debit Direct labor for $20,000 and credit Wages payable for the same amount.

Figure 7-9:
Journal
entries
to record
direct labor
cost.

Date	Accounts	Debit	Credit
Jan. 31, 2013	Direct labor	20,000	
	Wages payable		20,000

Direct labor	Wages payable
20,000			20,000

Illustration by Wiley, Composition Services Graphics

The debit to Direct labor (a debit account) increases that account's balance; the credit to Wages payable (a credit account) increases that account's balance.

Paying for overhead

Overhead costs are all product costs not included in direct materials and direct labor. They typically encompass indirect materials, indirect labor, property taxes on the factory, depreciation of factory equipment, factory maintenance, and the cost of factory supervision.

On January 31, National Snow Globe paid $30,000 for overhead. As shown in Figure 7-10, you debit Overhead for $30,000 and credit Cash for this amount.

Figure 7-10:
Journal entries to record payment for overhead.

Date	Accounts	Debit	Credit
Jan. 31, 2013	**Overhead**	**30,000**	
	Cash		**30,000**

Overhead		Cash	
30,000			**30,000**

Illustration by Wiley, Composition Services Graphics

Requisitioning raw materials

The Work-in-process inventory account accumulates all direct materials, direct labor, and overhead costs that a company puts into production.

On January 14, National Snow Globe received an order from the Johnny Gentile Library and Museum in Jupiter, Florida, for 5,000 snow globes. The factory manager numbered this job BRM-10.

On January 15, Supervisor Jane Smiley arrived at the warehouse with a materials requisition slip for job BRM-10, requesting that workers put $4,000 worth of raw materials into production. Logistics personnel delivered the goods to Jane's department. Jane then notes receipt of the goods on the job order cost sheet. (Check out Figure 7-1 and Figure 7-2 earlier in the chapter for a sample job order cost sheet and materials requisition slip, respectively.) Figure 7-11 illustrates the journal entry: You debit the Work-in-process inventory account and credit Raw materials inventory for $4,000.

Figure 7-11:
Journal entries to record requisition of materials for BRM-10.

Date	Accounts	Debit	Credit
Jan. 15, 2013	**Work-in-process inventory**	**4,000**	
	Raw materials inventory		**4,000**

Work-in-process inventory		Raw materials inventory	
4,000		**50,000**	**4,000**
		46,000	

Illustration by Wiley, Composition Services Graphics

Because of a previous transaction, the company already had $50,000 in its Raw materials inventory account. After this transfer shifts $4,000 from Raw materials inventory into Work-in-process inventory, the company has a remaining balance in Raw materials inventory of $46,000.

Utilizing direct labor

Amanda Carpa, an employee in Jane Smiley's department, spent six hours working on job BRM-10. Jane then notes the cost of hours worked by Amanda on the job order cost sheet. At the end of the day, she completes a time ticket. (Figure 7-3 earlier in the chapter illustrates a sample time ticket.) The company pays Carpa $10 per hour, so the total direct labor cost for six hours equals $60 (6 hours × $10 per hour). The journal entry in Figure 7-12 debits the Work-in-process inventory account and credits Direct labor for $60.

Date	Accounts	Debit	Credit
Jan. 15, 2013	Work-in-process inventory	60	
	Direct labor		60

Figure 7-12: Journal entries to apply direct labor to job BRM-10.

Work-in-process inventory	
4,000	
60	
Balance 4,060	

Direct labor	
20,000	
	60
Balance 19,940	

Illustration by Wiley, Composition Services Graphics

Applying overhead

Work through the four steps to apply overhead in this example:

1. **Add up total overhead.**

   National Snow Globe estimated that overhead would amount to $30,000 for the month.

2. **Identify one or more cost drivers.**

   The company evaluated its overhead, identifying two appropriate cost drivers. The company recorded $10,000 in a cost pool called Utilities.

Managers determined that the appropriate cost driver for this cost pool should be direct labor hours; as I note in the earlier section "Paying for direct labor," the activity level for this pool is 2,000 hours.

The company also recorded $20,000 in a cost pool called Setups. Management determined that the appropriate cost driver for this cost pool should be the number of setups, estimating that it would have a total of 50 setups during the month.

3. **Compute the overhead allocation rate for each cost pool.**

Divide estimated overhead in each cost pool by its cost driver activity level, as shown in Figure 7-13. For example, in the Utilities cost pool, the company expects to incur $10,000 worth of overhead. The company also expects to have employees work 2,000 direct labor hours. Therefore, the overhead application rate comes to $5 per hour. Each direct labor hour also comes with $5 worth of overhead. Similarly, the overhead cost pool for setups comes to $20,000, and the company plans to do 50 setups. Therefore, the company assigns $400 worth of overhead for each setup.

Figure 7-13:
Computing
overhead
allocation
rates for
National
Snow Globe.

Activity Cost Pool	Estimated Overhead	Estimated Cost Driver Activity Level	Overhead Application Rate
Utilities	$10,000	2,000 hours	$5/hour
Setups	20,000	50 setups	400/setup

Illustration by Wiley, Composition Services Graphics

4. **Apply overhead.**

To figure out the overhead assigned to job BRM-10, measure the activity level of each cost driver and then multiply it by its respective overhead allocation rate, as shown in Figure 7-14.

Because six hours of direct labor were expended to make BRM-10 and the overhead allocation rate for utilities is $5 per hour, assign $30 in overhead cost to BRM-10. The job entailed one setup (at an overhead allocation rate of $400 per setup), so assign another $400 worth of overhead to this job. Therefore, BRM-10 gets assigned a total of $430 worth of overhead.

Activity Cost Pool	Activity Level	Overhead Allocation Rate	Cost Assigned
Utilities	6 hours	$5/hour	$30
Setups	1 setup	400/setup	400
Total overhead			$430

Figure 7-14: Allocating overhead for National Snow Globe.

Illustration by Wiley, Composition Services Graphics

As soon as the company's accountants are able to estimate overhead assigned to the job, they add this cost to the job's job order cost sheet (see Figure 7-1 earlier in the chapter for a blank example).

The journal entry to allocate overhead would debit (increase) Work-in-process inventory and credit (decrease) Overhead (see Figure 7-15). This entry effectively moves the overhead cost of the products out of the overhead pools and into the cost of the goods that you make.

Date	Accounts	Debit	Credit
Jan. 31, 2013	*Work-in-process inventory*	*430*	
	Overhead		*430*

Work-in-process inventory		Overhead	
4,000		*30,000*	
60			
430			*430*

Figure 7-15: Journal entry to allocate overhead.

Illustration by Wiley, Composition Services Graphics

After you finish manufacturing the goods, add all the costs of making BRM-10 as shown in Figure 7-16. Remember to include direct labor, direct materials, and overhead costs, so that the total cost of job BRM-10 sums to $4,490.

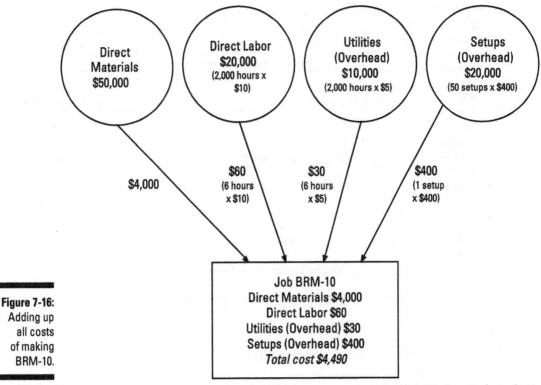

Illustration by Wiley, Composition Services Graphics

Figure 7-16:
Adding up
all costs
of making
BRM-10.

To record that you finished making the goods, transfer this cost from Work-in-process inventory to Finished goods inventory by debiting (increasing) Finished goods inventory and crediting (decreasing) Work-in-process inventory. Note how transactions in the books reflect what happens in the factory. As the goods are moved off the assembly line and into the finished goods warehouse, the accountants take their cost out of the account Work-in-process inventory and into the account Finished goods inventory. See Figure 7-17 for the journal entry to record this transfer.

Figure 7-18 provides a job order cost sheet for BRM-10. It illustrates how the company keeps track of direct materials, direct labor, and overhead costs throughout the production process.

Figure 7-17:
Journal entry to transfer goods from Work-in-process inventory to Finished goods inventory.

Date	Accounts	Debit	Credit
Jan. 31, 2013	Finished goods inventory	4,490	
	Work-in-process inventory		4,490

Work-in-process inventory			Finished goods inventory	
4,000				
60				
430	4,490		4,490	
0				

Illustration by Wiley, Composition Services Graphics

Job. No. _____ **BRM-10** _____

Item _____ **Singing Legend Snow Globes** _____

Customer _____ **Johnny Gentile Library and Museum** _____

Quantity _____ **5,000 units** _____

Date requested _____ **January 1, 2013** _____

Date	Direct Materials	Direct Labor	Overhead
January 15	$4,000.00		
January 15		$60.00	$430.00
Totals	4,000.00	60.00	430.00
Total cost			$4,490.00
Cost per unit			$0.898

Figure 7-18:
Job order cost sheet for job BRM-10.

Illustration by Wiley, Composition Services Graphics

When the products finally get sold, the cost of the products will be moved from Finished goods inventory to Cost of goods sold. Figure 7-19 illustrates the journal entry used to reflect this shift; it debits (increases) Cost of goods sold and credits (decreases) Finished goods inventory.

Date	Accounts	Debit	Credit
February 15	*Cost of goods sold*	*4,490*	
	Finished goods inventory		*4,490*

Figure 7-19:
Journal
entry to
record
the sale of
inventory.

Finished goods inventory		Cost of goods sold	
4,490		*4,490*	
	4,490		
0			

Illustration by Wiley, Composition Services Graphics

Chapter 8

Process Costing: Get In Line

*P*eople give Henry Ford credit for inventing the assembly line, which enabled him to produce thousands of identical Model T automobiles (in any color, as long as it's black, as Ford said) starting in 1908. Mass producing automobiles dramatically reduced their cost and price, making them afford-able for most families.

However, standardized production goes back much farther than Henry Ford. At the end of the 1700s, Eli Whitney started to manufacture standardized parts to make firearms, reducing costs and simplifying production. Workers no longer needed to spend time custom-fitting every part to work in each unit. If any part of one of Whitney's muskets broke, an equivalent part could easily replace it.

Today, the principles behind Whitney's standardized production and Ford's assembly line work hand-in-hand, allowing manufacturers to mass produce quality goods quickly at low cost. In modern mass production, a system called *process costing* keeps track of what was produced and how much it cost. In this chapter, I explain how companies accumulate costs in a process costing system and how they apply overhead to individual products made.

Comparing Process Costing and Job Order Costing

Some manufacturers make unique products, such as aircraft, made-to-order suits, or custom teddy bears. Others mass-produce large numbers of similar or identical items, such as soft drinks, sheets of paper, and boxes of cereal. To mass-produce products at a minimal cost, assembly lines move materials and partially finished goods from one station or department to the next until they get completed into finished goods.

Process costing handles the same types of manufacturing costs as job order costing, which I explain in Chapter 7. Both systems deal with tracking how manufacturing costs such as direct materials, direct labor, and overhead flow through work-in-process to finished goods and finally, when the goods are sold, to cost of goods sold.

As Chapter 7 describes, *job order costing* accumulates costs by job, using job order cost sheets that stay with the inventory as it flows through the production process. Process costing, on the other hand, accumulates costs by department. Process costing gives each department its own separate work-in-process (WIP) account for accumulating costs and tallies costs at the end of each fiscal period; job order costing uses only a single WIP account for all unfinished jobs and tallies the cost of a job when it's finished. Although job order costing measures the cost of each individual job, process costing measures the cost of work actually done on WIP during a period.

Unlike job order costing, which sends costs directly to individual jobs, process costing uses a two-step method:

1. Sending direct materials, direct labor, and overhead costs to departments

2. Sending the department costs to the units produced

Figure 8-1 illustrates the flow of this process.

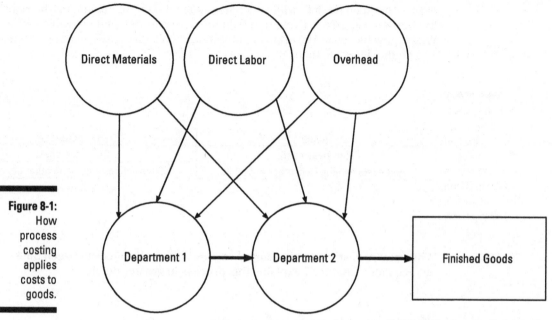

Figure 8-1:
How process costing applies costs to goods.

Keeping Process Costing Books

Before getting into the nitty-gritty of process costing, you may benefit from reviewing a few basics — namely, how to use debits and credits, how to keep track of the costs of goods that you make and sell, and how goods and their costs move through a typical production line.

Debiting and crediting

Remember that when costing goods, almost all accounts are either assets or expenses, such that in most cases, debits increase balances and credits decrease balances. Accordingly, when using T-accounts, increases go in the debit column on the left, while decreases go in the credit column on the right, as shown in Figure 8-2. (Note that liabilities, such as Accounts payable and Wages payable, go in the opposite direction. Debits decrease these accounts, and credits increase them.)

Figure 8-2:
Debits (to the left) increase, and credits (to the right) decrease.

Debits	Credits
Increase costs	Decrease costs
Add costs coming from other accounts	Subtract costs going to other accounts

Illustration by Wiley, Composition Services Graphics

When you're costing goods, journal entries transfer balances between different accounts. Chapter 7 explains this process in greater detail.

Keeping track of costs

Products have three different kinds of costs (as explained in Chapter 3):

- ✔ **Direct materials:** The cost of materials that you can easily trace to manufactured products. For example, if you're making peanut butter sandwiches, direct materials include three ounces of peanut butter and two slices of bread per sandwich.

- ✔ **Direct labor:** The cost of paying employees to make your products. Direct labor for making peanut butter sandwiches includes the cost of paying employees for the five minutes they take on average to prepare a single sandwich.

- ✔ **Overhead:** All other costs necessary to make your products. For peanut butter sandwiches, overhead includes the costs of running the kitchen, including utilities and cleaning.

Accountants need to first accumulate costs and then assign them to individual departments. The road map in Figure 8-3 shows how debits and credits steer through the accounts.

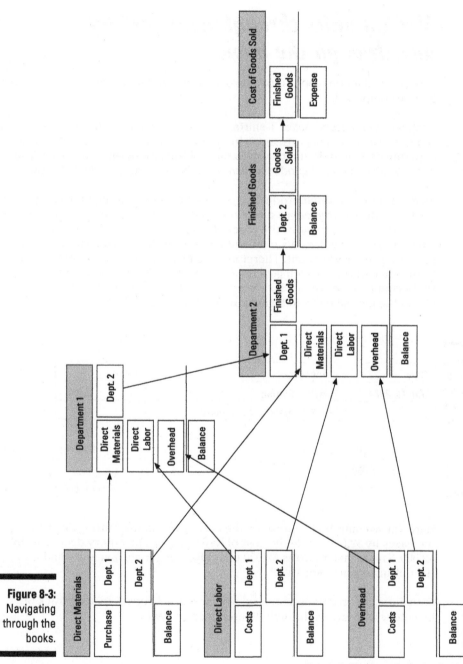

Figure 8-3:
Navigating
through the
books.

Moving units through your factory — and through the books

In mass production, goods move through different factory departments until they're completed.

Suppose your factory makes T-shirts. One department cuts the fabric and then sends it to a second department, which sews the cut pieces together. A third department then folds and packages the T-shirts into plastic bags. Then you can call the completed goods *finished goods* because they're ready for sale.

As goods move through production, their costs move through the company's books. As the factory moves direct materials into the Cutting department, use journal entries to move the cost of those direct materials out of the Raw materials inventory account and into the cutting department's work-in-process inventory account. Therefore, you debit/increase the account WIP Cutting department, which gets the direct materials, and you credit/decrease the account Raw materials inventory, which gave up the materials. Figure 8-4 shows the journal entry to transfer materials costing $2,000.

Figure 8-4:
How to transfer materials from raw materials into the Cutting department.

Date	Accounts	Debit	Credit
Jan. 10, 2013	**WIP – Cutting**	*2,000*	
	Raw materials inventory		*2,000*

WIP – Cutting		Raw materials inventory	
2,000			*2,000*

Illustration by Wiley, Composition Services Graphics

Here, the account that represents the cost of WIP in the Cutting department increases by $2,000, while the cost of Raw materials inventory decreases by $2,000. This transfer moves $2,000 out of Raw materials inventory and into the Cutting department's WIP.

From here, you continue to record similar journal entries to keep track of inventory as it moves through different departments.

Demonstrating Process Costing

Following an example of process costing in action can help you better understand the flow of the system.

Consider fictional company XYZ Computer, which manufactures inexpensive, disposable computers. Each computer unit must go through three different departments in XYZ's factory: Assembly, Testing, and Packaging. The following sections show you how XYZ uses process costing.

Buying raw materials

On February 3, XYZ purchases $100,000 worth of parts and other raw materials on account. As Figure 8-5 illustrates, debit Raw materials inventory for $100,000 and credit Accounts payable for $100,000.

Figure 8-5:
Journal entry to purchase materials.

Date	Accounts	Debit	Credit
Feb. 3, 2013	*Raw materials inventory*	*100,000*	
	Accounts payable		*100,000*

Raw materials inventory		Accounts payable	
100,000			*100,000*

Illustration by Wiley, Composition Services Graphics

The debit to Raw materials inventory increases this account. However, because Accounts payable is a liability, it carries a credit balance. Therefore, crediting Accounts payable (the amount of money that you owe to suppliers) increases the balance of this account.

Paying for direct labor

On February 28, XYZ records direct labor of $30,000 paid to employees, who worked 1,500 hours during this time. Figure 8-6 indicates the debit to Direct labor for $30,000 and credit to Cash for this amount.

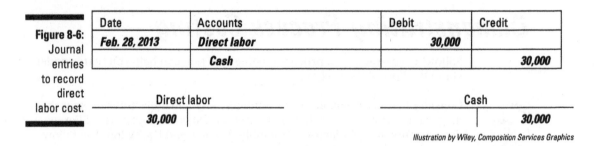

	Date	Accounts	Debit	Credit
Figure 8-6: Journal entries to record direct labor cost.	Feb. 28, 2013	Direct labor	30,000	
		Cash		30,000

Direct labor
30,000

Cash
30,000

Illustration by Wiley, Composition Services Graphics

Debiting Direct labor increases this account. Crediting Cash reduces the balance of cash on your books.

Incurring overhead

Overhead costs include all product costs except for direct materials and labor.

On February 28, XYZ pays $60,000 for overhead. Debit Overhead for $60,000 and credit Cash for this amount, as shown in Figure 8-7.

	Date	Accounts	Debit	Credit
Figure 8-7: Journal entry to record payment for overhead.	Feb. 28, 2013	Overhead	60,000	
		Cash		60,000

Overhead
60,000

Cash
60,000

Illustration by Wiley, Composition Services Graphics

Moving raw materials into production

Each department has its own WIP account to accumulate the costs of products being worked on in that department. (Check out the earlier section "Comparing Process Costing and Job Order Costing" for info on WIP.)

On February 5, XYZ employees move direct materials, consisting of raw materials and parts costing $60,000, out of storage and into the Assembly department. Another $10,000 goes to the Testing department and $5,000 to

Packaging. Figure 8-8 illustrates the journal entry: Debit each department's WIP account for the amount transferred, and credit Raw materials inventory for the total of $75,000.

Date	Accounts	Debit	Credit
Feb. 5, 2013	*WIP – Assembly*	*60,000*	
	WIP – Testing	*10,000*	
	WIP – Finishing	*5,000*	
	Raw materials inventory		*75,000*

Figure 8-8:
Journal
entry to
move mate-
rials into
the depart-
ments.

WIP – Assembly department	
60,000	

WIP – Testing department	
10,000	

WIP – Finishing department	
5,000	

Raw materials inventory	
100,000	*75,000*
25,000	

Illustration by Wiley, Composition Services Graphics

Remember that the company previously added $100,000 worth of direct materials and parts to its Raw materials inventory account. After this transfer, the company has $25,000 worth of raw materials remaining in its warehouse.

Using direct labor

In addition to direct materials, companies also have to keep track of direct labor and overhead costs. For direct labor, they keep track of how many hours are worked in each department and then allocate direct labor costs in proportion to the hours worked. As I indicate in "Paying for direct labor," XYZ paid direct labor costs of $30,000 to its employees, who worked 1,500 hours. These employees worked 900 hours in the Assembly department, 400 hours in the Testing department, and 200 hours in the Finishing department.

You figure that employees in this factory earn an average of $20 per hour ($30,000 ÷ 1,500 hours). Therefore, you assign the Assembly department direct labor costs of $18,000 (900 hours × $20 per hour). You assign the Testing department $8,000 (400 hours × $20 per hour) and the Finishing department $4,000 (200 hours × $20 per hour).

Figure 8-9 illustrates the journal entry: Debit each department's WIP account for the amount of direct labor allocated to it, and credit the account direct labor for the total $30,000.

Date	Accounts	Debit	Credit
Feb. 28 , 2013	WIP – Assembly	18 ,000	
	WIP – Testing	8,000	
	WIP – Finishing	4,000	
	Direct labor		30 ,000

Figure 8-9:
Journal entry to move the cost of direct labor into the departments.

WIP – Assembly
60 ,000
18,000

WIP – Testing
10,000
8,000

WIP – Finishing
5,000
4,000

Direct labor
30,000 | 30,000
0

Illustration by Wiley, Composition Services Graphics

This journal entry shifts all the direct labor costs — $30,000 — out of the direct labor account and into the individual departments where employees did the work.

Allocating overhead

Overhead consists of indirect materials, indirect labor, and other manufacturing costs that are difficult to trace to manufactured products. As Chapter 6 explains, you can use the following four-step process to allocate overhead:

1. **Add up estimated overhead.**

    XYZ Computer expects to incur $60,000 worth of overhead during the period (refer to "Incurring overhead" earlier in the chapter).

2. Identify cost drivers.

XYZ managers allocate overhead based on just one cost driver: the number of direct labor hours expected to be worked. In this example, employees are expected to work 1,500 hours. You can read about cost drivers in Chapter 5.

3. Compute overhead allocation rates.

Because XYZ has one cost driver, it needs only one overhead allocation rate. To compute this rate, divide estimated overhead ($60,000) by the total activity level of the cost driver (1,500 hours):

$$\text{Overhead allocation rate} = \frac{\text{Estimated overhead}}{\text{Cost driver activity level}}$$

$$= \frac{\$60,000}{1,500} = \$40.00$$

XYZ assigns $40 worth of overhead for every hour worked.

4. Apply overhead.

To figure out how much overhead goes to each department, multiply the overhead allocation rate by each department's direct labor hours, as shown in Figure 8-10.

Figure 8-10:
Applying overhead to individual departments.

Department	Direct Labor	Overhead Allocation Rate	Overhead Allocated
Assembly	900 hours	$40 per hour	$36,000
Testing	400 hours	40 per hour	16,000
Finishing	200 hours	40 per hour	8,000
Total			**$60,000**

Illustration by Wiley, Composition Services Graphics

For XYZ's departments, the more direct labor hours worked, the greater the share of overhead. Assembly gets hit with $36,000 worth of overhead, while Testing gets $16,000. The Finishing department gets $8,000 worth of overhead. Note that the total overhead allocated equals XYZ's estimated overhead incurred, or $60,000.

The journal entry to record this allocation, shown in Figure 8-11, debits each department's WIP account for its share of overhead and credits the account Overhead for the total of $60,000.

Date	Accounts	Debit	Credit
Feb. 28, 2013	*WIP – Assembly*	*36,000*	
	WIP – Testing	*16,000*	
	WIP – Finishing	*8,000*	
	Overhead		*60,000*

Figure 8-11: Journal entry to allocate overhead to the departments.

WIP – Assembly

60,000	
18,000	
36,000	

WIP – Finishing

5,000	
4,000	
8,000	

WIP – Testing

10,000	
8,000	
16,000	

Overhead

60,000	*60,000*
0	

Illustration by Wiley, Composition Services Graphics

This journal entry shifts $60,000 worth of overhead out of the Overhead account and into the individual departments that, in theory, benefited from it.

As Chapter 6 explains, companies that use activity-based costing apply the four steps just like XYZ does, except that they identify more than one cost driver and multiple overhead allocation rates.

Moving goods through the departments

After each department finishes working on its goods, the goods move on to the next department, ready for the next process. For the accountants, this shift requires preparing journal entries that move the goods from one department to the next.

Suppose XYZ's Assembly department sends goods costing $100,000 to the Testing department. Figure 8-12 provides the journal entry to record this transfer, reducing WIP in the Assembly department by $100,000 and increasing WIP in the Testing department by this amount.

Date	Accounts	Debit	Credit
Feb. 28, 2013	WIP – Testing	100,000	
	WIP – Assembly		100,000

Figure 8-12:
Journal entry to transfer goods from the Assembly department to the Testing department.

WIP– Assembly		WIP – Testing	
60,000	100,000	10,000	
18,000		8,000	
36,000		16,000	
		100,000	

Illustration by Wiley, Composition Services Graphics

Next, the Testing department sends goods costing $120,000 to the Finishing department. Figure 8-13 shows the journal entry to record this transfer, reducing the Testing department's WIP by $120,000 and increasing the Finishing department's WIP by $120,000.

Date	Accounts	Debit	Credit
Feb. 28, 2013	WIP – Finishing	120,000	
	WIP – Testing		120,000

Figure 8-13:
Journal entry to transfer goods from the Testing department to the Finishing department.

WIP – Testing		WIP – Finishing	
10,000	120,000	5,000	
8,000		4,000	
16,000		8,000	
100,000		120,000	

Illustration by Wiley, Composition Services Graphics

Finally, the Finishing department completes production of $110,000 worth of goods. The journal entry to record this completion, shown in Figure 8-14, moves $110,000 out of the WIP – Finishing account and into Finished goods inventory.

The total cost of each unit increases as the unit moves through the production process and accumulates more costs. However, total costs vary as the products move from one department to the next depending on how many units get transferred. That's why the Finishing department receives $120,000 worth of goods but transfers out only $110,000 worth of goods. This department's input of units must have exceeded its output.

Date	Accounts	Debit	Credit
Feb. 28, 2013	Finished goods inventory	110,000	
	WIP — Finishing		110,000

Figure 8-14: Journal entry for the Finishing department to complete goods.

WIP – Finishing

5,000	110,000
4,000	
8,000	
120,000	

Finished goods inventory

110,000	

Illustration by Wiley, Composition Services Graphics

Last but not least, the company needs to sell goods. Say XYZ sells computers that cost the company $90,000 to make for $130,000. XYZ records two entries, as shown in Figure 8-15. The first entry records the sale, debiting and increasing cash by $130,000 and crediting and increasing Sales revenue for the same amount. The second entry transfers the cost of the goods from the Finished goods inventory account to the Cost of goods sold account, so that it can be reported as an expense on the income statement.

Date	Accounts	Debit	Credit
Feb. 28, 2013	Cash	130,000	
	Sales revenue		130,000
	Cost of goods sold	90,000	
	Finished goods inventory		90,000

Figure 8-15: Journal entries to sell goods.

Cash			Sales revenue	
130,000				130,000
Cost of goods sold			Finished goods inventory	
90,000			110,000	90,000

Illustration by Wiley, Composition Services Graphics

The road map in Figure 8-16 illustrates how costs start in direct materials, direct labor, and overhead and then flow through the departments until they complete production and get sold.

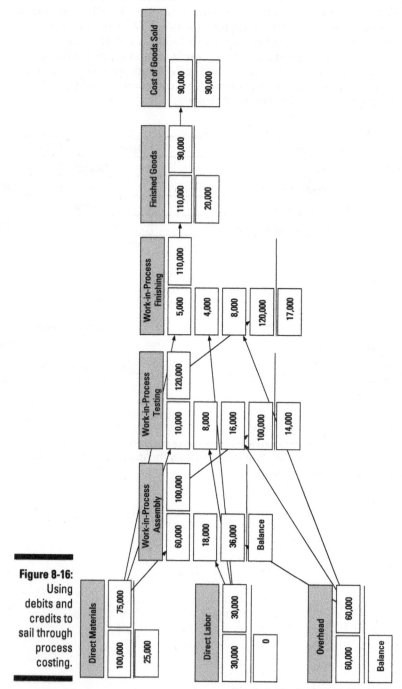

Figure 8-16:
Using debits and credits to sail through process costing.

Illustration by Wiley, Composition Services Graphics

Preparing a Cost of Production Report

Have you ever seen the circus clown trick where seemingly dozens of full-sized clowns climb into an unbelievably small car? They close the door and then drive around. You look carefully but don't see any hole in the floor under the car. Where did the clowns go? Clowns don't disappear.

Lucky for you, managerial accounting doesn't work this way. Inventory that comes into a production department must do one of two things: stay in the department or, when complete, move on to the next department. The same holds true for the cost of inventory: Costs must either stay in a department or move on to the next. To keep track of units and costs, managerial accounting uses a four-part document called the *cost of production report.*

Here's how the cost of production report breaks down:

- ✔ **Part 1: Units to account for.** Each department needs to account for the number of units that it was given responsibility for, including units in beginning WIP and units transferred in.

- ✔ **Part 2: Units accounted for.** Each department needs to explain what it did with the units listed in Part 1. How many units were transferred out? How many units remain in ending WIP? The total units to account for in Part 1 must equal the total units accounted for in Part 2.

- ✔ **Part 3: Costs to account for.** Each department then must account for the total cost of its units. *Costs to account for* includes the cost of beginning WIP and the cost of units transferred in.

- ✔ **Part 4: Costs accounted for.** Finally, each department must show what happened to the costs that it was given responsibility for (in Part 3). These costs either get transferred out or remain in ending WIP.

Part 1: Units to account for

The cost of production report first accounts for the number of units in the department's beginning WIP and transferred into the department during the period.

Suppose a toy factory makes clowns. The Balloon department attaches a set of balloons to each clown and then sends the units over to the next department, which, I suppose, pops the balloons.

The Balloon department started the month of April with 200 clowns, all WIP in need of balloons. During April, it received 2,500 clowns from direct materials. (The company buys these from a factory in China.) That means that the Balloon department had 2,700 units to account for:

$$\text{Units to account for} = \text{Beginning work-in-process units} + \text{Units started}$$
$$= 200 + 2,500$$
$$= 2,700$$

Part 2: Units accounted for

The second part of the report accounts for the units that the first part indicates the department is responsible for. During April, the Balloon department finished working on 1,900 clowns, sending them to the next department. At the end of April, the Balloon folks still had 800 clowns of WIP on the assembly line, waiting for their balloons. This progress means that the Balloon department has accounted for 2,700 units:

$$\text{Units accounted for} = \text{Units completed} + \text{Ending work-in-process units}$$
$$= 1,900 + 800$$
$$= 2,700$$

The number of units to account for must equal the number of units accounted for. This is a factory, not a circus.

To measure how much work each WIP department did, accountants use the term *equivalent units*. Equivalent units sum up the fractions of units actually completed. For example, if a department got halfway through two separate units, it would count that work as one equivalent unit.

I know what you're thinking: What's the difference? Suppose an assembly line has 24 toys that are 50 percent complete. Everywhere else in this book, these half-done toys count as 24 units because they'll eventually be sold as 24 toys. However, 24 toys that are only 50 percent complete comprise 12 equivalent units because that measure represents the amount of work that each WIP department actually did. They got 50 percent of the way through 24 units, which comes out to 12 equivalent units.

To compute the number of equivalent units of production, just add the total number of units completed and transferred out to the number of equivalent units of ending WIP:

$$\text{Equivalent units of production} = \text{Units completed} + \left(\begin{array}{c} \text{Units in ending} \\ \text{work-in-process} \end{array} \times \begin{array}{c} \text{Percentage} \\ \text{complete} \end{array} \right)$$

For example, suppose that the Theresa Toy Factory Assembly department made and finished 100 rubber ducks. As shown in Figure 8-17, it also had 30 units still in process left over at the end of the period, all half complete. These unfinished ducks equal 15 equivalent units (30 units × 0.5 complete). The total equivalent units of production equal 115:

$$\text{Equivalent units of production} = \text{Units completed} + \left(\begin{array}{c} \text{Units in ending} \\ \text{work-in-process} \end{array} \times \begin{array}{c} \text{Percentage} \\ \text{complete} \end{array} \right)$$
$$= 100 + (30 \times 50\%)$$
$$= 115$$

100 Completed Units:

30 Units, each 50% complete:

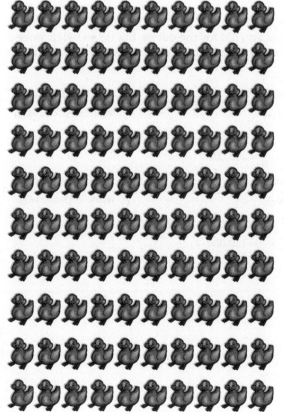

15 equivalent units (30 x 50%)

Figure 8-17:
Theresa Toy
Factory's
duck output.

Illustration by Wiley, Composition Services Graphics

You can also apply the equivalent units concept to direct labor and overhead costs. These costs are sometimes referred to as *conversion costs* because they're the costs of converting direct materials into finished goods.

The degree of completion with respect to direct materials may differ from conversion costs because direct materials usually get added at the beginning of the production process, whereas conversion costs get added throughout the production process. For example, maybe your inventory is 100 percent complete with respect to direct materials (because all the materials have been added) but only, say, 10 percent complete with respect to conversion costs. Therefore, the same inventory may actually have two different equivalent units of production: one for direct materials and another for conversion costs.

Now think about another example. The Turbo Paper Clip Company's Bending department bends paper clips into their proper shape. The Bending department transferred 100,000 completely bent paper clips into the Boxing department. At the end of the period, Bending had 40,000 units of WIP on hand that were 100 percent complete with respect to direct materials, but only 25 percent complete with respect to conversion costs.

To compute the equivalent units produced by the Bending department, apply the same formula as you did for the ducks, but do so twice: once for direct materials and a second time for conversion costs, as shown in Figure 8-18.

$$\text{Equivalent units of production}_{DM} = \text{Units completed}_{DM} + \left(\text{Units in ending work-in-process}_{DM} \times \text{Percentage complete}_{DM} \right)$$

$$= 100,000 + (40,000 \times 100\%)$$
$$= 140,000$$

$$\text{Equivalent units of production}_{CC} = \text{Units completed}_{CC} + \left(\text{Units in ending work-in-process}_{CC} \times \text{Percentage complete}_{CC} \right)$$

$$= 100,000 + (40,000 \times 25\%)$$
$$= 110,000$$

Figure 8-18:
Separate
equivalent
units for
direct mate-
rials and
conversion
costs.

	Equivalent Units	
	Direct Materials	**Conversion Costs**
Units transferred out	100,000	100,000
WIP at the end of the period:		
40,000 units x 100%	40,000	
40,000 units x 25%		10,000
Total equivalent units	140,000	110,000

Illustration by Wiley, Composition Services Graphics

Part 3: Costs to account for

In Part 3, you determine the total costs that were assigned to the department, including the cost of any beginning inventory; the cost of goods transferred from other departments; and any direct materials, direct labor, and overhead assigned directly to the department. You divide these total costs by the number of equivalent units the department produces to compute the cost per equivalent unit.

Adding up total costs

Consider the clown factory I discuss earlier in the chapter. The Balloon department started April with 200 units of beginning WIP, which cost $400 for direct materials. Another $5,000 worth of direct materials costs went into the department during April. Total direct materials costs equal $5,400.

The Balloon department's beginning WIP had $600 worth of conversion costs. Another $7,500 worth of conversion costs were allocated to the department during April, so total conversion costs came to $8,100.

As Figure 8-19 illustrates, total costs to account for are $13,500.

Figure 8-19:
Total costs
to account
for in the
Balloon
department.

	Direct Materials	**Conversion Costs**	**Total**
Beginning WIP	$400	$600	$1,000
Added during April	5,000	7,500	12,500
Costs to account for	$5,400	$8,100	$13,500

Illustration by Wiley, Composition Services Graphics

Dividing by equivalent units to get cost per equivalent unit

To determine the cost per equivalent unit, divide total cost by the number of equivalent units, with respect to both direct materials and conversion costs:

$$\text{Cost per equivalent unit} = \frac{\text{Total cost}}{\text{Number of equivalent units}}$$

During April, the Balloon department finished 1,900 clowns and sent them to the next department (refer to "Part 2: Units accounted for" for details). At the end of April, 800 clowns remained on the Balloon department's assembly line. These clowns were 62.5 percent complete with respect to direct materials and 32.5 percent complete with respect to conversion costs.

To find the number of equivalent units, add the number of completed units transferred out to the number of equivalent units remaining in WIP at the end of the month. As Figure 8-20 shows, the Balloon department made 2,400 equivalent units with respect to direct materials and 2,160 equivalent units with respect to conversion costs.

	Equivalent Units	
	Direct Materials	**Conversion Costs**
Units transferred out	1,900	1,900
WIP at the end of the period:		
800 units x 62.5%	500	
800 units x 32.5%		260
Total equivalent units	2,400	2,160

Figure 8-20: Separate equivalent units for direct materials and conversion costs.

Illustration by Wiley, Composition Services Graphics

Finally, to figure out the equivalent cost per unit, divide total cost by total equivalent units. Direct materials cost $2.25 per equivalent unit ($5,400 ÷ 2,400 units). Conversion costs came to $3.75 per equivalent unit ($8,100 ÷ 2,160 units), so total cost per equivalent unit is $6.

Part 4: Costs accounted for

Part 4 requires you to compute the *costs accounted for,* also called the *cost reconciliation schedule.* This schedule computes the cost of goods transferred out (based on the number of units transferred out times the cost per equivalent unit calculated in Part 3) plus the cost of WIP inventory remaining in the department at the end of the month.

The preceding section establishes that $13,500 worth of costs went into the Balloon department (refer to Figure 8-19). For your last and final trick, you have to prove that those $13,500 worth of costs either remain in the Balloon department or have moved on to the next department. Just follow these steps:

1. **Find the total cost of the units transferred out.**

   In this example, 1,900 units were transferred out of the Balloon department during April. Because these had a cost of $6 per equivalent unit, the total cost of these units comes to $11,400.

2. **Compute the separate costs of WIP for direct materials and for conversion costs.**

   With respect to direct materials, the Balloon department had 500 equivalent units of WIP at the end of April. These equivalent units cost $2.25 each, so the total cost of WIP at the end of April comes to $1,125.

   For conversion costs, the Balloon department had 260 equivalent units of WIP left over at the end of April. These equivalent units cost $3.75 each, so their total cost comes to $975. This amount, added to the cost of direct materials WIP above of $1,125, gives you total WIP of $2,100.

3. **Add the total cost of units transferred out to the cost of WIP.**

   As explained in Step 1, the department transferred costs of $11,400 to the next department. Furthermore, another $2,100 worth of costs remain in the department with WIP. Therefore, total costs accounted for (the sum of these figures) amounts to $13,500.

   Figure 8-21 demonstrates this step for the Balloon department.

Figure 8-22 provides a complete cost of production report that accounts for all the Balloon department's units and costs.

Costs transferred out (1,900 units x $6.00)		$11,400
Ending WIP		
Direct materials (500 units x $2.25)	$1,125	
Conversion costs (260 equivalent units x $3.75)	975	2,100
Costs accounted for		$13,500

Figure 8-21: Total costs accounted for.

Ballon Department
Cost of Production Report
April 2014

	Physical Units	Direct Materials	Conversion
Units to account for			
Beginning work-in-process (WIP)	200		
Units tranferred in	2,500		
Total units to account for	2,700		
Units accounted for			
Units completed and tranferred out	1,900	1,900	1,900
Ending work-in-process (WIP)			
Total units	800		
Equivalent units of direct materials			
(800 units x 62.5%)		500	
Equivalent units of conversion costs			
(800 units x 32.5%)			260
Total units accounted for	2,700	2,400	2,160

		Direct Materials	Coversion Costs	Total Costs
Costs to account for				
Beginning work-in-process (WIP)		$ 400	$ 600	$ 1,000
Added during April		5,000	7,500	12,500
Total costs to account for	(A) $	5,400	$ 8,100	$ 13,500
Number of equivalent units (from above)	(B)	2,400	2,160	
Cost per equivalent unit	(A)/(B) $	2.25	$ 3.75	$ 6.00

Costs accounted for
Cost of goods completed and transferred out
    (1900 units x $6.00) $ 11,400
Cost of ending work-in-process (WIP)
    Direct materials
        (480 units x $2.25) $ 1,125
    Conversion costs
        (320 units x $3.75) $ 975   2,100
Total costs accounted for $ 13,500

Figure 8-22:
Completed
cost of
production
report.

Illustration by Wiley, Composition Services Graphics

Part III
Using Costing Techniques for Decision-Making

The 5th Wave   By Rich Tennant

"We're using just-in-time inventory and just-in-time material flows, which have saved us from implementing our just-in-time bankruptcy plan."

In this part . . .

The costing techniques from Part II come into play in this part, where you see how to use them in order to make management decisions. You first need to understand contribution margin because it provides key insights into how specific transactions affect sales. Contribution margin helps you compute how much you need in sales to break even or achieve a target level of profit.

I also explain how to decide whether to invest in long-term assets, using time value of money techniques. I discuss using contribution margin techniques when you make more than one product; this analysis helps you to decide how much of each product you should make. Next, I explore setting prices and describe transfer pricing techniques that encourage different divisions of a company to work together.

Chapter 9

Straight to the Bottom Line: Examining Contribution Margin

Consider the following exchange:

"I've got a million-dollar idea. Everybody wants a Rolls Royce, but no one wants to pay for a Rolls Royce, right?"

"Yeah. They're way too expensive."

"Okay, here's my idea: I'm going to sell Rolls Royces but at a price that people can afford: just $999.95."

"But making a Rolls Royce costs a lot of money. How will you ever earn a profit?"

"Who cares? At these prices, I can sell so many cars, I'll make it up in volume."

As this discussion shows, when you have to make a business decision about what to sell, how much of it to sell, or how much to charge, you first need to understand how your decision will affect net income, which is your profit. Suppose you sell one Rolls Royce for $999.95. How does that sale affect your net income? Now suppose you sell 1,000 Rolls Royce cars at this price. How does that sales volume affect net income?

Contribution margin simplifies these decisions. In this chapter, I show you how to calculate contribution margin and how to apply it to different business decisions, using both graphs and formulas. I describe how to prepare something called a *cost-volume-profit analysis,* which explains how the number of products sold affects profits. I demonstrate how to prepare a *break-even analysis,* which indicates exactly how many products you must sell in order to break even and start earning a profit.

Suppose you set a *target profit,* a goal for net income this period. In this chapter, I show you how to estimate the number of units you need to sell in order to meet your target profit. I also explain how to measure something called *margin of safety,* or how many sales you can afford to lose before your profitability drops to zero. Finally, I explain and demonstrate *operating leverage,* which measures a company's riskiness.

Computing Contribution Margin

Contribution margin measures how sales affects net income or profits. To compute contribution margin, subtract variable costs of a sale from the amount of the sale itself:

Contribution margin = Sales – Variable costs

For example, if you sell a gadget for $10 and its variable cost is $6, the contribution margin for the sale would be $4 ($10 – $6 = $4). Selling this gadget would increase your profit by $4.

When computing contribution margin, subtract all variable costs, including variable manufacturing costs and variable selling, general, and administrative costs. Don't subtract any fixed costs. As I explain in Chapter 2, you compute gross profit by subtracting cost of goods sold from sales. Because cost of goods sold usually includes a mixture of fixed and variable costs, gross profit doesn't equal contribution margin.

You can calculate contribution margin in three forms, which I discuss in the following sections:

- ✔ In total
- ✔ Per unit
- ✔ As a ratio

Contribution margin, in any of its forms, explains how different factors in the company — sales price, sales volume, variable costs, and fixed costs — interact. This understanding helps you make better decisions when planning sales and costs.

Figuring total contribution margin

Total contribution margin measures the amount of contribution margin earned by the company as a whole. You calculate it by using this formula:

Total contribution margin = Total sales – Total variable costs

To determine overall profitability, compare total contribution margin to fixed costs. Net income equals the excess of contribution margin over fixed costs.

You can use total contribution margin to create something called a *contribution margin income statement.* This document is different from a multi-step income statement (shown in Figure 9-1), where you first subtract cost of goods sold from sales and then subtract selling, general, and administrative costs.

Sales	$1,000
Less: Cost of goods sold	600
Gross profit	400
Less: Selling, general, and administrative expenses	100
Operating income	300
Less: Provision for income taxes	100
Net income	$200

Figure 9-1:
Multi-step income statement.

Illustration by Wiley, Composition Services Graphics

A contribution margin income statement first subtracts the variable costs and then subtracts fixed costs, as shown in Figure 9-2. Here, variable costs include variable costs of both manufacturing and selling. Likewise, fixed costs include more manufacturing and selling costs.

Sales	$1,000
Less: Variable costs	400
Contribution margin	600
Less: Fixed costs	300
Operating income	300
Less: Provision for income taxes	100
Net income	$200

Figure 9-2:
Contribution margin income statement.

Illustration by Wiley, Composition Services Graphics

The contribution margin income statement makes understanding cost behavior and how sales will affect profitability easier. In Figure 9-2, the company earned $1,000 in sales, $400 of which went toward variable costs. This scenario resulted in $600 of contribution margin.

These amounts — sales, variable costs, and contribution margin — change in proportion to each other. If sales were to increase by 10 percent, then variable costs and contribution margin would also increase by 10 percent; $1,100 in sales would increase variable costs to $440 and contribution margin to $660. On the other hand, fixed costs always remain the same: The $300 in fixed costs will be $300 regardless of any increase or decrease in sales and contribution margin.

The contribution margin income statement presents the same net income figure as a traditional income statement. However, the contribution margin income statement is not in accordance with *Generally Accepted Accounting Principles* (GAAP), the set of rules companies must use for external reporting. Managers can internally use a contribution margin income statement to better understand their own companies' operations.

Calculating contribution margin per unit

Contribution margin per unit measures how the sale of one additional unit would affect net income. You calculate it by subtracting variable costs per unit from sales price per unit, as in this formula:

Contribution margin per unit = Sales price per unit – Variable costs per unit

Say a company sells a single gadget for $100, and the variable cost of making the gadget is $40. Contribution margin per unit on this gadget equals $60 (100 – 40 = 60). Therefore, selling the gadget increases net income by $60.

Increasing the sales price doesn't affect variable costs because the number of units manufactured, not the sales price, is what usually drives variable manufacturing costs. Therefore, if the gadget company raises its sales price to $105, the variable cost of making the gadget remains at $40, and the contribution per unit increases to $65 per unit ($105 – $40 = $65). The $5 increase in sales price goes straight to the bottom line as net income.

Working out contribution margin ratio

Contribution margin ratio measures the percentage of sales that would increase net income. To calculate it, divide contribution margin by sales, either in total or per unit:

$$\text{Contribution margin ratio} = \frac{\text{Total contribution margin}}{\text{Total sales}}$$

or

$$\text{Contribution margin ratio} = \frac{\text{Contribution margin per unit}}{\text{Sales price per unit}}$$

Suppose a gadget selling for $100 per unit brings in $40 per unit of contribution margin. Its contribution margin ratio is 40 percent:

$$\text{Contribution margin ratio} = \frac{40}{100} = 40\%$$

To find out how sales affect net income, multiply the contribution margin ratio by the amount of sales. In this example, $1,000 in gadget sales increases net income by $400 ($1,000 × 40 percent = $400).

Preparing a Cost-Volume-Profit Analysis

Contribution margin indicates how sales affects profitability. When running a business, a decision-maker needs to consider how four different factors affect net income:

- Sales price
- Sales volume
- Variable cost
- Fixed cost

Cost-volume-profit analysis helps you understand different ways to meet your net income goals. In the following sections, I explain cost-volume-profit analysis by using graphical and formula techniques. I pay special attention to computing net income based on different measures of contribution margin: total contribution margin, contribution margin per unit, and the contribution margin ratio.

The graphs provide a helpful way to visualize the relationship among cost, volume, and profit. However, when solving problems, you'll find that plugging numbers into formulas is much quicker and easier.

Drafting a cost-volume-profit graph

Figure 9-3 visually describes the relationship among cost, volume, and profit.

Pemulis Basketballs sells basketballs for $15 each. The variable cost per unit of the basketballs is $6. Pemulis had total fixed costs of $300 per year.

In this figure, fixed costs are represented by a horizontal line because no matter the sales volume, fixed costs stay the same. Total variable costs are a diagonal line, starting at the origin (the point in the lower-left corner of the graph where there are zero sales). Total costs (the sum of total variable costs and total fixed costs) are a diagonal line starting at the $300 mark because when the company makes and sells zero units, total costs equal the fixed costs of $300. Total costs then increase with volume. Finally, total sales forms a diagonal line starting at the origin and increasing with sales volume.

Figure 9-4 shows when the company will earn net income or incur a loss. When the sales curve exceeds total costs, the company earns net income (represented by the shaded right side of the X in Figure 9-4). However, if total sales is too low to exceed total costs, then the company incurs a net loss (the shaded left side of the X). The higher the sales volume — that is, the more sales volume moves to the right of the graph — the higher the company's net income.

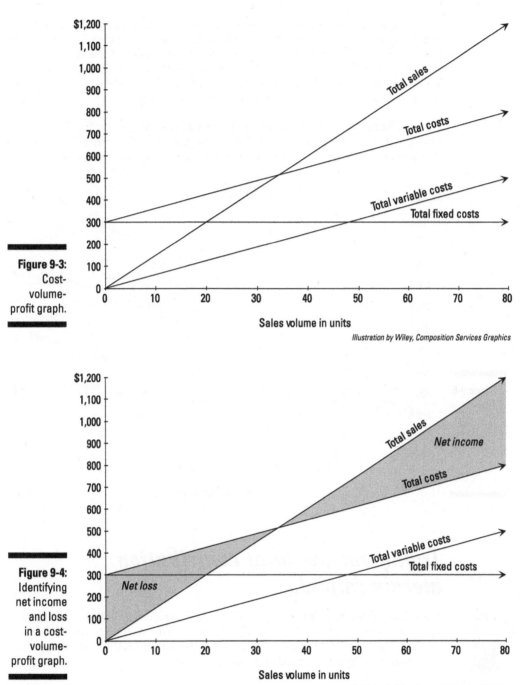

Figure 9-3:
Cost-
volume-
profit graph.

Sales volume in units

Illustration by Wiley, Composition Services Graphics

Figure 9-4:
Identifying
net income
and loss
in a cost-
volume-
profit graph.

Sales volume in units

Illustration by Wiley, Composition Services Graphics

Dropping numbers into the chart shows exactly how much income can be earned at different sales levels. Assuming Pemulis has a sales price of $15 per unit, a variable cost per unit of $6, and total fixed costs of $300, what happens if Pemulis sells 60 basketballs? Total sales come to $900 (60 units × $15). Total variable costs multiply to $360 (60 units × $6). Add these total variable costs to total fixed costs of $300 to get total costs of $660.

Figure 9-5 illustrates these amounts. Total sales ($900) sits on the Total sales line. Total costs ($660) sits on the Total cost line. The difference between these amounts ($240) represents the net income from selling 60 units.

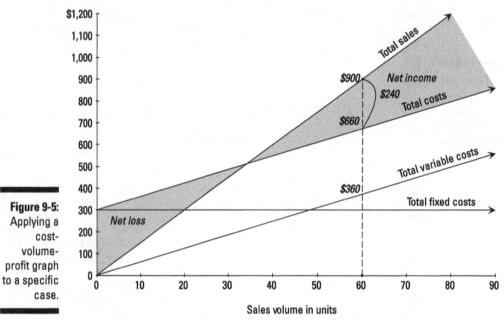

Figure 9-5: Applying a cost-volume-profit graph to a specific case.

Illustration by Wiley, Composition Services Graphics

Trying out the total contribution margin formula

The following formula, based on total contribution margin, follows the same structure as the contribution margin income statement. (Flip to the earlier section "Figuring total contribution margin" for details on total contribution margin and its related income statement.)

Net income = Total contribution margin − Fixed costs

Assume that Pemulis Basketballs sells 60 units for $15 each for total sales of $900 (see the preceding section for more on the origins of this example). The variable cost of each unit is $6 (so total variable costs come to $6 × 60, or $360), and total fixed costs are $300. Using the contribution margin approach, you can find the net income in two easy steps:

1. **Calculate total contribution margin.**

   Use the formula that I provide earlier in the chapter to compute total contribution margin, subtracting total variable costs from total sales:

   Total contribution margin = Total sales − Total variable costs
   $$= (60 \times \$15) - (60 \times \$6)$$
   $$= \$540$$

   This total contribution margin figure indicates that selling 60 units increases net income by $540.

2. **To calculate net income, subtract the fixed costs from the total contribution margin.**

   Just plug in the numbers from Step 1:

   Net income = Total contribution margin − Fixed costs
   $$= \$540 - \$300$$
   $$= \$240$$

   Subtracting fixed costs of $300 from total contribution margin of $540 gives you net income of $240.

Practicing the contribution margin per unit formula

If you know the contribution margin per unit (which I cover in "Calculating contribution margin per unit" earlier in the chapter), the following approach lets you use that information to compute net income. Here's the basic formula equating net income with contribution margin per unit:

Net income = (Sales volume × Contribution margin per unit) − Fixed costs

Say Pemulis Basketballs now wants to use this formula. It can simply plug in the numbers — 60 units sold for $15 each, variable cost of $6 per unit, fixed costs of $300 — and solve. First compute the contribution margin per unit:

$$\text{Contribution margin per unit} = \text{Sales price per unit} - \text{Variable costs per unit}$$
$$= \$15 - \$6$$
$$= \$9$$

Next, plug contribution margin per unit into the net income formula to figure out net income:

$$\text{Net income} = (\text{Sales volume} \times \text{Contribution margin per unit}) - \text{Fixed costs}$$
$$= (60 \times \$9) - \$300$$
$$= \$240$$

Eyeing the contribution margin ratio formula

If you want to estimate net income but don't know total contribution margin and can't find out the contribution margin per unit, you can use the contribution margin ratio to compute net income.

As I note in the earlier section "Working out contribution margin ratio," you can compute contribution margin ratio by dividing total contribution margin by total sales. So if your contribution margin is 540 and your sales is 900, your contribution margin ratio is 60 percent:

$$\text{Contribution margin ratio} = \frac{\text{Total contribution margin}}{\text{Total sales}} = \frac{\text{Contribution margin per unit}}{\text{Sales price per unit}}$$
$$= \frac{540}{900} = 60\%$$

This means that 60 cents of every sales dollar directly increases net income. After you know the contribution margin ratio, you're ready for the net income formula:

$$\text{Net income} = (\text{Sales} \times \text{Contribution margin ratio}) - \text{Fixed costs}$$

To calculate net income for the earlier example company, plug the contribution margin ratio of 60 percent into the formula:

$$\text{Net income} = (\text{Sales} \times \text{Contribution margin ratio}) - \text{Fixed costs}$$
$$= (\$900 \times 60\%) - \$300$$
$$= \$240$$

Generating a Break-Even Analysis

How much do you need to sell in order to break even? The *break-even point* (BE) is the amount of sales needed to earn zero profit — enough sales so that you don't earn a loss, but insufficient sales to earn a profit. In this section, I look at a couple of different ways — graphs and formulas — to analyze where your break-even point falls.

Drawing a graph to find the break-even point

In a cost-volume-profit graph, the break-even point is the sales volume where the total sales line intersects with the total costs line. This sales volume is the point at which total sales equals total costs.

Suppose that, as with the basketball example earlier in the chapter, a company sells its products for $15 each, with variable costs of $6 per unit and total fixed costs of $300. The graph in Figure 9-6 indicates that the company's break-even point occurs when the company sells 34 units.

For many products (like basketballs) you can only sell whole units. Therefore, if you sell whole units, the break-even point must always be a whole number. This fact means that if break-even analysis results in some fractional volume of sales (such as 33.33333 units), you should always round *up* (in this case, to 34 units), even if the fraction is closer to the lower whole number than the higher number. If your break-even point equals 33.0001, round it up to 34. If you rounded down (to 33 units), then the actual sales volume would be below the break-even point, and at this volume level, your company would report a net loss.

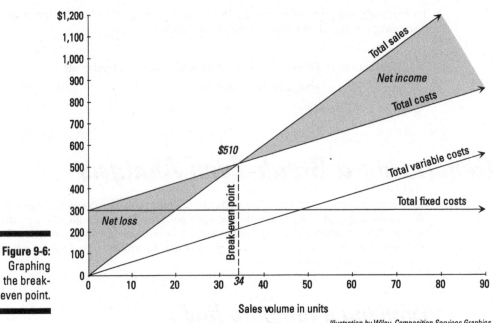

Figure 9-6:
Graphing
the break-
even point.

Employing the formula approach

When you need to solve actual problems, drawing graphs isn't always practical. In that case, you want to rely on the three formulas that use contribution margin to measure net income. (I lay out these formulas in "Preparing a Cost-Volume-Profit Analysis" earlier in the chapter.)

The break-even point is where net income is zero, so just set net income equal to zero, plug whatever given information you have into one of the equations, and then solve for sales or sales volume. Better yet: At the break-even point, total contribution margin equals fixed costs.

Suppose a company has $30,000 in fixed costs. How much total contribution margin does it have to generate in order to break even?

$$\text{Net income} = \text{Total contribution margin} - \text{Fixed costs}$$
$$0 = \text{Total contribution margin}_{BE} - \text{Fixed costs}$$
$$0 = \text{Total contribution margin}_{BE} - \$30{,}000$$
$$\$30{,}000 = \text{Total contribution margin}_{BE}$$

Here, too, at the break-even point, total contribution margin equals fixed costs of $30,000. Now suppose a company has contribution margin per unit of $6 and fixed costs of $600. What's the break-even point in units?

$$\text{Net income} = (\text{Sales volume} \times \text{Contribution margin per unit}) - \text{Fixed costs}$$
$$0 = (\text{Sales volume}_{BE} \times \text{Contribution margin per unit}) - \text{Fixed costs}$$
$$0 = (\text{Sales volume}_{BE} \times \$6) - \$600$$
$$\frac{\$600}{\$6} = \text{Sales volume}_{BE}$$
$$100 \text{ units} = \text{Sales volume}_{BE}$$

Another company has a contribution margin ratio of 40 percent and fixed costs of $1,000. Sales price is $1 per unit. What's the break-even point in dollars?

$$\text{Net income} = (\text{Sales} \times \text{Contribution margin ratio}) - \text{Fixed costs}$$
$$0 = (\text{Sales}_{BE} \times \text{Contribution margin ratio}) - \text{Fixed costs}$$
$$0 = (\text{Sales}_{BE} \times 40\%) - \$1,000$$
$$\frac{\$1,000}{40\%} = \text{Sales}_{BE}$$
$$\$2,500 = \text{Sales}_{BE}$$

You can express break-even point in units or dollars. If your formula gives you units and you want dollars, multiply the number of units by the sales price. If your formula gives you dollars and you want units, just divide by the sales price.

Shooting for Target Profit

If you have set a specific goal for net income, contribution margin analysis can help you figure out the needed sales. This goal for net income is called target profit.

To compute target profit, just adapt one of the three net income formulas. (Head to the earlier section "Preparing a Cost-Volume-Profit Analysis" to see these formulas.) Then simply plug target profit into one of these formulas as net income.

For example, say a company is pushing to earn $20,000 in profit and has to pay $10,000 in fixed costs. How much total contribution margin does the company need to generate in order to make its target profit of $20,000?

$$\text{Net income} = \text{Total contribution margin} - \text{Fixed costs}$$
$$\$20,000 = \text{Total contribution margin}_{\text{Target}} - \$10,000$$
$$\$30,000 = \text{Total contribution margin}_{\text{Target}}$$

Total contribution margin of $30,000 will result in $20,000 worth of net income.

Now suppose a company has set its target profit for $2,000, earns contribution margin per unit of $5, and incurs fixed costs of $500. How many units must the company sell?

$$\text{Net income} = \left(\text{Sales volume} \times \text{Contribution margin per unit}\right) - \text{Fixed costs}$$
$$\$2,000 = \left(\text{Sales volume}_{\text{Target}} \times \text{Contribution margin per unit}\right) - \text{Fixed costs}$$
$$\$2,000 = \left(\text{Sales volume}_{\text{Target}} \times \$5\right) - \$500$$
$$\frac{\$2,500}{\$5} = \text{Sales volume}_{\text{Target}}$$
$$500 \text{ units} = \text{Sales volume}_{\text{Target}}$$

If the company wants to earn $2,000 in profit, it needs to sell 500 units.

Consider another company with a contribution margin ratio of 40 percent and fixed costs of $1,000. The company is looking to earn $600 in net income. How much does that company need in sales?

$$\text{Net income} = \left(\text{Sales} \times \text{Contribution margin ratio}\right) - \text{Fixed costs}$$
$$\$600 = \left(\text{Sales}_{\text{Target}} \times \text{Contribution margin ratio}\right) - \text{Fixed costs}$$
$$\$600 = \left(\text{Sales}_{\text{Target}} \times 40\%\right) - \$1,000$$
$$\frac{\$1,600}{40\%} = \text{Sales}_{\text{Target}}$$
$$\$4,000 = \text{Sales}_{\text{Target}}$$

Don't confuse dollars with units. The formula that uses contribution margin per unit gives you sales in units. However, the formula that uses contribution margin ratio gives you sales in dollars. To translate between these units, just multiply or divide by the sales price as I describe earlier in the chapter.

Observing Margin of Safety

Margin of safety is the difference between your actual or expected profitability and the break-even point. It measures how much breathing room you
have — how much you can afford to lose in sales before your net income
drops to zero. When budgeting, compute the margin of safety as the difference between budgeted sales and the break-even point. Doing so will help
you understand the likelihood of incurring a loss. Turn to Chapters 14 and 15
for more information about budgeting.

Using a graph to depict margin of safety

Figure 9-7 shows you how to visualize margin of safety with a graph. In this
example, margin of safety is the difference between current or projected
sales volume (60 units) and break-even sales volume (34 units), or 26 units.
Sales would have to drop by 26 units for existing net income of $240 to
completely dry up.

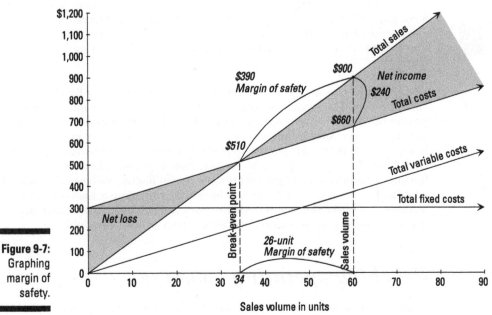

Figure 9-7:
Graphing
margin of
safety.

Making use of formulas

To compute margin of safety directly, without drawing pictures, first calculate the break-even point and then subtract it from actual or projected sales. You can use dollars or units:

$$\text{Margin of safety (in dollars)} = \text{Sales}_{\text{Actual}} - \text{Sales}_{\text{BE}}$$
$$\text{Margin of safety (in units)} = \text{Unit sales}_{\text{Actual}} - \text{Unit sales}_{\text{BE}}$$

For guidance on finding the break-even point, check out the earlier section "Generating a Break-Even Analysis."

You can compute margin of safety either in sales dollars or in units, but be consistent. Don't subtract break-even sales in units from actual sales in dollars!

Taking Advantage of Operating Leverage

Operating leverage measures how changes in sales can affect net income. For a company with high operating leverage, a relatively small increase in sales can have a fairly significant impact on net income. Likewise, a relatively small decrease in sales for that same company will have a devastating effect on earnings.

Operating leverage is typically driven by a company's blend of fixed and variable costs. The larger the proportion of fixed costs to variable costs, the greater the operating leverage. For example, airlines are notorious for their high fixed costs. Airlines' highest costs are typically depreciation, jet fuel, and labor — all costs that are fixed with respect to the number of passengers on each flight. Their most significant variable cost is probably just the cost of the airline food, which, judging from some recent flights I've been on, couldn't possibly be very much. Therefore, airlines have ridiculously high operating leverage and unspeakably low variable costs. A small drop in the number of passenger-miles can have a dreadful effect on an airline's profitability.

Graphing operating leverage

In a cost-volume-profit graph (see Figure 9-3 earlier in the chapter), operating leverage corresponds to the slope of the total costs line. The more horizontal the slope of this line, the greater the operating leverage. Figure 9-8 compares the operating leverage for two different entities, Safe Co., which has lower operating leverage, and Risky Co., which has higher operating leverage.

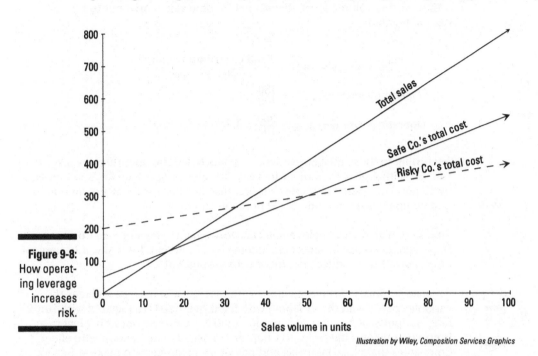

Figure 9-8: How operating leverage increases risk.

Sales volume in units

Illustration by Wiley, Composition Services Graphics

In this example, Risky Co. has higher fixed costs and lower variable costs per unit than Safe Co. Therefore Risky's total cost line is more horizontal than Safe's total cost line. Accordingly, Risky has the potential to earn much higher income with the same sales volume than Safe does. Because its fixed costs are so high, Risky also has the potential to incur greater losses than Safe does.

Looking at the operating leverage formula

The formula for operating leverage is

$$\text{Operating leverage} = \frac{\text{Total contribution margin}}{\text{Net income}}$$

Suppose that Safe Co. and Risky Co. each earn sales of $400 on 50 units. Assume that on these sales, Safe Co. has $150 in contribution margin and

Risky has $300 in contribution margin. Safe Co. has fixed costs of $50, while Risky Co. has fixed costs of $200. Safe's net income comes to $100 ($150 – $50). At this volume level, Risky's net income also works out to be $100. Here's the math:

$$\text{Operating leverage} = \frac{\text{Total contribution margin}}{\text{Net income}}$$

$$\text{Operating leverage}_{\text{Safe Co.}} = \frac{150}{100} = 1.5$$

$$\text{Operating leverage}_{\text{Risky Co.}} = \frac{300}{100} = 3.0$$

According to these measures, Risky Co. has twice the operating leverage of Safe Co. Although a 10-percent increase in sales boosts Safe Co.'s net income by 15 percent, a similar 10-percent increase in sales for Risky Co. increases that company's net income by 30 percent!

That said, high operating leverage can work against you. For Safe Co., a 10-percent decrease in sales cuts income by 15 percent; for Risky, a 10-percent decrease in sales reduces net income by 30 percent.

Because automation replaces labor with machines, it usually replaces the variable costs (from direct labor) with fixed overhead (associated with running equipment). As such, automation tends to increase operating leverage. However, outsourcing (refer to Chapter 11) usually has the opposite effect. Companies that close factories and pay other companies to make goods for them replace fixed costs (needed to run factories) with variable costs (used to pay other companies to make the goods).

Chapter 10

Capital Budgeting: Should You Buy That?

*A*fter a big project is already underway, managers can't just go to the customer service desk with their receipts and ask to get their money back. Before investing big bucks in a long-term project, then, managers must carefully plan all the project's details and determine that it will deliver reasonable returns for the company. This planning means estimating the future cash flows that the project will bring in and coming to a reasonable determination that the project's cash inflows will exceed its cost.

In this chapter, I show you several techniques for making decisions about whether to pursue long-term capital projects. First, I review the idea of incremental and opportunity costs — how a project may change some costs but not others. Then I describe an easy technique called payback period for determining how long a project will take to become profitable. I describe time value of money concepts to explain how to estimate the net present value and the internal rate of return of a long-term capital project. Finally, I discuss why you also need to consider nonquantitative factors, such as product safety or employee loyalty, when making decisions about budgeting capital.

If you're new to time value of money, read this chapter in order. Each section takes a step toward helping you understand this topic.

Identifying Incremental and Opportunity Costs

As I explain in Chapter 3, when faced with two or more alternatives, *incremental costs* are those costs that change depending on which alternative you choose. Suppose you want to buy a new bicycle. Incremental costs of buying the bike include the actual price of the bike plus any accessories. You also need to pay for gas and tolls to drive to and from the bike store — another incremental cost. On the other hand, the cost of buying lunch after purchasing the bike isn't an incremental cost because you need to pay for that regardless of whether you buy the bike (and if there's one thing accountants know, it's that there's no such thing as a free lunch).

As you analyze budgeting decisions, take special care to consider only incremental costs and to ignore all other costs.

Choosing one option may mean you lose money because you turned down another alternative. These incremental costs are called *opportunity costs*. For example, say you choose to take the day off from work to go bike shopping, losing $100 in income. That lost income is an opportunity cost. When considering decisions to invest in long-term projects, one of the most significant opportunity costs is how much you could have earned by investing your money elsewhere.

When analyzing for incremental costs (and especially for opportunity costs), remember that they're expected to happen in the future. That's how you know that you can't include *sunk costs* (costs that you incurred in the past; refer to Chapter 3). For example, say you already bought a new bike last week that you really liked and that just got stolen. The cost of the missing bike is a sunk cost. Because you can't change sunk costs, you can ignore them completely. It doesn't matter how much that stolen bike cost you — it's gone.

Keeping It Simple: The Cash Payback Method

Companies invest in capital projects — buying big things like factories, equipment, and vehicles — to earn profits and a return on their investment. Therefore, managers need tools and techniques to evaluate different capital projects and decide which ones to invest in and which ones to avoid.

One such tool is the *cash payback method,* which estimates how long a project will take to cover its original investment. You can calculate the cash payback method whether you have equal payments each period or unequal payments. The main benefit of the cash payback method is that you can calculate it on the fly to quickly screen out investments.

Although it's quick and easy, the cash payback method doesn't account for the full profitability of the project; it ignores any payback earned after the cash payback period ends. Furthermore, because this approach neglects the time value of money, managers should use a more sophisticated model, such as the net present value method I describe later in the chapter, before investing company funds into any project.

Using the cash payback method with equal annual net cash flows

The cash payback method uses the following formula to compute how long a given project will take to pay for itself. When computing cash payback period, annual net cash flow should include all revenues arising from the new project less expected incremental costs. Note that *net* means "to offset," and *net cash flows* means that you're subtracting cash outflows from cash inflows (or vice versa). Therefore, to compute annual net cash flow, you estimate any potential revenues and then add in savings in materials, labor, and overhead associated with the new project. Offset any additional costs associated with the new project against these cash inflows.

The following formula works in a situation where each year's net cash flows from the investment are expected to be equal:

$$\text{Cash payback period} = \frac{\text{Cost of investment}}{\text{Annual net cash flow}}$$

Simply divide the cost of the investment — how much you initially paid for the investment — by the estimated net cash flow the investment generates each year. The higher the cash payback period, the longer the period you need to recover your investment.

For example, suppose you need to decide whether to buy a new computer costing $500; you expect the computer to increase your net cash flow by $300 per year. Plug the numbers into the formula:

$$\text{Cash payback period} = \frac{\text{Cost of investment}}{\text{Annual net cash flow}}$$

$$= \frac{500}{300} = 1.67 \text{ years, or one year and eight months}$$

Here you can see that the computer would take one year and eight months to pay for itself.

When making investment decisions, compare the cash payback period of one project with that of another and select projects that offer the quickest cash payback period. Suppose a less-expensive computer has a cash payback period of only nine months; compared to one year and eight months, the nine-month cash payback period suggests that the less-expensive computer is probably a better investment for your company.

Using the cash payback method when annual net cash flows change each year

When you are computing cash payback period, remember to include all revenues arising from the new project less expected incremental costs in each year's net cash flows. When preparing this computation, the net cash flow will probably vary each year. If so, just project the net cash flows that you expect to realize or incur each year.

For example, suppose that your new $500 computer is expected to yield different net cash flows each year, as shown in Figure 10-1.

Figure 10-1:
Computing cash payback period when net cash flows change each year.

Year	Initial Investment	Net Cash Flow	Cumulative Net Cash Flows
2013	($500)		
2014		$200	$200
2015		150	350
2016		400	750
2017		200	950

Illustration by Wiley, Composition Services Graphics

The computer will be fully paid off in 2016, when cumulative net cash flows of $750 exceed the initial investment of $500. This result amounts to a three-year payback period.

When computing net cash flows, use cash flow rather than accrual income amounts. For example, use projected cash receipts from customers rather than sales. Because depreciation expense doesn't require cash payments, ignore it completely.

It's All in the Timing: The Net Present Value (NPV) Method

Over time, the value of money changes. Given the choice between receiving $1,000 today and receiving $1,000 a year from now, most people would take the cash now because the value of money decreases with time. The later the cash flow, the less it's worth. Understanding and estimating how the value of money changes over time is the premise for evaluating the *time value of money,* an extremely important financial tool for making investment decisions.

Net present value techniques use time value of money tools to estimate the current value of a series of future cash flows. For example, suppose you hit the lottery, winning $1 million a year for the next 20 years. The state lottery board will publicize your winnings as a $20 million prize, but that figure is misleading. After all, time value of money principles say that the $1 million received a year from now is somewhat less valuable than the $1 million received today. The next installment, two years from now, would be worth even less than that, and so on. Therefore, simply multiplying $1 million by 20 years disingenuously overstates the amount of the prize.

In fact, the net present value of a 20-year series of annual payments of $1 million (assuming a 5-percent interest rate and that the first payment is received immediately) is equal to $13,085,321. (If you're wondering how I figured this out, read the later section "Calculating NPV with a series of future cash flows.") In other words, $1 million a year for the next 20 years is really worth $13,085,321 today.

Because net present value (NPV) techniques consider changes in the value of money, they offer an informative tool for managers making capital project decisions. After all, new investments, like a winning lottery ticket, should be expected to yield future cash inflows.

You have several options for computing the time value of money:

- ✔ Tables (found online and at the back of most managerial accounting textbooks)
- ✔ Formulas (which require familiarity with exponents)
- ✔ Microsoft Excel spreadsheets (which entail understanding how to use certain Excel formulas, such as NPV)
- ✔ Financial calculators (which have idiosyncratic commands explained in their instruction manuals)

In this section, I use the formula approach because it doesn't require you to look up tables, run Excel, or buy a new calculator. Don't worry; the formulas aren't difficult to remember.

Because the value of money decreases over time, use the variable *PV* (present value) to measure a cash flow today and the variable *FV* (future value) to estimate the value of a cash flow at some point in the future. Set the interest rate as variable *i*, expressed as a decimal (for example, 12 percent interest equals 0.12). The following sections walk you through time value of money and NPV calculations for various scenarios.

Calculating time value of money with one payment for one year

Consider a company that has $100 right now, on which it can earn 12-percent interest:

$$PV = \$100$$
$$i = 0.12$$

To determine the future value of this investment after one year, just multiply the present value by one plus the interest rate:

$$PV(1+i) = FV$$
$$100(1+0.12) = FV$$
$$100 \times 1.12 = FV$$
$$\$112 = FV$$

This formula works in both directions. Suppose that you know that you need $500 one year from now, and the expected interest rate is 11 percent. To figure out the present value, plug the $500 future value into the formula:

$$PV(1+i) = FV$$
$$PV(1+0.11) = 500$$
$$PV = \frac{500}{1.11}$$
$$PV = \$450.45$$

In this case, if you start with $450.45 today and put it away to earn 11-percent interest for one year, you'll have $500 one year from now.

To simplify the math in time value of money problems, and to avoid having to memorize long formulas, focus on the interest factor of "one plus the interest rate," or $(1 + i)$. Use this factor to convert back and forth between present and future values: To get the future value, multiply this factor by the present value. If you need the present value, divide the future value by this factor.

For example, if the interest rate is 12 percent, you focus on the interest rate factor, which equals 1.12, or $(1 + 0.12)$. If present value were equal to $100, the future value would equal $100 × 1.12, or $112. Working in the opposite direction, the present value of $112 is just $112 ÷ 1.12, or $100.

Finding time value of money with one payment held for two periods or more

Obviously, companies hold most long-term investments for longer than one year. To determine the future value of this investment for longer periods of time, just multiply the interest factor by itself for each year the investment is held. In other words, take the interest factor to the power of the number of years' held, n:

$$PV(1+i)^n = FV$$

Suppose a company invests $400 today for five years, at an interest rate of 12 percent. What's the future value of this investment?

$$PV = \$400$$
$$i = 12\%$$
$$n = 5$$
$$PV(1+i)^n = FV$$
$$400(1+0.12)^5 = FV$$
$$400 \times 1.76 = FV$$
$$\$705 = FV$$

Investing $400 today and holding it for five years at 12 percent will eventually give you $705. You can also use this formula to find the present value required to reach a known future value. If you know that you need to have exactly $900 four years from now (that's the future value) and that the expected interest rate is 9 percent, you can plug these values into the formula to figure out the present value:

$$i = 9\%$$
$$n = 4$$
$$FV = \$900$$
$$PV(1+i)^n = 900$$
$$PV(1+0.09)^4 = 900$$
$$PV \times 1.41 = 900$$
$$PV = \frac{900}{1.41}$$
$$PV = \$638$$

Therefore, if you sock away $638 now at 9-percent annual interest, you'll have $900 in four years.

As with the one-year version of the formula in the preceding section, treat the unit of $(1 + i)^n$ as a single factor to avoid using long formulas to convert between present value and future value.

In these examples, I apply time value of money formulas based on year-long periods, designating the variable n to measure the number of years. For more-precise results, apply time value of money formulas based on shorter periods of time, such as months or even days. The variable n, then, would measure the number of months or days. That said, the interest rate, or i, always measures the interest rate per period. Therefore, if n equals one year, an annual interest rate of 12 percent would be apropos. However, if n equals one month, you should also express the interest rate by months — say, as 1 percent per month (12 percent divided by 12 months). Bankers call this *monthly compounding.* To try daily compounding, where *n* equals one day, express the interest rate in days. For example, 12 percent divided by 365 days equals 0.0329 percent per day, so that i = 0.000329.

Calculating NPV with a series of future cash flows

Most capital projects are expected to provide a series of cash flows over a period of time. The following sections walk you through the individual steps necessary for calculating NPV when you have a series of future cash flows: estimating future net cash flows, setting the interest rate for your NPV calculations, computing the NPV of these cash flows, and evaluating the NPV of a capital project.

Estimating annual net cash flows

To estimate each year's net cash flow, add cash inflows from potential revenues to expected savings in materials, labor, and overhead from the new project. Here, include cash savings resulting from incremental costs eliminated by the project. From this sum, subtract any additional costs you'll need to pay because of the new project. Cash inflows should be set as positive amounts, while cash outflows should be set as negative.

Net means that you're offsetting each year's expected cash inflows against its expected cash outflows. If a year's expected cash inflows exceed the outflows, congratulations! You're going to have a net cash inflow. On the other hand, if a year's expected cash inflows fall short of expected outflows, you have an expected net cash outflow. Sometimes it happens to the best of us.

When estimating annual net cash flows, companies usually account for a *depreciation tax shield,* which results from tax savings on the depreciation of project assets. To compute this figure, multiply the tax depreciation expense for the year by the company's expected tax rate that year. Then, because this amount represents tax savings each year, add the result to your expected cash inflows.

Setting the interest rate

Before you can determine the NPV of the cash flows, you need to set an interest rate. For these purposes, companies usually estimate their *cost of capital,* the average interest rate the company must pay to borrow money from creditors and raise equity from stockholders.

Managers use many different terms to describe the interest rate in a net present value calculation, including the following:

- ✔ Cost of capital
- ✔ Cutoff rate
- ✔ Discount rate
- ✔ Hurdle rate
- ✔ Required rate of return

Technically, theoretical differences among these terms do exist, but for all intents and purposes in this book, I treat these terms as being synonymous with the interest rate, or *i*.

Computing the net present value of a series of annual net cash flows

To determine the present value of these cash flows, use time value of money computations with the established interest rate (see the preceding section) to convert each year's net cash flow from its future value back to its present value. Then add these present values together. Remember to preserve the sign of each year's net cash flow, such that positive net cash inflows get converted into positive net present values and net cash outflows get converted into negative net present values.

Suppose that Sombrero Corporation expects a new project to yield $500 one year from now, $600 in two years, and then $750 in three years. The company's cost of capital is 12 percent. Figure 10-2 illustrates how to convert each of these future values to present value so you can determine total net present value. According to this figure, the total present value of these future cash flows equals $1,458.59.

Year	Future Value A	Factor B	Present Value A/B
1	$500	$(1 + 0.12)$	$446.43
2	600	$(1 + 0.12)^2$	478.32
3	750	$(1 + 0.12)^3$	533.84
			$1,458.59

Figure 10-2: Computing the present value of a series of cash flows.

Illustration by Wiley, Composition Services Graphics

Evaluating the NPV of a capital project

To evaluate the NPV of a capital project, simply estimate the expected net present value of the future cash flows from the project, including the project's initial investment as a negative amount (representing a payment that needs to be made right now). If a project's NPV is zero or a positive value, you should accept the project. If the NPV is negative, it represents a loss, and you should reject the project.

Suppose Corporation X is evaluating a project costing $3,000. Managers expect the project to yield $700 one year from now, $800 in two years, $900 in three years, and $1,200 in four years. The company's cost of capital is 11 percent. Figure 10-3 illustrates how to estimate the net present value of X's project.

Figure 10-3:
Computing the net present value of Corporation X's project.

Year	Future Value A	Factor B	Present Value A/B
0			($3,000.00)
1	$700	$(1 + 0.11)$	630.63
2	800	$(1 + 0.11)^2$	649.30
3	900	$(1 + 0.11)^3$	658.07
4	1,200	$(1 + 0.11)^4$	790.48
Net Present Value			($271.52)

Illustration by Wiley, Composition Services Graphics

The net present value of X's project comes to –$271.52, indicating that the company would lose $271.52 on this project. Therefore, managers should reject the project.

Measuring Internal Rate of Return (IRR)

When evaluating a capital project, *internal rate of return* (IRR) measures the estimated percentage return from the project. It uses the initial cost of the project and estimates of the future cash flows to figure out the interest rate. In general, companies should accept projects with IRR that exceed the cost of capital and reject projects that don't meet that guideline.

Using the NPV method (which I outline in the earlier section "Calculating NPV with a series of future cash flows"), you can figure out internal rate of return through trial and error — plug different interest rates into your formulas until you figure out which interest rate delivers an NPV closest to zero.

Consider Corporation X's proposed project costing $3,000. Managers project positive net cash inflow of $700 one year from now, $800 in two years, $900 in three years, and $1,200 in four years. An interest rate of 11 percent yields an NPV of –$271.52 (as illustrated in Figure 10-3 earlier in the chapter). Recompute the NPV, using a lower interest rate such as 10 percent, as shown in Figure 10-4.

Figure 10-4:
Estimating the IRR of Corporation X's project with a 10-percent interest rate.

Year	Future Value A	Factor B	Present Value A/B
0			($3,000.00)
1	$700	$(1 + 0.10)$	636.36
2	800	$(1 + 0.10)^2$	661.16
3	900	$(1 + 0.10)^3$	676.18
4	1,200	$(1 + 0.10)^4$	819.62
Net Present Value			($206.68)

Illustration by Wiley, Composition Services Graphics

This rate results in an NPV of –$206.68. No good. Try a much lower interest rate, like 7 percent, as shown in Figure 10-5.

Figure 10-5:
Estimating the IRR of Corporation X's project with a 7-percent interest rate.

Year	Future Value A	Factor B	Present Value A/B
0			($3,000.00)
1	$700	$(1 + 0.07)$	654.21
2	800	$(1 + 0.07)^2$	698.75
3	900	$(1 + 0.07)^3$	734.67
4	1,200	$(1 + 0.07)^4$	915.47
Net Present Value			$3.10

Illustration by Wiley, Composition Services Graphics

The extremely low net present value of $3.10 for this experiment indicates that the internal rate of return for this project is about 7 percent.

Computing internal rate of return may require estimating the NPV for several different interest rates and estimating an interest rate to one-tenth of 1 percent, judging which rate results in the lowest NPV. Microsoft Excel offers powerful functions for computing internal return of return, as do many financial calculators.

Granted, using trial and error to compute IRR may be frustrating. This process can be all the more daunting because IRR usually leads managers to make the same decision as NPV does. Any project with positive NPV will also have IRR that exceeds the cost of capital. However, NPV values are difficult to compare across different projects. Naturally, a large project (with a large investment) should have a higher NPV than a smaller project (with a smaller investment). However, IRR takes into account the size of the investment, allowing you compare different-sized projects alongside each other.

Considering Nonquantitative Factors

As my mom would say, some things in life just can't be measured (though as an accounting professor, I have a really hard time understanding that). However, projections of future cash flows do inherently ignore certain factors that can't be monetized, such as the following:

- ✔ Better customer loyalty
- ✔ Enhanced safety
- ✔ Stronger employee morale
- ✔ Improved quality
- ✔ Protection of the environment

Ignore these kinds of factors at your peril.

For example, say you're evaluating a new factory expansion project and arrive at a negative NPV, causing you to reject the project. But the new expansion would have saved the company from outsourcing jobs overseas, helped employee morale, and improved community relations.

Evaluating such qualitative factors when making decisions requires a measure of personal judgment, which is different for every decision-maker. If employee morale is important to you, you may choose to expand the factory in spite of the negative NPV. When looking over the numbers for any capital project, think about other factors that the analysis doesn't account for but that you consider to be important.

Chapter 11

Reality Check: Making and Selling More than One Product

....

In This Chapter

▶ Finding the break-even point when you make more than one product

▶ Maximizing limited capacity

▶ Deciding whether to discontinue a product line

....

*E*arlier chapters in this book assume that a company makes just one product and that the company has the ability to make and sell as much of that product as it wants. This scenario keeps things simple but isn't necessarily realistic.

Welcome to reality. Most companies sell many products — often hundreds or even thousands of different models — and usually have *limited capacity* (only enough machinery, space, and workers to produce a restricted amount of finished goods during a time period).

In this chapter, I show you how to figure out the break-even point when you make and sell more than one product. I explain how to determine which products to make when limited capacity prevents you from producing as much as you can sell. Because profits and break-even points sometimes force you to make hard decisions, I also discuss how to decide when to outsource or discontinue a product.

Preparing a Break-Even Analysis with More than One Product

As I explain in Chapter 9, managers often want to know how much they need to sell in order to break even or in order to earn a target level of profit. To get this information, managers derive something called a *break-even point* (BE) — the amount of sales necessary to earn zero profit.

Why bother? Because knowing the break-even point helps you set sales targets.

To figure out the break-even point when you make and sell more than one product, follow these steps, which I outline in the following sections:

1. **Compute the contribution margin ratio for each product.**
2. **Estimate the sales mix.**
3. **Calculate the weighted average contribution margin ratio (WACMR).**
4. **Divide total fixed costs by WACMR to get the break-even point in dollars.**

Step 1: Computing contribution margin ratio

Contribution margin, as I explain in Chapter 9, measures how sales impact net income. As it comes in, contribution margin offsets fixed costs. After the total contribution margin exceeds fixed costs, it begins to increase profits above zero. (Of course, if contribution margin falls short of fixed costs, then the company incurs a net loss.)

To compute a company's total contribution margin, subtract variable costs from sales:

Contribution margin = Sales – Variable costs

Contribution margin tells you how a company's sales affects profits. For example, if a given sale creates $50,000 worth of contribution, that money will cover fixed costs and then go straight to the bottom line, net income.

One particular measure of contribution margin is the *contribution margin ratio,* which you compute by dividing total contribution margin by total sales. For example, a contribution margin of $300, with total sales of $400, works out as a contribution margin ratio of 75 percent:

$$\text{Contribution margin ratio} = \frac{\text{Total contribution margin}}{\text{Total sales}}$$

$$= \frac{\$300}{\$400} = 75\%$$

Take a look at Figure 11-1. It shows how 75 percent of the sales price goes to cover variable costs, while the other 25 percent, the contribution margin ratio, goes toward fixed costs and then net income.

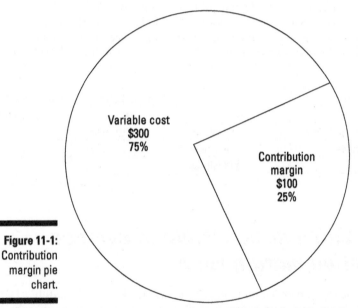

Variable cost
$300
75%

Contribution
margin
$100
25%

Figure 11-1:
Contribution
margin pie
chart.

Illustration by Wiley, Composition Services Graphics

You can also calculate contribution margin ratio on a per-unit basis, dividing a given product's contribution margin per unit by its sales price.

Consider a gadget that sells for $1,000, with a variable cost of $550. The gadget's contribution margin is $1,000 – $550 = $450. Each gadget sold increases net income by $450. To compute the contribution margin ratio, divide contribution margin per unit by the sales price per unit:

$$\text{Contribution margin ratio} = \frac{\$450}{\$1,000} = 45\%$$

Here, the contribution margin ratio of 45 percent means that 45 percent of the sales price goes straight to the bottom line.

Step 2: Estimating sales mix

Sales mix is the relative percentage of sales of each product. To figure out the sales mix, divide the sales of each type of product by total sales. The sales mix percentage of all products should always add up to 100 percent.

Suppose that fictional Acme Company sold $8 million worth of rocket-powered products and $2 million worth of giant rubber bands. To figure out the sales mix, divide the sales of each type of product by total sales. As shown in Figure 11-2, Acme's sales mix percentage of rocket-powered products is 80 percent, while its sales mix percentage of giant rubber bands is 20 percent.

	Product	Sales	Total Sales	Sales Mix Percentage
Figure 11-2: Estimating Acme's sales mix.		**(A)**	**(B)**	**(A)/(B)**
	Rocket-powered products	$2 million	$10 million	20%
	Giant rubber bands	8 million	10 million	80%
	Total	**$10 million**		**100%**

Illustration by Wiley, Composition Services Graphics

Step 3: Calculating weighted average contribution margin ratio

The *weighted average contribution margin ratio* (WACMR), affectionately known as "Wack 'em 'er," is an average of all products' contribution margin ratios, weighted by sales. To compute WACMR, multiply each product's sales mix percentage by its contribution margin ratio. Then add all the products together.

Suppose that rocket-powered products have a contribution margin ratio of 30 percent, while giant rubber bands have a contribution margin ratio of 60 percent. (This scenario means that the rocket-powered products are a loss leader for giant rubber bands. A *loss leader* attracts customers to the business in order to encourage them to buy more profitable products.)

As Figure 11-3 shows, even though Acme sells two classes of products with widely different contribution margin ratios, the average contribution margin ratio for all products sold — WACMR — equals 36 percent.

Figure 11-3:
Multiplying contribution margin ratio by sales mix to find WACMR.

Product	Sales Mix Percentage	Contribution Margin Ratio	WACMR
Rocket-powered products	80%	30%	24%
Giant rubber bands	20%	60%	12%
Total	100%		36%

Illustration by Wiley, Composition Services Graphics

Step 4: Getting to break-even point

To figure out the break-even point in sales dollars, divide total fixed costs by WACMR.

In the preceding section, you discover that Acme has a WACMR of 36 percent. Now suppose that the company also has fixed costs of $3.6 million. Plug this information into the following formula to determine the break-even point:

$$\text{Total sales}_{BE} = \frac{\text{Total fixed costs}}{\text{WACMR}}$$
$$= \frac{\$3,600,000}{36\%}$$
$$= \$10,000,000$$

Acme's break-even point is therefore $10 million worth of sales. When Acme achieves this level of sales, its contribution margin will have covered its fixed costs, and the company will have earned zero profit. After it earns more sales, the excess of contribution margin over fixed costs results in positive net income.

Here I present break-even point in dollars. Because products can vary widely in cost and sales price, computing break-even point in units usually doesn't make sense for companies; you may as well add apples and bananas. If you do need to find a unit-based break-even point, first calculate sales mix as the percentage of units sold rather than the percentage of sales dollars. Then multiply that sales mix by the contribution margin per unit. To get a WACMR per unit, add all these figures together. Divide fixed costs by this per-unit WACMR to arrive at the break-even point.

Coping with Limited Capacity

You can't always get what you want. Unfortunately, companies usually have limited resources, such as limits on space, on the number of workers, or even on the machine capacity needed to produce goods. This reality means that in order to best use limited production capabilities, managers must choose which products to make and sell.

Suppose Charlie's Burger Restaurant is constrained by the size of its 1,000-square-inch cooking grill. Because the restaurant is open eight hours a day, Charlie's has a maximum of 8,000 square-inch-hours of grill time available per day (1,000 square inches times eight hours). To keep things simple, I call these units of grill time.

Suppose that one medium-cooked Deluxe Burger requires eight units of grill time. Charlie's maximum capacity of medium-cooked burgers, therefore, equals the total capacity of 8,000 units of grill time divided by the 8 units needed for each burger. Therefore, in theory at least, Charlie's can produce a maximum of 1,000 medium-cooked Deluxe Burgers a day.

As long as Charlie's customers demand fewer than 1,000 Deluxe Burgers a day, capacity is no problem. Charlie's cook can make as many burgers as customers order.

However, when a company doesn't have enough capacity to meet its needs, it must carefully consider the best way to use its constrained resource. Here, if Charlie's customers demand more than 1,000 burgers a day (or, for that matter, more food at any one time than can fit on the cooking grill during that time span), managers must decide how to allocate the restaurant's limited cooking space.

Given that your business has to deal with at least one constraint that limits your ability to make and sell the products your customers want, how can you adjust your sales to make the best possible use of the constraint? A simple technique of dividing contribution margin by a measure of the constrained resource indicates which products squeeze the most profitability out of constrained resources. Following this technique helps you choose which products deliver the most profitability.

Say that Charlie's Burger Restaurant has four total items on the menu, with the following contribution margins and grill time requirements per order:

Item	Contribution Margin	Grill Time
Deluxe Burger	$4.50	8 units
Juicy Grilled Chicken	$4.00	12 units
Puffy Hot Dog	$2.00	3 units
Vegetarian Pasta Primavera	$6.00	0 units

First, find each product's contribution margin per unit of constrained resource by dividing each product's contribution margin per unit by the amount of constrained resource needed to make it. For example, in Figure 11-4, I divide the contribution margin of each product by the number of units of grill time needed.

Figure 11-4:
Measuring contribution margin per unit of constrained resource.

	Contribution Margin per Unit Sold	Units of Grill Time Needed	Total Contribution Margin per Unit of Constrained Resources
	(A)	(B)	(A)/(B)
Deluxe burger	$4.50	8 minutes	$0.56
Juicy grilled chicken	$4.00	12 minutes	$0.33
Puffy hot dogs	$2.00	3 minutes	$0.67
Vegetarian pasta primavera	$5.00	0 minutes	NA

Illustration by Wiley, Composition Services Graphics

If Charlie's cook is making Juicy Grilled Chicken, each unit of grill time yields only $0.33 worth of contribution margin. When he's cooking Puffy Hot Dogs, each unit of grill time yields $0.67. Cooking Deluxe Burgers results in $0.56 of contribution margin per unit of grill time.

Therefore, if grill time is constrained, Charlie's wants to sell as many Puffy Hot Dogs as possible because they have the highest contribution margin per unit of constrained resource (a staggering $0.67 per unit of grill time). The cook should then dedicate any remaining grill space to Deluxe Burgers ($0.56 per unit of grill time). If the restaurant can meet the demand for hot dogs and deluxe burgers, the cook can make room for the Juicy Grilled Chicken. (If not, he may just want to pretend he's run out of chicken.)

Now don't forget the Vegetarian Pasta Primavera. Because this dish doesn't require any time on the grill at all, it offers the most effective way around the constraint. Even though the grill limits your production and sales of hamburgers, chicken, and hot dogs, it can't limit your production and sales of Vegetarian Pasta Primavera. It's the perfect candidate for Special of the Day.

A useful management tool called the theory of constraints, which I describe in Chapter 19, provides more advanced techniques to help managers maximize the benefits from limited resources.

Deciding When to Outsource Products

Sometimes paying another company to make the product — *outsourcing* — is more profitable for a company than making the product in its own factory is. Although news reports tend to focus on outsourcing to other countries, outsourcing actually refers to any time you pay another company to do something that you used to do yourself — regardless of where the actual work gets done.

A decision to outsource focuses strictly on expenses and should not affect revenues. Therefore, to make an outsourcing decision, you compare the cost of making a product with the cost of paying another company for it. Choose whichever option is less costly.

Suppose that the fictional Red Socks company produces a line of socks called Duds. Managers project that making 50,000 Duds this year will cost $150,000, as shown in Figure 11-5.

Direct materials	$20,000
Direct labor	25,000
Variable overhead	45,000
Fixed overhead	60,000
Total manufacturing costs	$150,000

Figure 11-5: The cost of making Duds.

Illustration by Wiley, Composition Services Graphics

Royals Corp. is willing to make and sell Duds to Red Socks for just $2.50 per unit. This option reduces Red Socks's fixed overhead costs by 90 percent, to $6,000. To decide whether to outsource the product to Royals, compare Red Socks's costs under both the make and the buy scenarios. Remember to focus only on *incremental costs* — costs that change depending on which alternative you choose. Ignore any other costs or revenues.

Multiplying Royals' $2.50 price per unit times 50,000 units, Red Socks knows it would need to pay $125,000 to outsource Duds. Now compare the two scenarios, as shown in Figure 11-6. As shown there, direct materials, direct labor, and variable overhead all disappear if Royals takes over production. However, Red Socks still needs to pay $6,000 for fixed costs, and, of course, pay $125,000 to Royals.

Figure 11-6:
Comparing the cost of making and buying Duds.

	Make	Buy (Outsource)
Direct materials	$20,000	
Direct labor	25,000	
Variable overhead	45,000	
Fixed overhead	60,000	6,000
Cost of buying		125,000
Total man	$150,000	$131,000

Illustration by Wiley, Composition Services Graphics

This analysis indicates that making Duds would cost Red Socks $150,000, while it can pay just $131,000 to outsource this product, saving $19,000.

When making decisions to outsource, be careful to consider *opportunity costs,* or how you can lose money by choosing one alternative over another. By outsourcing the money-losing alternative, you may be able to use your limited capacity to produce a more profitable product. (Flip to Chapter 3 for details on opportunity costs.)

When faced with an outsourcing decision, think about qualitative factors that are difficult to measure in dollars and cents. For example, outsourcing may adversely affect product quality, customer satisfaction, or corporate image.

Eliminating Unprofitable Products

Managers sometimes must decide whether to eliminate certain products or even a segment of their operations. For example, Keebler discontinued Hydrox Cookies a few years ago, ending the Oreo versus Hydrox debate once and for all.

A decision to discontinue a product line or segment requires you to consider how your decision affects both revenues and expenses. Focus on revenues that will change as a result of your decision and on incremental costs. Then choose the option that is more profitable (or perhaps just less unprofitable).

If you want to find out what will happen if you eliminate a particular product, compare two contribution margin income statements: one that assumes that you continue with the product and one that assumes you drop it. (Chapter 9 explains how to prepare a contribution margin income statement — which is different from a conventional multi-step income statement, where you first subtract gross profit from sales revenue, and then subtract other expenses.)

The Great Soda Corp. is thinking about discontinuing a soft drink line called Fizzy!. The company expects to be able to sell just 1,200 cases of Fizzy! this year, at a price of $10 per case. The cost of making Fizzy! is shown in Figure 11-7. Note that fixed costs here are unavoidable. If The Great Soda Corp. stops making Fizzy!, that line's fixed costs will get allocated to other products the company makes.

Figure 11-7:
Projected income from making and selling Fizzy!.

Sales (1,200 cases x $10)		$12,000
Direct materials	$2,000	
Direct labor	1,000	
Variable overhead	7,000	
Fixed overhead	5,000	
Total manufacturing costs		$15,000
Projected net loss from Fizzy!		($3,000)

Illustration by Wiley, Composition Services Graphics

Figure 11-8 provides the contribution margin income statement analysis for The Great Soda Corp.'s Fizzy! dilemma. If the company continues with Fizzy!, the numbers keep going as projected. However, if it drops Fizzy!, all costs except fixed costs go away.

When it comes to profitability, it turns out Fizzy! is a no-win situation. Continuing to make Fizzy! means The Great Soda Corp. loses $3,000. However, eliminating Fizzy! causes the company to lose $5,000. Therefore, The Great Soda Corp. isn't in a situation where it can maximize profits; instead, it has to minimize its losses. Eliminating Fizzy! increases losses by $2,000, so the smart decision is for The Great Soda Corp. to keep making Fizzy!. (Fizzy! fans, rejoice!)

Figure 11-8:
Comparing
scenarios
for Fizzy!.

	Continue	Eliminate
Sales	$12,000	
Direct materials	(2,000)	
Direct labor	(1,000)	
Variable overhead	(7,000)	
Contribution margin	$2,000	$0
Fixed costs	(5,000)	(5,000)
Effect on net income	(3,000)	(5,000)

Illustration by Wiley, Composition Services Graphics

Now set aside talk of profitability and focus on contribution margin, which addresses this dilemma quite nicely. Making Fizzy! provides a positive contribution margin of $2,000 — so the company should continue to make it and keep the contribution margin flowing.

As with all decisions, consider qualitative factors. Eliminating an unprofitable brand may alienate customers or reduce demand for complementary products.

Chapter 12

The Price Is Right: Knowing How Much to Charge

*H*ave you ever seen the game show *The Price Is Right?* The host challenges contestants to guess the prices of different pieces of merchandise. Guessing the right price can win you cash and all sorts of valuable prizes. Even if you get the price wrong, you still walk away with your novelty nametag and maybe a chance to spin a giant wheel.

The stakes get a lot higher when you're naming prices in the real business world. Prices that are too high will scare away customers. Too low, and losses may wipe out your business. Prices must be low enough to lure customers but high enough to cover your costs and help you earn a profit. Therefore, before setting a price, you must understand both market forces and the cost structure of your business.

In this chapter, I explain how to use your knowledge of cost behavior to make pricing decisions. Absorption cost pricing takes into account all variable and fixed costs of manufacturing a product. Many businesses use cost-plus pricing — adding a markup to absorption cost — as well as variable cost pricing, which ignores fixed costs. Target costing sets the product price from the outset and then forces managers to design and make products so that they can be profitably sold at that price.

Differentiating Products

Product differentiation allows consumers to see differences among different companies' products, which makes them willing to spend more money for some brands than for others. Hence, a company that successfully differentiates its products can charge a higher price than its competitors, making it a *price maker.* Companies that don't differentiate their products need to use low prices to get a leg up on the competition. Marketers call these companies *price takers.*

Customers usually have trouble seeing any difference among the products offered by different mainstream supermarkets. Therefore, all supermarkets — price takers — need to price their products competitively in line with each other. On the other hand, premium supermarkets such as Whole Foods have done a brilliant job of differentiating themselves from competitors, so much so that customers often pay significantly more money to shop there. Whole Foods is a price maker.

Regardless of how well a company differentiates its products, its prices must take into account both market forces and the company's own cost behavior.

Taking All Costs into Account with Absorption Costing

Absorption costing (sometimes also called *full costing*) is the predominant method for costing goods the companies manufacture and sell. United States Generally Accepted Accounting Principles (GAAP) require all U.S. companies to use absorption costing in their financial statements. International accounting standards have similar requirements worldwide.

Absorption costs include all *product costs* — the costs of making products. Product costs include a variable component that increases and decreases with volume and a fixed component that doesn't change regardless of how much or how little you produce.

The costs of *direct materials,* raw materials that you can directly trace to the manufactured product, are variable. After all, the more units you make, the more direct materials you need to make them. The same goes for *direct labor,* the cost of paying employees to make your products.

Overhead costs, such as the miscellaneous costs of running a factory, usually consist of a mixture of fixed and variable costs. Absorption costing requires you to spread out the fixed costs over all units produced. (Flip to Chapter 3 for details on direct and overhead costs.)

Suppose your factory makes T-shirts. Each T-shirt requires $8 worth of variable costs (direct materials, direct labor, and variable overhead), and your factory pays $100,000 for fixed costs each year for rent and utilities. This year, you plan to make 50,000 T-shirts. How much will each T-shirt cost?

According to absorption costing, the cost of a T-shirt includes both variable and fixed components. You know that the variable component per shirt is $8.

The fixed component of $100,000 applies to all the shirts, however, so you need to spread it out among them. Divide the total fixed costs of $100,000 by the number of units you plan to produce (50,000) to get a fixed cost per unit of $2. Therefore, each T-shirt includes $8 worth of variable costs and $2 worth of fixed costs, resulting in total cost per unit of $10.

As I explain in Chapter 4, businesses use total cost per unit to report the value of inventory on their balance sheets and cost of goods sold on their income statements.

Pricing at Cost-Plus

Many retailers and manufacturers set their prices at *cost-plus* by adding a fixed markup to their absorption cost. Cost-plus pricing ensures that prices are high enough to meet profit goals. Figure 12-1 illustrates how cost-plus pricing computes the sales price by adding markup to a product's fixed and variable costs.

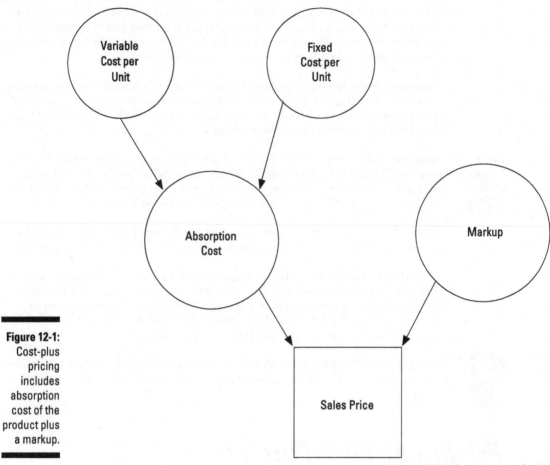

Figure 12-1:
Cost-plus pricing includes absorption cost of the product plus a markup.

Computing fixed markups

To figure out the markup for cost-plus pricing, divide total desired profit by the number of units produced.

For example, suppose that Saint Company wants to earn $100,000 on the production of 100 Model 51 Robots:

$$\frac{\text{Desired profit}}{\text{Units produced}} = \text{Markup}$$

$$\frac{\$100,000}{100} = \text{Markup}$$

$$\$1,000 = \text{Markup}$$

Dividing the desired profit by units produced results in a planned markup of $1,000 per unit. To set the price, add this planned markup to the cost. Assume that Saint's cost to produce each robot is $4,000:

$$\text{Cost} + \text{Markup} = \text{Sales price}$$

$$\$4,000 + \$1,000 = \text{Sales price}$$

$$\$5,000 = \text{Sales price}$$

If Saint Company wants to earn a total of $100,000, it should set the price at $5,000 per unit.

Setting a cost-plus percentage

Because companies often sell many different products at different prices, they commonly use a *cost-plus percentage* or *percentage markup on cost* that applies to all their products. To figure this percentage, you divide the markup, in dollars, by the expected sales price. Then, to determine the products' sales prices, you apply this percentage to all products, or to different categories of products.

For example, Saint Company's Model 51 Robot has a $1,000 markup on a sales price of $5,000.

$$\frac{\text{Markup}}{\text{Sales price}} = \text{Cost-plus percentage}$$

$$\frac{\$1,000}{\$5,000} = \text{Cost-plus percentage}$$

$$20\% = \text{Cost-plus percentage}$$

Here, Saint earns a 20-percent cost-plus percentage. The company can then apply the same cost-plus percentage to set the prices of other products. For example, another robot, Model 6, costs Saint Company $6,500 to produce. The markup on this robot amounts to $1,300 ($6,500 × 20 percent), pricing it at $7,800 ($6,500 + $1,300).

Considering problems with cost-plus pricing

Cost-plus pricing works because it's easy to use. However, it carries a few drawbacks. First, it ignores market factors. Just because you like to mark up your merchandise 20 percent doesn't necessarily mean your customers are willing to pay this price or that your competitors will cooperate with you by setting their prices even higher.

Second, because cost-plus pricing relies on absorption costing, it treats fixed costs as though they were variable. Saint Company wants to sell 100 Model 51 Robots, which means it can distribute its fixed costs over 100 units. However, the fixed costs remain the same regardless of how many units Saint actually sells; if the company sells only 50 robots, the fixed costs are spread over fewer units (50 robots rather than 100), and the cost per unit rises. Here, if production drops to 50 robots, then the cost per unit increases to $6,000 per unit. This change puts Saint into a tight bind. Figure 12-2 shows how this miscalculation causes Saint's profits to vaporize into a $50,000 loss.

Figure 12-2: Cost-plus pricing gone wild.

	The Plan	What Actually Happened
Number of units sold	100	50
Sales price	$5,000	$5,000
Cost per unit	4,000	6,000
Total sales	500,000	250,000
Cost of sales	400,000	300,000
Gross profit (loss)	100,000	(50,000)

Illustration by Wiley, Composition Services Graphics

Saint originally assumes it will make and sell 100 units. Based on this assumption, it projects an average cost of $4,000 per unit, a markup of $1,000, and a sales price of $5,000. However, if Saint makes and sells only 50 units, the average cost balloons to $6,000 per unit. Stuck with a sales price of $5,000, Saint loses $50,000.

Look on the bright side: If your sales volume is higher than you expected, then it will have a disproportionately *positive* effect on income — delivering profits way beyond your wildest dreams.

Extreme Accounting: Trying Variable-Cost Pricing

Variable-cost pricing offers an adventurous variation on cost-plus pricing (refer to the earlier section "Pricing at Cost-Plus"). Instead of adding a markup on total cost, *variable-cost pricing* adds a markup on just the variable cost. It disregards fixed costs altogether. Figure 12-3 compares variable-cost pricing with boring old cost-plus pricing. In the following sections, I show you how variable-cost pricing works and point out the drawbacks of using this system.

Figure 12-3: Comparing cost-plus (a) and variable-cost pricing (b).

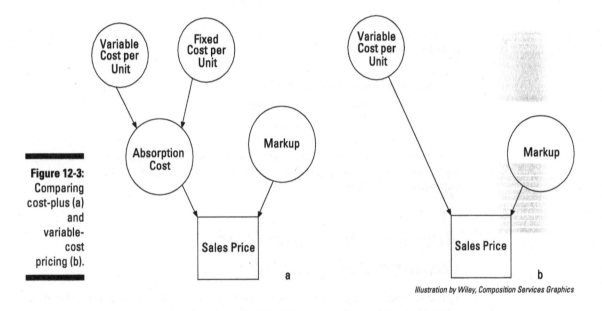

Illustration by Wiley, Composition Services Graphics

Working out variable-cost pricing

When you use variable-cost pricing, your markup must cover both the desired profit and expected fixed costs. Therefore, to figure out your markup, divide the total desired profit plus expected fixed costs by the number of units produced.

Suppose that Sparl Industries makes the Red Rover model. The entire production run of Red Rover requires $900,000 worth of fixed costs. Each unit costs another $90,000 in variable costs. Sparl wants to earn $400,000 in profit on the production and sale of 20 units of this model.

First, figure out how much markup you need on each unit to cover both the desired profit and the fixed costs:

$$\frac{\text{Desired profit} + \text{Fixed costs}}{\text{Units produced}} = \text{Markup}$$

$$\frac{\$400,000 + \$900,000}{20} = \text{Markup}$$

$$\$65,000 = \text{Markup}$$

The markup is $65,000 per unit. Now set the price at this planned markup plus the variable cost:

$$\text{Variable cost} + \text{Markup} = \text{Sales price}$$

$$\$90,000 + \$65,000 = \text{Sales price}$$

$$\$155,000 = \text{Sales price}$$

According to this analysis, if Sparl Industries wants to earn $400,000 in profit and cover $900,000 worth of fixed costs by selling 20 units, it should set the sales price at $155,000.

Avoiding the hazards of variable-cost pricing

Variable-cost pricing is especially useful for companies pricing special orders when they have excess capacity, meaning they have sufficient resources to produce more goods. However, when operating at full capacity, variable-cost pricing may be hazardous to the health of your business.

Suppose that you operate a hotel with vacant rooms. Each room has a variable cost of $10/night, and a fixed cost of $90/night. Cost-plus pricing requires you to base your price on a total cost of $100/night. However, variable-cost pricing allows you to base your price on a variable cost of just $10/night.

If your hotel has vacancies (read: excess capacity) and a customer walks in without a reservation, offering to pay $52 for a room for the night, variable-cost pricing indicates you should take the guy in. After all, $52 exceeds the variable cost of $10, increasing your profits by $42. (Cost-plus pricing tells you to throw the customer out. Each room costs $100/night. Why would you willingly lose $48?) But if your hotel is completely booked, the only way to house the $52 customer would be to throw a full-price-paying customer out on the street, reducing revenue.

Variable-cost pricing poses another severe danger: To earn a profit, your sales must exceed costs. Because variable-cost pricing doesn't fully account for fixed costs, it can trick managers into setting prices so low that they hurt profits, or worse yet, cause net losses. As I explain in the preceding example, occasionally selling a room for $52 may increase your profits. However, selling too many rooms at such low prices (even if you're never at full capacity) will cause you to lose a lot of money.

Bull's-Eye: Hitting Your Target Cost

Many industries use *price points* — special "magic" price levels that customers expect to pay. You've probably seen these prices in the store: $99.99, $26.99, $19.95, and so on. Understanding customer expectations and competitor pricing, manufacturers design products specifically so that the products can be produced and sold at the magic price points.

Although traditionally you first design the product and then set the price, target costing requires you to set the price before you design the product. After you know the price, you can engineer the product so that its cost is low enough to ensure that you earn the expected profit margin. Done right, target costing avoids problems caused by products that are priced too high for consumers or too expensive to make. It engineers the price, the profit margin, and the cost right into the product.

Calculating your target cost

With target costing, the company starts with market price and markup and uses that information to figure out the product's cost and specifications. (In contrast, cost-plus pricing starts with the product cost and desired profit and uses that information to set the price. You can read about cost-plus pricing earlier in the chapter.)

To figure out the target cost, subtract the desired profit from the market price:

Market price – Desired profit = Target cost

Figure 12-4 illustrates how this process works.

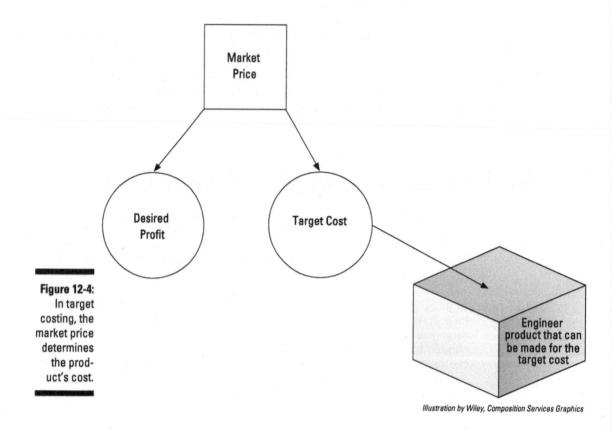

Figure 12-4:
In target costing, the market price determines the product's cost.

Consider this completely true example from my own life: Last week, I went to Costco to buy a new desktop computer. Believe it or not, that ginormous store was selling only four different desktop models, costing $599.99, $749.99, $999.99, and $1,299.99. Because I wanted to spend $750.00, I took the $749.99 model.

As of this writing, Costco's financial statements indicate that the company sets prices so that gross profit equals 10.51 percent of the company's sales price. An inventory item that sells for $100 typically includes $10.51 worth of gross profit ($100 × 10.51 percent), costing the company $89.49 ($100.00 – $10.51).

The company's desired profit on my computer model equals $78.82 ($749.99 × 10.51 percent). Plug it into the formula:

$$\text{Market price} - \text{Desired profit} = \text{Target cost}$$
$$\$749.99 - \$78.82 = \text{Target cost}$$
$$\$671.17 = \text{Target cost}$$

The math indicates that Costco should pay $671.17 for computers that it can sell for $749.99.

Target costing works both for retailers (like Costco) and for manufacturers (like Hewlett-Packard, maker of my new computer). Therefore, after Costco determines that it's willing to pay $671.17 for these computers, HP needs to figure out how to make computers with all the right bells and whistles that it can sell for $671.17.

Hewlett-Packard works to earn a 22.7-percent profit margin on sales. Therefore, the company's desired profit equals $152.36 ($671.17 × 22.7 percent):

$$\text{Market price} - \text{Desired profit} = \text{Target cost}$$
$$\$671.17 - \$152.36 = \text{Target cost}$$
$$\$518.81 = \text{Target cost}$$

After subtracting desired profit of $152.36 from its expected sales price of $671.17, Hewlett-Packard works out that it needs to engineer and produce computers that cost $518.81. Armed with this knowledge, the engineers pick and choose various specifications and features to cook up a computer that costs exactly this amount.

Knowing when to use target costing

Target costing works especially well for companies whose products aren't well-differentiated (such as electronic accessories and economy automobiles), where price is often a key consideration for customers selecting which brand to buy. This technique ensures that the company can sell a competitive product with all the features — and the price — that customers expect.

Chapter 13

Spreading the Wealth with Transfer Prices

My three sons love to cut deals. Yesterday, Levi sold David three action figures for $1, payable whenever David collects the $5 that Aaron owes him for his old watch. Aaron, meanwhile, is still waiting for the $5.37 balance from Levi for an old, torn-up *Harry Potter* book. These deals often require complex computations involving not only time value of money (a dollar today is worth more than a dollar tomorrow) but also cost, market value, and opportunity costs. Negotiations can stretch on for days or even weeks and sometimes employ tactics that probably wouldn't hold up in court. My boys attach great importance to these prices because they can substantially increase their net worth.

Similarly, divisions within companies must sometimes haggle in order to make deals to buy and sell merchandise among themselves. For example, if one company owns both a retail store and a factory that sells its wares to the retailer, then someone somewhere has to set a price, called the *transfer price*.

In this chapter, I explain how to set transfer prices and describe the most commonly used technique: having the divisions negotiate a transfer price among themselves. I also explain how to use other transfer pricing techniques, such as cost-based pricing and market-based pricing.

Pinpointing the Importance of Transfer Pricing

Companies usually organize themselves into divisions that provide different goods or services and often do business with each other. For example, a clothing retailer may own several clothing factories; the retailer and each factory can be treated as separate divisions, sort of like companies within a company. Separate divisions of an oil company may produce, refine, and sell gasoline. Many large entertainment companies own film studios, movie theaters, and cable networks. The movie theaters and cable networks both feature movies and shows produced by the film studio.

In order to manage these divisions, most larger companies *decentralize,* treating each division as its own business earning its own net income. As these different divisions do business with each other, buying and selling different products, the transfer prices they set play a critical role in determining how they'll share profits.

Suppose Jeffrey and Sandy both work for Dorothy. Jeffrey makes T-shirts that Sandy retails to customers. Each T-shirt costs Jeffrey $5 in variable costs per unit and $30,000 worth of fixed costs a year. Sandy sells each shirt to the end-customer for $10. However, to do so, she must pay an additional $1 commission per shirt, and $25,000 a year in fixed costs. Sandy expects to sell 50,000 shirts to outside customers.

At what price should Jeffrey sell Sandy the shirts? Pick a number: How about $8? Figure 13-1 uses contribution margin, as explained in Chapter 9, to describe how this price impacts both divisions' profits. Remember that the contribution-margin income statement starts with sales and then subtracts variable costs, resulting in contribution margin. Then, to arrive at net income, you subtract fixed costs.

Figure 13-1 indicates that at a price of $8 per unit, Jeffrey enjoys contribution margin per unit of $3, leaving Sandy with only $1 per unit. Now multiply this contribution margin per unit by total sales volume for each division and then subtract fixed costs. Jeffrey gets $120,000 worth of net income, while Sandy gets just $25,000.

Try a different sales price: $5.50. Figure 13-2 shows what happens: With a per unit price of $5.50, the shoe is on the other foot. Won't Jeffrey be disappointed to learn that he earns only $0.50 in contribution margin per unit, while Sandy earns $3.50 per unit? Jeffrey incurs a $5,000 net loss, while Sandy earns $150,000 in net income for the year.

	Jeffrey (makes shirts)	Sandy (sells them)
Jeffrey's sales price (comes from Sandy)	$8.00	
Sandy's sales price (comes from customers)		$10.00
Jeffrey's variable cost	(5.00)	
Sandy's variable cost of buying shirts from Jeffrey		(8.00)
Sandy's variable cost of sales commissions		(1.00)
Contribution margin per unit	$3.00	$1.00
Volume	50,000 shirts	50,000 shirts
Total contribution margin	$150,000	$50,000
Total fixed costs	(30,000)	(25,000)
Net income	$120,000	$25,000

Figure 13-1: Selling shirts at a transfer price of $8.

Illustration by Wiley, Composition Services Graphics

	Jeffrey (makes shirts)	Sandy (sells them)
Jeffrey's sales price (comes from Sandy)	$5.50	
Sandy's sales price (comes from customers)		$10.00
Jeffrey's variable cost	(5.00)	
Sandy's variable cost of buying shirts from Jeffrey		(5.50)
Sandy's variable cost of sales commissions		(1.00)
Contribution margin per unit	$0.50	$3.50
Volume	50,000 shirts	50,000 shirts
Total contribution margin	$25,000	$175,000
Total fixed costs	(30,000)	(25,000)
Net income (loss)	($5,000)	$150,000

Figure 13-2: How a transfer price of $5.50 affects Jeffrey and Sandy's profits.

Illustration by Wiley, Composition Services Graphics

Higher transfer prices shift income from the purchasing division (Sandy) to the selling division (Jeffrey). This discrepancy may lead to some discord.

Note: For clarity, throughout this chapter I use the terminology of a *selling division* that sells product to a *purchasing division,* as illustrated in Figure 13-3.

Figure 13-3:
Selling
division
transfers
product
to the
purchasing
division.

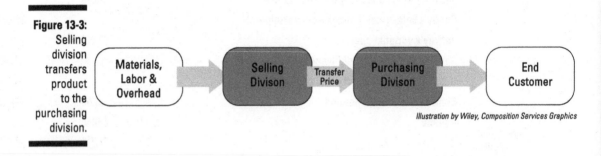

Illustration by Wiley, Composition Services Graphics

The fundamental problem here is how to set the transfer price so that the two divisions split profits. A higher price gives more profit to the selling division, while a lower price gives a larger share of profit to the purchasing division. Consider a few different approaches to address this problem, which I cover in this chapter:

- ✔ **Negotiation:** Let the selling and purchasing divisions fight over a price.

- ✔ **Cost-based transfer price:** The boss (Dorothy, in the T-shirt example), sets the transfer price equal to the selling division's variable cost or total cost, adding a reasonable markup.

- ✔ **Market-based transfer price:** The boss sets the transfer price equal to the shirts' market value, the amount that the selling division can sell them to outside customers for.

- ✔ **Centralize:** The boss declares martial law. She does away with all transfer pricing schemes and no longer computes separate profit for each division. Instead, she evaluates the selling division based on its total expenses and evaluates the purchasing division on its total sales.

Negotiating a Transfer Price

To negotiate a transfer price between two divisions, lock the managers of the selling and purchasing divisions into a room and don't let them out until they agree on a number or discover that no mutually beneficial price is possible.

Of course, these negotiations aren't based on numbers the purchasing and selling divisions have pulled out of thin air. Each side has to do its research first. In order to prepare itself with a minimum transfer price, the selling division needs to carefully consider its cost structure and other sales opportunities. Similarly, the purchasing division must figure out the maximum transfer price it's willing to pay. The negotiated price winds up falling somewhere in the middle.

In the following sections, assume that the selling and purchasing divisions must do business together. The selling division doesn't have the option to sell its goods to some outside buyer. Likewise, the purchasing division has no choice but to buy from the selling division.

Finding the selling division's minimum transfer price

The selling division's primary objective should be to add more money to its *contribution margin,* the difference between sales and variable cost, as I explain in Chapter 9. Therefore, as long as the selling division has excess capacity, it should be willing to sell its wares to the purchasing division for any value that will give it a contribution margin of zero or higher — a price that won't hurt its profits. The minimum transfer price should equal variable cost so that the selling division is willing to transfer goods to the purchasing division as long as the transfer price is equal to or exceeds this value.

In the T-shirt example (refer to the previous section), Jeffrey has a variable cost of $5 per T-shirt. Any transfer price over $5 results in positive contribution margin and increases Jeffrey's profits. At a minimum, Jeffrey must cover his variable costs on the deal. Ideally, however, he wants to earn more — enough to cover his fixed costs and earn a healthy profit.

Setting the purchasing division's maximum transfer price

Like the selling division, the purchasing division doesn't want to lose money on any deal. Therefore, the purchasing division should be willing to pay any price that results in contribution margin greater than or equal to zero.

In the earlier T-shirt example, Sandy's sales price to customers is $10 per shirt. Because Sandy refuses to pay any variable cost that results in a negative contribution margin, she needs to figure out where to draw the line on price so that contribution margin equals zero:

$$\text{Contribution margin per unit} = \text{Sales price per unit} - \text{Variable costs per unit}$$
$$0 = \$10 - \text{Variable costs per unit}$$
$$\$10 = \text{Variable costs per unit}$$

Sandy can afford to pay no more than $10 in variable costs. Remember that she also must pay $1 commission for each T-shirt sold, a variable cost. Therefore, she has a maximum of $9 left to pay Jeffrey ($10 – $1). Therefore, the maximum transfer price that Sandy can afford comes to $9.

Note that this "purchase" price is so high that Sandy's sales price only covers her variable costs, but not her fixed costs. Sandy certainly would prefer to pay a lower price so that her revenues cover both her variable and fixed costs.

Trying to meet in the middle

At this point, the selling and purchasing departments are ready to sit down and talk. Both divisions play a role in setting prices that make each of them — and the company as a whole — profitable. In the T-shirt example, Jeffrey knows he can't sell the T-shirts for any amount less than $5. Sandy won't pay more than $9.

If the seller's minimum price exceeds the purchaser's maximum price, both parties agree *not* to cut a deal. After all, neither of them wants to lose money. What if Jeffrey's minimum transfer price is $5 but Sandy's maximum transfer price is only $3? A sales price of $2 would make Sandy happy but force Jeffrey to lose $3 per shirt. A sales price of $7 would make Jeffrey happy but would cause Sandy to lose money. A compromise of $4 would force both divisions to lose money. They'd have to abandon the deal, a decision that would be in the best interest of the company as a whole.

Negotiated prices may be unduly affected by each party's ability (or inability) to negotiate, causing divisions led by weak negotiators to earn less than divisions led by more-aggressive negotiators. Furthermore, clashing egos or lack of trust between negotiating partners can cause divisions to avoid transactions that would have been profitable for the company as a whole.

Managing with full capacity

If the selling division is operating at maximum capacity and has only a limited number of goods to sell, any goods sold to another division mean giving up sales to an outside customer. This scenario entails *opportunity costs* — the cost of losing profits because you choose a different alternative (turn to Chapter 3 for more on this topic). Therefore, the selling division's minimum transfer price in this scenario equals its variable cost plus any contribution margin it would've earned from existing customers (that is, the opportunity cost of not selling to other customers).

Sylvia farms corn, and her business partner Herbert runs a restaurant. Corn costs $1 per ear to grow, and a sufficient demand exists, so Sylvia will have no problem selling her entire crop. Sylvia must choose whether to sell to her partner Herbert for his restaurant or to a local dealer. She can sell corn to the local dealer for $2 per ear as long as she pays additional variable sales commissions of $0.20 per ear.

Sylvia's minimum price when negotiating with Herbert equals her variable cost plus the contribution margin she'd earn from existing customers. If she sells to the corn dealer, her contribution margin equals $0.80 (as shown in Figure 13-4): $2 per ear less $1 variable cost to grow and $0.20 variable sales commission. Therefore, her minimum transfer price for the deal with Herbert equals $1.80 ($1 cost plus $0.80 contribution margin earned from existing customers).

Figure 13-4: Sylvia's contribution margin when selling to the outside.		
Sales price (per ear)		$2.00
Variable costs:		
Cost of growing corn		(1.00)
Sales commissions		(0.20)
Contribution margin		$0.80

Illustration by Wiley, Composition Services Graphics

Selling to another division rather than selling to an outside customer can also affect variable costs. For example, suppose that fictional company Big Paper has two divisions: One manufactures raw paper, and the other makes paper bags out of raw paper. When selling to other divisions, the raw-paper division's usual cost of $100/roll drops to $95/roll because of savings in shipping costs. This savings in variable cost reduces the raw-paper division's minimum transfer price by $5.

However, selling to another division may increase cost instead. Perhaps the internal purchasing division demands higher-quality materials than an outside customer would.

Transferring Goods between Divisions at Cost

Establishing standard and agreed-upon guidelines for transfer pricing can help managers avoid arbitrary or expensive negotiation. After all, separately negotiating every transaction increases the amount of costly and time consuming bureaucracy. One such approach to cutting out negotiation is to base the transfer price on the selling division's own manufacturing cost. The following sections offer a few options.

Setting the transfer price at variable cost

One simple approach to setting a transfer price is to use the item's variable cost. After all, in a negotiation, this amount would have been the seller's minimum price anyway.

Suppose that Ernie's Western Dairy has two divisions: Milk and Ice Cream. The Milk division produces milk for a variable cost of $3 per gallon. The Ice Cream division processes milk into ice cream for an additional variable cost of $1 per gallon. Its ice cream sells for $6 per gallon.

Variable cost gives Ernie's a transfer price of $3 per gallon. Figure 13-5 shows how this price affects the two divisions' contribution margins.

Figure 13-5:		Milk	Ice Cream
Ernie's	Milk's sales price (the transfer price)	$3.00	
Western	Ice Cream's sales price (to customers)		$6.00
Dairy sets			
the transfer	Milk's variable cost	(3.00)	
price at	Ice Cream's variable cost of buying product from Milk		(3.00)
variable	Ice Cream's variable cost of sales commissions		(1.00)
cost.	Contribution margin per unit	$0.00	$2.00

Illustration by Wiley, Composition Services Graphics

Figure 13-5 shows how setting the contribution margin at Milk's variable cost of $3 shifts all the profits from the Milk division to the Ice Cream division, such that Milk earns no contribution margin per unit (left column), while Ice Cream earns $2 per unit (right column). If Ernie's evaluates the Milk division on its profitability, then the Milk division needs to find a better customer than the Ice Cream division — one that provides more contribution margin. Selling to an outside customer for a slightly higher price would improve Milk's profitability.

Establishing the transfer price at variable cost plus a markup

In order for both divisions to share profits more equally, managers may prefer to set the transfer price at variable cost plus a markup. At Ernie's Western Dairy (introduced in the preceding section), President Ernie Hill decides to set the transfer price at variable cost plus a $1 markup, resulting in a transfer price of $4 ($3 variable cost plus $1 markup). To see how the Milk and Ice Cream divisions now share profits, take a look at Figure 13-6. Fair is fair, and now the two divisions split their contribution margins equally: $1 goes to each.

Figure 13-6: Ernie's Western Dairy sets the transfer price at variable cost plus markup.		**Milk**	**Ice Cream**
	Milk's sales price (the transfer price)	$4.00	
	Ice Cream's sales price (to customers)		$6.00
	Milk's variable cost	(3.00)	
	Ice Cream's variable cost of buying product from Milk		(4.00)
	Ice Cream's variable cost of sales commissions		(1.00)
	Contribution margin per unit	$1.00	$1.00

Illustration by Wiley, Composition Services Graphics

Setting the transfer price at variable cost plus markup can lead to problems, though. Suppose that the Ice Cream division receives a special order to supply a local summer camp with 1,000 gallons of ice cream. Competitors offer to sell ice cream for $4.80 per gallon. How low can Ernie's Western Dairy Ice Cream division go?

The Ice Cream division figures that its variable costs equal the $4 transfer price plus another $1 in sales commissions. That makes $5, well over the competitors' price of $4.80. Therefore, Ice Cream division would probably skip this opportunity.

And yet, if you consider the real cost of the ice cream, Ernie's would have been better off if Ice Cream had cut its price. After all, because making a gallon of milk costs the Milk division only $3, total cost for the ice cream is really $4 ($3 variable cost to the Milk division plus $1 sales commission). Ernie's could've bid $4.75 per gallon on the summer camp account and still earned $0.75 contribution margin on each gallon sold.

Setting the transfer price at variable cost plus a markup, therefore, can lead to decisions that aren't in the best interest of the company as a whole. To avoid this scenario, Milk division must share its information about the real cost of the milk, even if that cost is lower than the transfer price. Furthermore, the divisions sometimes need to forgo their own profits in order to do what's most profitable for the whole company.

Basing transfer price on full cost

A company may set the transfer price at *full cost* (also known as *absorption cost*), which is the sum of variable and fixed costs per unit. In order to ensure that the selling division earns a profit, they can also add a markup.

Suppose that HOO Water Company produces both spring water and soft drinks. The Clor division produces spring water, and the Shpritz division makes soft drinks. HOO managers encourage Clor and Shpritz to work together so that Shpritz division uses Clor division's spring water to make its soft drinks. However, Clor division also sells its water to outside customers for $0.75 per gallon. In order to minimize costs, Shpritz can also buy water from suppliers other than Spring.

This year, Clor division plans to produce 100,000 gallons of spring water but has the ability to produce more water if it can sell it. Clor's water carries variable cost of $0.30 per gallon and must cover fixed costs of $40,000.

Shpritz division plans to make 60,000 gallons of soft drinks; it can buy the water from Shpritz or from an outside vendor. In addition to the cost of the water, Shpritz must pay $0.40 per gallon for flavorings and other additives to produce each gallon of soft drink. Shpritz also pays fixed costs of $30,000 per year. Shpritz's soft drink sells for $2 per gallon.

First, compute Clor's's full cost. Fixed costs amount to $40,000 needed to produce 100,000 gallons of spring water. The fixed cost per unit, then, comes to $0.40 per gallon ($40,000 ÷ 100,000 gallons). Clor's variable costs equal $0.30 per gallon; add that to the fixed cost per unit to get a total cost of $0.70 per gallon, the transfer price.

Figure 13-7 explains what happens when Clor supplies Shpritz with 60,000 worth of spring water for a transfer price of $0.70 per gallon and the rest to outside customers for $0.75 per gallon.

	Clor	Shpritz
Clor's sales to outside customers (40,000 gallons x $0.75)	$30,000	
Clor's sales to Shpritz (60,000 gallons x $0.70)	42,000	
Shpritz' sales of soft drinks (60,000 gallons x $2.00)		120,000
Clor's variable costs (100,000 gallons x $0.30)	(30,000)	
Shpritz's variable costs of buying spring water from Clor (60,000 gallons x $0.70)		(42,000)
Shpritz's variable costs of flavorings and other additives (60,000 gallons x $0.40)		(24,000)
Total contribution margin	$42,000	$54,000
Fixed costs	(40,000)	(30,000)
Net income of each division	$2,000	$24,000
HOO Water's total net income		$26,000

Figure 13-7: Best-case scenario: Clor sells spring water to Shpritz for $0.70 per gallon.

Illustration by Wiley, Composition Services Graphics

Here, Clor receives $30,000 in revenues from outside customers and $42,000 in revenues from Shpritz. Subtracting Clor's variable costs of $30,000 and fixed costs of $40,000 results in net income of $2,000. Shpritz takes in revenues of $120,000 from its soft drinks. Of this amount, it must pay $42,000 to Clor and $24,000 in other variable costs. Shpritz must also pay $30,000 worth of fixed costs, resulting in net income of $24,000 for Shpritz. HOO Water, which owns both divisions, earns a total income of $26,000 from both products.

Decisions to base transfer price on full cost can trick division managers into making bad decisions that hurt the overall company's profitability. Suppose another company, Malcolm Water, sells water for $0.65 per gallon. (In case you're wondering, Malcolm Water can charge less money for its water because its water is of poorer quality.) Shpritz division must choose between paying $0.70 per gallon to Clor division or $0.65 per gallon to Malcolm.

On one hand, Shpritz may prefer to do business with Clor just because both companies have the same parent. However, if HOO pays $0.70 a gallon to make water but only $0.65 to buy it from Malcolm, shouldn't HOO just buy the water from the cheaper outside vendor and save $0.05 per gallon?

Not necessarily. Figure 13-8 illustrates the fiasco that occurs when Shpritz attempts to save money by buying its water from Malcolm.

	Clor	Shpritz
Clor's sales to outside customers (40,000 gallons x $0.75)	$30,000	
Shpritz's sales of soft drinks (60,000 gallons x $2.00)		120,000
Clor's variable costs (40,000 gallons x $0.30)	(12,000)	
Shpritz's variable costs of buying spring water from Malcolm (60,000 gallons x $0.65)		(39,000)
Shpritz's variable costs of flavorings and other additives (60,000 gallons x $0.40)		(24,000)
Total contribution margin	$18,000	$57,000
Fixed costs	(40,000)	(30,000)
Net income of each division	($22,000)	$27,000
HOO Water's total net income		$5,000

Figure 13-8: Shpritz buys water from an outside vendor for $0.65 per gallon.

Illustration by Wiley, Composition Services Graphics

Shpritz's decision to try to cut costs reduces HOO Water's overall profitability by $21,000. No question about it: Shpritz's profitability goes up. Because the decision to outsource reduces the variable cost of buying water from $42,000 to $39,000, the net income of Shpritz rises to $27,000.

However, Shpritz's decision hurts Clor and ultimately reduces HOO Water's total profitability. Clor's sales to Shpritz of $42,000 completely dry up. Its variable costs also drop from $30,000 to $12,000. However, Clor's fixed costs of $40,000 remain the same, forcing Clor to suffer a loss of $22,000. HOO Water's overall profits fall from $26,000 to just $5,000. Basing the transfer price on full cost has led Shpritz to make decisions that hurt the company's overall profitability.

Positioning Transfer Price at Market Value

Setting the transfer price at market value solves many of the problems that crop up with the other methods described earlier in this chapter. If an outside market exists for the transferred goods, managers can set the transfer price equal to the listed market value of the goods. This listed market value is often readily available through listings published with commodity markets. These published listings eliminate the need for negotiations.

When the selling division operates at full capacity, market pricing usually encourages both divisions to do what's in the best interest of the whole company. When the transfer price equals market value, the selling division doesn't care who it sells to as long as the sale maximizes its revenue and profit. The purchasing division doesn't care who it buys from; it, too, makes choices to earn the highest revenue and profit possible. As each division maximizes its revenues and profits, so too does the whole company.

However, when the selling division has excess capacity, making additional sales in-house to the purchasing division increases the selling division's revenues and helps cover its fixed costs. In this scenario, market-value pricing may encourage the purchasing division to buy cheaper goods from outside sources instead of buying higher-priced goods from the selling division. (The full-cost and markup pricing strategies earlier in the chapter may also have this effect.) This move hurts the selling division's sales and profitability, possibly also damaging the whole company's performance.

Centralizing your business

Most managers think of transfer pricing as a necessary evil: You can't run your business without it, yet it often creates new problems that encourage managers to make decisions that aren't in the best interest of the company.

That said, no hard-and-fast rule requires companies to evaluate each division based on net income. That is, perhaps transfer pricing isn't as necessary an evil as it seems. Instead, managers may choose to evaluate selling divisions on their costs, eliminating the need for transfer prices that set revenues and net income. Similarly, evaluators may gauge purchasing divisions based on sales to outside customers and ignore their expenses (which would be based on the transfer price), at least for evaluation purposes. A company can also combine different divisions, eliminating the need for any transfer prices.

Part IV
Planning and Budgeting

The 5th Wave   By Rich Tennant

"Sorry, Cedric, the King cut my budget for additional fools. He said the project already had enough fools on it."

In this part . . .

This part explains how to prepare the *master budget,* a financial plan that projects how the company will meet its profit and cash flow goals. I also explain how to flex your budget — how to create a master budget that you can change in response to underlying circumstances.

Chapter 14

Master Budgets: Planning for the Future

*T*wo summers ago, I took my three Jersey boys on a cross-country camping trip, visiting Yellowstone National Park, Yosemite National Park, and Grand Canyon National Park. Along the way, we took detours through Chicago; Bozeman, Montana; San Francisco; Palo Alto; Beverly Hills; Las Vegas; Phoenix; San Antonio; and Miami Beach (not a typo).

Planning took about four months. After some negotiations, we agreed to the three primary destinations. Then we worked out an itinerary spreadsheet that specified driving times, side trips, and where we'd sleep every day over seven weeks. I used this itinerary to prepare a detailed budget, estimating the cost of food, gas, campsites, motels, and long-lived equipment. Finally, we booked it.

Don't worry; I'm not bringing up my vacation so I can show you my photo slideshow. I tell this story to illustrate that whether you're taking a road trip or running a Fortune 500 company, you need to plan for the future. This chapter clues you in on how to prepare a *master budget* (which uses realistic sales goals to plan your company's production level, cash flow, and profitability) for manufacturers, retailers, and service companies.

 Budgeting helps you plan your business — by identifying your goals and how you'll reach them — as well as control your business by measuring the likelihood that you'll be able to reach your goals. If you're not convinced yet, consider that budgeting does the following:

- ✔ Establishes measurable objectives for different parts of your company
- ✔ Signals when your company may get sidetracked by problems
- ✔ Motivates employees
- ✔ Coordinates different activities
- ✔ Determines whether you'll have adequate resources
- ✔ Helps you allocate resources throughout your business

In a big organization, poor planning can cause fatal errors: Your business may run out of inventory or cash.

Preparing a Manufacturer's Master Budget

Welcome to the world of Bizarro Accounting, where everything goes backward. Normally, a business must first buy materials, find labor, pay overhead, make goods, and finally sell them. But in the world of Bizarro Accounting, where people prepare budgets, you move in the opposite direction. Start with your sales. Don't use an accurate number based on actual receipts from the prior year. Instead, come up with a realistic ballpark estimate of next year's sales.

After you (sort of) know next year's sales, keep working backward. To make all these sales, what quantity of goods must your factory produce? Then figure out the direct materials, direct labor, and overhead needed to make all these goods.

From here, estimate your cash flows. No, not last year's cash flows. Next year's cash flows. Start with cash payments: How much will you need to pay in order to make all the goods that you plan to produce next year? Then look at inflows: Where will you generate the cash inflows needed to support production? Will you need to borrow money next year? Finally, prepare the rest of next year's financial statements.

Feeling like you're lost in Bizarro Accounting? Figure 14-1 provides a map of the master budget process I lay out in the following sections, starting with sales and then working its way down to a cash flows budget and other budgeted financial statements.

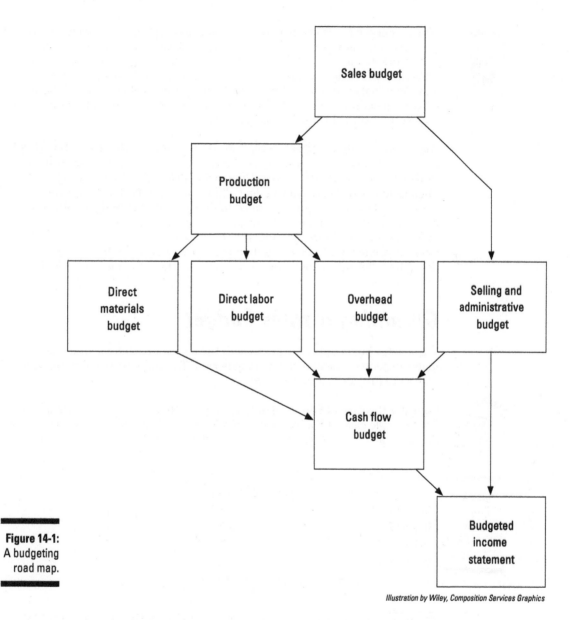

Illustration by Wiley, Composition Services Graphics

Figure 14-1:
A budgeting
road map.

When compared to budgeting, ordinary accounting is pretty cut and dried. In ordinary accounting, you record, classify, and report what happened. No guesswork; boom, you're done. However, in order to create a master budget, different parts of an organization need to negotiate and work out estimates and plans that coordinate all parts of the business. This process involves more than adding — different groups need to work together until they create a budget that works best for the organization.

For example, a draft of the master budget may indicate that the sales budget is too low to make the company profitable. So make the sales department rework the sales budget, perhaps increasing prices and lowering volume. Then redo the whole master budget all over again to find out what will happen. In fact, you're going to need to do and redo the budget until you create a budget based on realistic assumptions that generates manageable cash flow and maximizes net income. This document becomes your road map, so you need it to be accurate and to mark a clear route to your destination. The following sections break down the parts of the master budget.

Obtaining a sales budget

The master budget process starts with the sales department, which estimates expected sales for the coming period. The *sales budget* uses this information to project total sales revenue.

Consider the case of Forever Tuna, a company that processes and cans tuna fish. A single case of Forever Tuna sells for $100. Figure 14-2 provides the Sales department's projection of the next four quarters' sales.

Figure 14-2:		**Expected Unit Sales**
Projected	Quarter 1	4,000
sales of	Quarter 2	5,000
Forever	Quarter 3	6,000
Tuna.	Quarter 4	7,000

Illustration by Wiley, Composition Services Graphics

To create a sales budget that projects total sales for the next year, multiply expected unit sales by the sales price as shown in Figure 14-3.

Forever Tuna, Inc.

Sales Budget

For the Year Ended December 31, 2013

Figure 14-3:
How much
will Forever
Tuna sell
next year?

	Quarter 1	Quarter 2	Quarter 3	Quarter 4	Year
Expected unit sales	4,000	5,000	6,000	7,000	22,000
Sales price	$100	$100	$100	$100	$100
Total sales	$400,000	$500,000	$600,000	$700,000	$2,200,000

Illustration by Wiley, Composition Services Graphics

Generating a production budget

If you plan to sell inventory, you need some inventory to sell. That's why you need a production budget. The *production budget* computes the number of units the company needs to produce in order to meet its sales budget. To prepare a production budget, you estimate how much inventory the company wants to keep in stock at the end of each period.

To prepare a production budget, start with the formula for inventory flow that I present in Chapter 4:

Beginning + Inputs – Ending = Outputs

Chapter 4 shows you how to apply this formula to calculate the number of units sold, the number of units manufactured, cost of goods sold, and cost of goods manufactured.

But in master budgeting, you know the outputs (how many units you need) — just check out the sales budget. And you can find beginning and ending units on the company's estimates of inventory needed at the end of each period. Therefore, the missing number you're after in the production budget is inputs. How many units do you need to make? Rearrange the formula like so:

Inputs = Outputs + Ending – Beginning

Plug the numbers in for Forever Tuna's first quarter. According to the sales budget in Figure 14-3, the company plans to sell 4,000 units in the first quarter and 5,000 units in the second quarter. Managers keep inventory equal to 10 percent of the following period's sales. The company starts its first quarter in 2013 with 400 units. At the end of the first quarter, it needs 500 units (that is, 5,000 units projected to be sold in the second quarter times 10 percent).

Inputs = Outputs + Ending – Beginning

Inputs = 4,000 + 500 – 400

Inputs = 4,100 units

The company needs to produce 4,100 units.

A full-blown production budget computes this information for a whole year. As indicated in the sales budget shown in Figure 14-2, Forever Tuna projects unit sales of 4,000 in Quarter 1 of 2013. The production budget is shown in Figure 14-4.

Forever Tuna, Inc.
Production Budget
For the Year Ended December 31, 2013

	Quarter 1	Quarter 2	Quarter 3	Quarter 4	Year
Expected unit sales	4,000	5,000	6,000	7,000	22,000
Add: desired ending finished goods	500	600	700	750	2,550
Less: beginning finished goods units	(400)	(500)	(600)	(700)	(2,200)
Required units to produce	4,100	5,100	6,100	7,050	22,350

Figure 14-4: How much inventory will Forever Tuna make next year?

Illustration by Wiley, Composition Services Graphics

The number of beginning units in one period always equals the number of ending units in the prior period. Similarly, the cost of beginning inventory always equals the cost of ending inventory in the last period.

Setting a direct materials budget

Making inventory? You need to get direct materials (as well as direct labor and overhead, which I cover in the next sections). First tackle the *direct materials budget,* which specifies the amount of direct materials that the company must buy in order to meet its production budget. To prepare this document (using the budget formula I introduce in "Generating a production budget"), you need to know the following:

- ✔ **The level of production:** You find this info in the production budget.

- ✔ **The beginning direct materials inventory:** To get this information, go to the production budget for the most recently completed period.

- ✔ **The ending direct materials inventory the company wants:** Set this target at a level that ensures you have enough direct materials to feed production in the next period.

- ✔ **The direct materials that go into your products:** Base this figure on how you designed your products.

- ✔ **The cost of direct materials:** Obtain this projected price from the purchasing department.

The outputs are the level of production already noted in the existing production budget. For Forever Tuna's level of production, use the production budget in Figure 14-4. Assume the company started its first quarter with 2,460 pounds of direct materials inventory. Managers like to have 10 percent of the following period's direct materials in inventory at the beginning of each period. Because the company estimates that it'll need 40,000 pounds of direct materials in the first quarter of 2014, it'll need ending direct materials of 4,000 pounds at the end of the fourth quarter (which is 10 percent of 40,000). Six pounds of tuna fish go into every case of Forever Tuna. The company pays $10 per pound for tuna fish.

To compute the direct materials needed for production, multiply the number of finished goods units to be produced by the cost per unit. This calculation gives you the total direct materials needed for production. Next, following the budget formula, add desired ending direct materials and subtract beginning direct materials, to get the total direct material purchases needed. Multiply this amount by the cost of the direct material units to arrive at the total cost of direct materials. Figure 14-5 provides the direct materials budget for Forever Tuna.

This direct materials budget indicates that the company needs to purchase $252,000 worth of direct materials in the first quarter; $312,000 in the second quarter; $371,700 in the third quarter; and $420,700 in the fourth quarter.

Forever Tuna, Inc.
Direct Materials Budget
For the Year Ended December 31, 2013

	Quarter 1	Quarter 2	Quarter 3	Quarter 4	Year
Units to be produced (from Production Budget)	4,100	5,100	6,100	7,050	
Direct materials per unit (lbs.)	6	6	6	6	
Total direct materials needed for production (lbs.)	24,600	30,600	36,600	42,300	
Add: desired ending direct materials (lbs.)	3,060	3,660	4,230	4,000	
Less: beginning direct materials (lbs.)	(2,460)	(3,060)	(3,660)	(4,230)	
Direct material purchases (lbs.)	25,200	31,200	37,170	42,070	
Cost per pound	$10.00	$10.00	$10.00	$10.00	
Cost of direct material purchases	$252,000	$312,000	$371,700	$420,700	$1,356,400

Figure 14-5: What quantity of materials must Forever Tuna buy next year?

Illustration by Wiley, Composition Services Graphics

Working on a direct labor budget

In order to convert direct materials into finished goods, you need direct labor. The *direct labor budget* tells you how many direct labor hours of work you'll need, indicating whether you have enough workers or need to hire more.

To prepare a direct labor budget, multiply the number of units to be produced (from the production budget) by the direct labor time needed to make each unit. Then multiply that result by the average direct labor cost per hour.

In the Forever Tuna example from the preceding sections, the company's production budget (Figure 14-4) indicates the number of units to be produced. Assume making a single case of Forever Tuna takes half an hour of direct labor. The company pays, on average, $12 per direct labor hour. The direct labor budget in Figure 14-6 multiplies the number of units produced each quarter by the direct labor time per unit, by the direct labor cost per hour.

Forever Tuna, Inc.
Direct Labor Budget
For the Year Ended December 31, 2013

	Quarter 1	Quarter 2	Quarter 3	Quarter 4	Year
Units to be produced (from Production Budget)	4,100	5,100	6,100	7,050	
Direct labor hours per unit	½	½	½	½	
Total direct labor hours needed	2,050	2,550	3,050	3,525	
Direct labor cost per hour	$12.00	$12.00	$12.00	$12.00	
Cost of labor	$24,600	$30,600	$36,600	$42,300	$134,100

Figure 14-6:
How much will Forever Tuna need to pay workers next year?

Illustration by Wiley, Composition Services Graphics

The direct labor budget indicates that the company can expect to pay a total of $134,100 for direct labor next year.

Building an overhead budget

The *overhead budget* estimates the coming year's total overhead costs and sets an overhead allocation rate. (As I explain in Chapter 3, *overhead* consists of the costs of making products above and beyond direct materials and direct labor.) To prepare it, you need detailed information about the company's overhead, including an analysis of fixed and variable components of the overhead (refer to Chapter 5).

Chapter 6 explains how accountants allocate overhead to products by spreading overhead costs out over all of the units produced, like peanut butter on sandwiches. To find the *overhead allocation rate,* divide total overhead by the *cost driver,* a factor that you expect to vary with overhead. For the overhead budget, set the number of direct labor hours as the cost driver:

$$\text{Overhead allocation rate} = \frac{\text{Estimated total overhead}}{\text{Estimated total direct labor hours}}$$

Then, for each product, multiply the overhead allocation rate by the direct labor hours required.

Don't confuse the overhead allocation rate with variable overhead per unit or per direct labor hour. Variable overhead per unit is used to compute variable cost per unit when calculating contribution margin (see Chapter 9). Variable overhead per direct labor hour is used in theory of constraints (turn to Chapter 19).

For the earlier Forever Tuna example, assume that the company has variable overhead equal to $5 per direct labor hour. The company must pay an additional $200,000 per year in fixed overhead. Use the number of direct labor hours computed in the direct labor budget (in Figure 14-4 earlier in the chapter), to estimate total variable costs. Then add in fixed costs of $50,000 per quarter ($200,000 divided by four quarters) as shown in Figure 14-7.

Forever Tuna, Inc.
Overhead Budget
For the Year Ended December 31, 2013

	Quarter 1	Quarter 2	Quarter 3	Quarter 4	Year
Direct labor hours (from Direct Labor Budget)	2,050	2,550	3,050	3,525	
Variable overhead per unit	$4	$4	$4	$4	
Total variable overhead	$8,200	$10,200	$12,200	$14,100	
Total fixed overhead	50,000	50,000	50,000	50,000	
Total overhead	$58,200	$60,200	$62,200	$64,100	$244,700
Number of direct labor hours	2,050	2,550	3,050	3,525	11,175
Overhead allocation rate per direct labor hour ($244,700 / 11,175 hours)					$21.90
Number of units produced (from Production Budget)					22,350
Overhead cost per unit ($244,700 / 22,350 units)					$10.95

Figure 14-7: How much overhead will Forever Tuna pay next year?

Illustration by Wiley, Composition Services Graphics

Adding up the product cost

A critical step in the budgeting process is to compute *projected product cost,* or the expected cost of each unit made during the budget period. (Turn to Chapter 3 for more on product costs.) To calculate Forever Tuna's projected product cost, add together the costs of direct materials per unit, direct labor per unit, and overhead per unit, as shown in Figure 14-8.

Figure 14-8: Forever Tuna's product cost per unit.				
Direct materials per unit	$60.00	From Direct Materials Budget	(6 lbs. x $10 each)
Direct labor per unit	6.00	From Direct Labor Budget	(½ hour x $12 each)
Overhead per unit	10.95	From Overhead Budget	
Total cost per unit	$76.95		

Illustration by Wiley, Composition Services Graphics

On average, each unit costs $76.95 to make.

Product cost per unit helps you to prepare the budgeted income statement. Furthermore, this information is very useful for setting prices (see Chapter 12).

Fashioning a selling and administrative budget

Sales don't happen by themselves, especially when it comes to canned seafood product. If you plan to sell 22,000 cases of vacuum-packed tuna, you can't just sit around waiting for customers. Instead, you need a sales force, paid with a combination of salaries and commissions. You may also have to pay freight to ship goods to customers. And then you've got advertising, office salaries, and all the costs that come with running a sales office.

The *selling and administrative expense budget* predicts the amount of selling and administrative expenses (abbreviated S&A) needed to generate the sales forecasted in the sales budget. To prepare this budget, you need detailed information about the company's S&A; you then divide S&A costs into fixed and variable components.

Forever Tuna plans to sell 22,000 cases of product, as projected by the Sales department in Figure 14-2 earlier in the chapter. Suppose an account analysis indicates that Forever Tuna has variable S&A costs of $5 per unit. The company pays fixed S&A costs equal to $90,000 per year ($22,500 per quarter). Figure 14-9 shows how to combine fixed and variable S&A expenses to create an S&A budget.

Forever Tuna, Inc.
Selling and Administrative Budget
For the Year Ended December 31, 2013

	Quarter 1	Quarter 2	Quarter 3	Quarter 4	Year
Budgeted sales in units (from Sales Budget)	4,000	5,000	6,000	7,000	
Variable S&A per unit	$5	$5	$5	$5	
Total variable S&A	$20,000	$25,000	$30,000	$35,000	
Total fixed S&A	22,500	22,500	22,500	22,500	
Total S&A	$42,500	$47,500	$52,500	$57,500	$200,000

Figure 14-9: Forever Tuna's S&A budget.

Illustration by Wiley, Composition Services Graphics

The S&A budget indicates that Forever Tuna's managers expect to pay $200,000 worth of S&A expenses next year.

Creating a cash budget

The *cash budget* summarizes all your cash inflows and outflows for the period, adding cash receipts and subtracting cash payments. Positive cash projections assure you that your company will have enough cash to make it through the next period. If your cash budget comes out negative, though, you may have to start all over again from the beginning. Do not pass go, do not collect $200.

Before you can prepare a cash budget, however, do some homework to estimate cash receipts and cash payments. I walk you through the cash budgeting process in the following sections.

Predicting cash receipts

Some customers pay their bills quickly, but others take advantage of the credit you give them, paying more slowly. This delay means that predicted sales, as enumerated in the production budget (refer to the earlier section "Generating a production budget"), don't always immediately translate into cash flows.

Forever Tuna's accountants estimate that, on average, the company collects 40 percent of sales in the same month as the sale, 35 percent in the following month, and the remaining 25 percent two months after the sale. The company had $230,000 worth of accounts receivable on December 31, 2013, of which it collected $155,000 in the first quarter and the remaining $75,000 in the second quarter. Figure 14-10 provides a schedule of expected cash receipts, which computes when the company expects to receive payments for each quarter's sales.

Forever Tuna, Inc.
Schedule of Expected Cash Receipts
For the Year Ended December 31, 2013

	Sales	Quarter 1	Quarter 2	Quarter 3	Quarter 4
Accounts receivable, 12/31/2013		$155,000	$75,000		
Quarter 1	$400,000	160,000	140,000	$100,000	
Quarter 2	500,000		200,000	175,000	$125,000
Quarter 3	600,000			240,000	210,000
Quarter 4	700,000				280,000
Total collections	$2,200,000	$315,000	$415,000	$515,000	$615,000

Figure 14-10:
Forever Tuna's predicted cash receipts.

Quarter 1 sales collected in Quarter 1: $400,000 x 40% = $160,000;
Quarter 1 sales collected in Quarter 2: $400,000 x 35% = $140,000;
Quarter 1 sales collected in Quarter 3: $400,000 x 25% = $100,000;
Quarter 2 sales collected in Quarter 2: $500,000 x 40% = $200,000;
Quarter 2 sales collected in Quarter 3: $500,000 x 35% = $140,000;
Quarter 2 sales collected in Quarter 4: $500,000 x 25% = $125,000;
Quarter 3 sales collected in Quarter 3: $600,000 x 40% = $240,000;
Quarter 3 sales collected in Quarter 4: $600,000 x 35% = $210,000;
Quarter 4 sales collected in Quarter 4: $700,000 x 40% = $280,000.

Illustration by Wiley, Composition Services Graphics

The schedule of expected cash receipts indicates that Forever Tuna will probably receive $315,000 from its customers in the first quarter; $415,000 in the second quarter; $515,000 in the third quarter; and $615,000 in the fourth quarter.

Predicting cash payments

Just as you give customers the luxury of paying their bills over several quarters, so too do your suppliers probably give you time to pay yours.

Forever Tuna's policy is to pay half its accounts payable in the same quarter as the purchase and half in the following quarter. The company pays 75 percent of its S&A expense in the same quarter and 25 percent in the following quarter. The company had $105,375 worth of accounts payable on December 31, 2012, and paid that entire amount in the first quarter of 2013. The direct materials budget in Figure 14-5 earlier in the chapter provides the amount of direct materials that the company plans to purchase next year, and the S&A budget in Figure 14-9 indicates how much the company plans to spend on S&A.

For the company's schedule of estimated cash payments, look at Figure 14-11, which computes the payments to be made for purchases and S&A next year.

Forever Tuna, Inc.
Schedule of Expected Cash Payments
For the Year Ended December 31, 2013

		Quarter 1	Quarter 2	Quarter 3	Quarter 4
Accounts payable, 12/31/2012	$105,375	$105,375			
Quarter 1	Purchases $252,000	$126,000	$126,000		
	S&A $42,500	31,875	10,625		
Quarter 2	Purchases $312,000		156,000	156,000	
	S&A $47,500		35,625	11,875	
Quarter 3	Purchases $371,700			185,850	185,850
	S&A $52,500			39,375	13,125
Quarter 4	Purchases $420,700				210,350
	S&A $57,500				43,125
Total payments		$263,250	$328,250	$393,100	$452,450

Quarter 1 purchases paid in Quarter 1: $252,000 x 50% = $126,000;
Quarter 1 purchases paid in Quarter 2: $252,000 x 50% = $126,000;
Quarter 1 S&A paid in Quarter 1: $42,500 x 75% = $31,875;
Quarter 1 S&A paid in Quarter 2: $42,500 x 25% = $10,625;
Quarter 2 purchases paid in Quarter 2: $312,000 x 50% = $156,000;
Quarter 2 purchases paid in Quarter 3: $312,000 x 50% = $156,000;
Quarter 2 S&A paid in Quarter 2: $47,500 x 75% = $35,625;
Quarter 2 S&A paid in Quarter 3: $47,500 x 25% = $11,875;
Quarter 3 purchases paid in Quarter 3: $371,700 x 50% = $185,850;
Quarter 3 purchases paid in Quarter 4: $371,700 x 50% = $185,850;
Quarter 3 S&A paid in Quarter 3: $52,500 x 75% = $39,375;
Quarter 3 S&A paid in Quarter 4: $52,500 x 25% = $13,125;
Quarter 4 purchases paid in Quarter 4: $420,700 x 50% = $210,350;
Quarter 4 S&A paid in Quarter 4: $57,500 x 75% = $43,125

Figure 14-11:
Forever Tuna's predicted cash payments.

This schedule of expected cash payments indicates that Forever Tuna expects to pay $263,250 in the first quarter; $328,250 in the second quarter; $393,100 in the third quarter; and $452,450 in the fourth quarter for purchases and S&A.

Piecing together your cash budget

To prepare a cash budget, combine information about every cash inflow and outflow from the schedule of estimated cash receipts, the schedule of estimated cash payments, and any other budgets that involve cash flows (such as the direct labor budget, the overhead budget, and/or income tax payment info).

In addition to the cash flows listed in Figures 14-10 and 14-11, Forever Tuna must pay for direct labor and overhead, which it does immediately, as incurred. The company also must make quarterly income tax payments of $5,000. It started the year with $50,000 worth of cash. The cash budget culminates this project, as shown in Figure 14-12.

Forever Tuna, Inc.
Cash Budget
For the Year Ended December 31, 2013

	Quarter 1	Quarter 2	Quarter 3	Quarter 4
Beginning cash	$50,000	$13,950	$4,900	$23,000
Cash receipts (from Schedule of Estimated Cash Receipts, Figure 14-10)	315,000	415,000	515,000	615,000
Cash payments for purchases and S&A (from Schedule of Estimated Cash Payments, Figure 14-11)	(263,250)	(328,250)	(393,100)	(452,450)
Cash payments for direct labor (from Direct Labor Budget, Figure 14-6)	(24,600)	(30,600)	(36,600)	(42,300)
Cash payments for overhead (from Overhead Budget, Figure 14-7)	(58,200)	(60,200)	(62,200)	(64,100)
Cash payments for income taxes	(5,000)	(5,000)	(5,000)	(5,000)
Ending cash	$13,950	$4,900	$23,000	$74,150

Figure 14-12: Forever Tuna's cash budget.

Illustration by Wiley, Composition Services Graphics

Note how the amount of ending cash at the bottom of each column of the budget rolls forward to become beginning cash in the next quarter (at the top of the budget).

This cash budget indicates that Forever Tuna sure is cutting it close. Although the company starts with $50,000 worth of cash, its cash reserves drop to $5,800 by the end of the second quarter. This reserve level means that an error or some unexpected cash payment greater than $5,800 would cause the company to run out of cash in the middle of the year.

Constructing a budgeted income statement

Another key test of a budget is the *budgeted income statement.* Here, you can check to see whether all the predictions and assumptions you made about sales, materials, direct labor, overhead, and S&A will bear fruit next year to generate net income. Like the cash budget, a budgeted income statement that predicts a loss indicates that you need to take the master budget back to the drawing board.

A budgeted income statement looks like any other income statement, except that it's for next year rather than last year. After all, you're still in the backwards Bizarro Accounting world of budgeting.

Figure 14-13 illustrates Forever Tuna's budgeted income statement, drawing figures from the other budgets prepared throughout the chapter. The company's income tax rate is 28 percent. Following the multi-step format (refer to Chapter 9), it starts with sales revenue and then subtracts cost of goods sold to arrive at gross profit. Then it subtracts S&A expenses to arrive at operating income; adds interest or dividend revenue; and subtracts interest or dividend expense to arrive at income before income taxes. Finally, it subtracts income tax expense to arrive at net income.

Forever Tuna, Inc.

Budgeted Income Statement

For the Year Ended December 31, 2013

Sales	$2,200,000	*(Sales Budget, Figure 14-3)*
Cost of goods sold	1,692,900	*(See below)*
Gross profit	507,100	
Selling and administrative expenses	200,000	*(S&A Budget, Figure 14-9)*
Income from operations	307,100	
Income tax expense	85,988	*(307,100 x 28%)*
Net income	$221,112	

Figure 14-13:
Forever
Tuna's
budgeted
income
statement.

Computation of Cost of goods sold:

22,000 units x $76.95 each

22,000 units comes from the Sales Budget, Figure 14-3

$76.95 cost per unit comes from Figure 14-8

Illustration by Wiley, Composition Services Graphics

Whew! The budgeted income statement indicates that, if all the assumptions of the budget hold true, Forever Tuna will report $221,112 worth of net income next year.

Many companies also prepare a budgeted balance sheet based on the prior year's balance sheet and the budgets for next year.

Applying Master Budgeting to Nonmanufacturers

Manufacturers aren't the only companies that need master budgeting. Retailers and service providers have to plan ahead, too. The following sections give you some tips on how to adapt the manufacturer's master budgeting process for other industries.

Budgeting a retailer

Remember that a retailer buys and sells goods. Unlike a manufacturer, it doesn't make goods. Therefore, it just operates stores or warehouses, not factories.

Even without all the burdens of manufacturing, retailers still must prepare budgets. However, their merchandise purchases budget replaces the need for a production budget, direct materials budget, and overhead budget. A retailer uses its merchandise purchases budget to prepare a schedule of cash payments in order to complete its cash budget.

The merchandise purchases budget uses the same budget formula as the manufacturer's budget does:

Beginning + Inputs − Ending = Outputs

Here, the retailer wants to know inputs — how much merchandise to buy. The outputs equal the budgeted cost of goods sold. Ending means the desired balance of ending inventory, and beginning reflects the existing balance of inventory at the beginning of the period. You can apply this formula in total, for separate quarters or months, or even for individual products.

Pickers, Inc., owns a chain of mall stores that sell clothing. The company's inventory on December 31, 2012, equaled $250,000. The company budgets predict cost of goods sold in 2013 of $325,000 and desired ending inventory on December 31, 2013, of $210,000. Figure 14-14 shows how the company estimates the merchandise purchases needed for next year.

Figure 14-14:
Pickers' planned merchandise purchases.

Pickers, Inc.
Merchandise Purchases Budget
For the Year Ended December 31, 2013

Budgeted cost of goods sold	325,000
Ending merchandise inventory	210,000
Less: beginning merchandise inventory	(250,000)
Budgeted merchandise purchases	$285,000

Illustration by Wiley, Composition Services Graphics

This merchandise purchases budget indicates that Pickers needs to purchase $285,000 worth of merchandise during the period.

Coordinating a service company's budget

Service companies, such as law offices, limousine services, and cellphone companies, sell services rather than products. Like manufacturers and retailers, service companies also need to prepare budgets. However, service companies need to focus on their direct labor budgets because direct labor usually comprises most of these companies' expenses. Overstaffing (hiring too many workers) can drag down profits. Understaffing can cause employees to work excessive overtime or even force the company to turn down business.

For a service company, the direct labor budget feeds right into the cash budget and the budgeted income statement. Service companies usually have no need for production or overhead budgets.

Chapter 15

Flexing Your Budget: When Plans Change

. . . .

In This Chapter

▶ Using a budget to control your business

▶ Looking at variances and their causes

▶ Creating a flexible budget

. . . .

In Chapter 14, I talk about how carefully I planned a cross-country camping trip with my sons. To tell you the truth, things didn't quite go as planned, and my famed budget spreadsheet turned out not to be so accurate. A 30-percent increase in the price of gas added more than $1,000 to the cost of the trip. And although I had timed the trip to drive 600 miles per day, I didn't take into account stops for coffee, restrooms, or motion sickness. Changes in time zones gave us three additional hours when driving west, which we lost on the way home. Worse yet, the kids didn't care for my *Power Rangers* videos, a problem alleviated when the VHS player and offending videos mysteriously disappeared somewhere in Indiana or Illinois. Needless to say, this loss caused further expenses (a new DVD player and movie collection).

As my road trip attests, budgets don't have to be set in stone. This chapter explains how to use flexible budgets to manage your business's operations.

Controlling Your Business

Budgeting helps you plan your business's operations. However, you also need to *control* your business — to monitor what's actually happening. Controlling involves constantly comparing actual activity to your budget and carefully analyzing and understanding any differences. To accomplish this task, you need budget reports that compare your budgets (what should have happened) to what actually happened.

For example, suppose your company budgeted $100,000 for sales in the first quarter. Actual sales for the quarter come up short, at only $70,000. First, call the sales manager to find out what happened. (A computer snafu accidentally canceled customer orders.) Then, take corrective action. (Fix your computer and call your customers to apologize.) Finally, adjust your future plans. (Cut next quarter's production estimates.)

As I explain in Chapter 14, master budgeting provides the basic template for this analysis, offering projections for sales, expenses, production levels, and cash flows to help you plan for future periods. However, its major flaw is that it's *static* — it projects only one scenario based on a single set of sales estimates. It can't change.

Therefore, a $30,000 difference throws off more than just your sales budget. It also necessitates changing your production, purchases, direct labor, overhead costs, and selling and administrative expenses, ruining the entire planning process and making it impossible for you to make future comparisons between your budgets and actual results.

Enter the flexible budget. As activity levels change, you can easily adjust a flexible budget so that you can continue to use it to plan and control your business.

Dealing with Budget Variances

One of the benefits of flexible budgeting is that it helps you to understand the reasons for your company's *variances,* the differences between actual and budgeted amounts. The next section gives you the lowdown on the flexible budgeting process, but first I go a little deeper into the issue of variances.

Always indicate whether a variance is favorable or unfavorable. A variance is usually considered *favorable* if it improves net income and *unfavorable* if it decreases income. Therefore, when actual revenues exceed budgeted amounts, the resulting variance is favorable. When actual revenues fall short of budgeted amounts, the variance is unfavorable. On the other hand, when actual expenses exceed budgeted expenses, the resulting variance is unfavorable; when actual expenses fall short of budgeted expenses, the variance is favorable.

Accountants usually express favorable variances as positive numbers and unfavorable variances as negative numbers, as I do in this chapter and in Chapter 17. However, some accountants and managerial accounting textbooks avoid expressing any variance values as negative but always notate whether a variance is favorable or unfavorable. Still other accountants (and textbooks) call variances positive when the actual amount exceeds budget and negative when the actual amount falls short of budget. Here, a positive variance for sales would be favorable because sales were higher than expected. However, a positive variance for costs would be unfavorable because costs were higher than expected (hurting net income). In this chapter, and in Chapter 17, I always express variances as positive when they are favorable to income and negative when they are unfavorable to income. Even so, take special care, as I do, to indicate whether each variance is favorable or unfavorable to net income.

Management should investigate the cause of significant budget variances. Here are some possibilities:

- **Changes in conditions:** For example, a supplier may have raised prices, causing the company's costs to increase.

- **The quality of management:** Special care to reduce costs can result in favorable variances. On the other hand, management carelessness can drive up unfavorable variances.

- **Lousy budgeting:** An unrealistically ambitious budget is likely to cause negative variances.

Don't be fooled into thinking that favorable budget variances are always good news. Cost-cutting measures reflected in a favorable variance may actually hurt the quality of finished products. Senior managers may have preferred that the company had spent more for better materials and sold higher-quality goods.

Many managers use a system called *management by exception.* They investigate the largest variances, whether favorable or unfavorable, and ignore the rest. This strategy helps focus managers on potential problem areas in operations. Chapter 16 explains more about how to assign responsibility for budget variances.

Implementing a Flexible Budget

To compute variances that can help you understand why actual results differed from your expectations, creating a flexible budget is helpful. A *flexible budget* adjusts the master budget for your actual sales or production volume.

For example, your master budget may have assumed that you'd produce 5,000 units; however, you actually produce 5,100 units. The flexible budget rearranges the master budget to reflect this new number, making all the appropriate adjustments to sales and expenses based on the unexpected change in volume.

To prepare a flexible budget, you need to have a master budget, really understand cost behavior, and know the actual volume of goods produced and sold.

Consider Kira, president of the fictional Skate Company, which manufactures roller skates. Kira's accountant, Steve, prepared the overhead budget shown in Figure 15-1.

Skate Company
Overhead Budget
For the Year Ended December 31, 2013

Budgeted production	100,000	units
Indirect materials	$50,000	
Indirect labor	40,000	
Supervisory salaries	100,000	
Rent	80,000	
Utilities	40,000	
Depreciation	20,000	
Total overhead	$330,000	

Figure 15-1: Skate's static overhead budget.

Illustration by Wiley, Composition Services Graphics

Skate had a great year; actual sales came to 125,000 units. However, much to the disappointment of Steve and Kira, the overhead budget report, shown in Figure 15-2, reported major overruns. For each category of overhead, Steve computed a variance, identifying unfavorable variances in indirect materials, indirect labor, supervisory salaries, and utilities.

Skate Company
Overhead Budget Report
For the Year Ended December 31, 2013

	Budget	Actual	Variance	Favorable/ Unfavorable
Production (units)	100,000	125,000		
Indirect materials	$50,000	$60,000	($10,000)	Unfavorable
Indirect labor	40,000	45,000	(5,000)	Unfavorable
Supervisory salaries	100,000	105,000	(5,000)	Unfavorable
Rent	80,000	80,000	-0-	
Utilities	40,000	45,000	(5,000)	Unfavorable
Depreciation	20,000	20,000	-0-	
Total overhead	$330,000	$355,000	($25,000)	Unfavorable

Figure 15-2: Skate's overhead budget report.

Illustration by Wiley, Composition Services Graphics

Skate's total overhead exceeded budget by $25,000. Steve made the elementary mistake of treating variable costs as fixed. After all, portions of overhead, such as indirect materials, appear to be variable costs. If Skate increased production from 100,000 units to 125,000 units, these variable costs should also increase. In other words, comparing the $60,000 actual cost of making 125,000 units to the $50,000 budgeted cost of making just 100,000 units makes no sense. You're comparing apples and oranges.

Instead, Steve should flex the budget to determine how much overhead he should have, assuming that the company makes 130,000 units. The following sections show you how.

Separating fixed and variable costs

Some costs are *variable* — they change in response to activity levels — while other costs are *fixed* and remain the same. For example, direct materials are variable costs because the more goods you make, the more materials you need. On the other hand, some overhead costs, such as rent, are fixed; no matter how many units you make, these costs stay the same. To determine whether a cost is variable or fixed, think about the nature of the cost and evaluate it by using the techniques in Chapter 5.

For Skate, an analysis indicates that indirect materials, indirect labor, and utilities are variable costs. On the other hand, supervisory salaries, rent, and depreciation are fixed. Steve recomputes variable costs with the assumption that the company makes 125,000 units, as shown in Figure 15-3.

	Original Budget	Variable Cost per Unit	Flexible Budget
		Original budget/ 100,000	Average cost x 125,000
Production	100,000 units		125,000 units
Indirect materials	$50,000	$0.50	62,500
Indirect labor	40,000	0.40	50,000
Utilities	40,000	0.40	50,000
Total	$130,000	$1.30	$162,500

Figure 15-3: Flexing variable overhead costs.

Illustration by Wiley, Composition Services Graphics

In the original budget, making 100,000 units resulted in total variable costs of $130,000. Dividing total cost of each category by the budgeted production level results in variable cost per unit of $0.50 for indirect materials, $0.40 for indirect labor, and $0.40 for utilities.

To compute the value of the flexible budget, multiply the variable cost per unit by the actual production volume. Here, Figure 15-3 indicates that the variable costs of producing 125,000 should total $162,500 (125,000 units × $1.30).

Comparing the flexible budget to actual results

The next step is to combine the variable and fixed costs in order to prepare a new overhead budget report, inserting the new flexible budget results into the overhead budget report as shown in Figure 15-4.

Skate Company
Overhead Budget Report (Flexible)
For the Year Ended December 31, 2013

	Flexible Budget	Actual	Variance	Favorable/ Unfavorable
Production (units)	125,000	125,000		
Variable Costs				
Indirect materials	$62,500	$60,000	$2,500	Favorable
Indirect labor	50,000	45,000	5,000	Favorable
Utilities	50,000	45,000	5,000	Favorable
Total variable costs	$162,500	$150,000		
Fixed Costs				
Supervisory salaries	100,000	105,000	(5,000)	Unfavorable
Rent	80,000	80,000	-0-	
Depreciation	20,000	20,000	-0-	
Total fixed costs	$200,000	$205,000		
Total overhead	$362,500	$355,000	$7,500	Favorable

Figure 15-4:
Skate's flexible overhead budget.

Illustration by Wiley, Composition Services Graphics

Look at that! After you adjust for the change in production level, Skate's variance is suddenly favorable. Actual overhead of $355,000 was $7,500 less than the $362,500 flexible budget.

Part V

Using Managerial Accounting for Evaluation and Control

The 5th Wave   By Rich Tennant

"If we cut our dividend, reduce inventory, and time travel to the 13th century, we should be able to last another year."

In this part . . .

You can use the budget to evaluate and control performance. After all, making budgetary plans for next year isn't enough; you have to make sure your plan is followed. In this part, I introduce *responsibility accounting* — how to assign responsibility to different parts of the organization. Then I explain *variance analysis,* a set of techniques that identify unexpected events, measure how they affect income, and help assign responsibility for them. I also discuss the *balanced scorecard,* which uses a wide-ranging set of measures to determine whether a company's strategy is in place as planned, and introduce you to the theory of constraints.

Chapter 16

Responsibility Accounting

. . . .

In This Chapter

▶ Organizing to implement strategy

▶ Handing over authority and establishing accountability

▶ Evaluating the performance of responsibility centers

. . . .

*A*h, teenage driving, one of the great rites of passage. The teen reaches driving age, passes the road test, and then asks for the keys. Along with the keys comes authority — not only the authority to drive a car but also the authority to go more places and to take family and friends there, too.

With this new authority comes responsibility (to drive carefully, to follow the law, and to obey any other rules parents try to enforce) and limits (driving the old pickup is okay, but keep away from the sports car). When the young driver oversteps these limits, it becomes time for accountability.

Just as a parent can't hand over the keys to the car without setting some degree of accountability, a manager can't delegate authority over a division of the company without also establishing accountability. *Responsibility accounting* is the primary tool to establish accountability throughout an organization; it involves ensuring that subordinates receive the authority to perform tasks and are held accountable for their performance. Organizations usually have a hierarchical structure in which individual managers report to more-senior managers, who in turn report to top managers. In this chapter, I look at how a company's strategy ties to its corporate organization and then delve into how divisions are classified based on what they're held responsible for.

Linking Strategy with an Organization's Structure

Companies and other organizations establish *goals* that they plan to meet, such as benchmarks for sales, profitability, new products, and even employee satisfaction. Ideally, all employees know the organization's goals and understand their roles in meeting them. The plan to meet the company's goals is called the *strategy*.

Managers should structure the company's operations to support its strategy to meet the company's goals. Doing so usually means breaking the strategy down into smaller tasks that different managers and departments can take responsibility for performing. In the typical chain of command for a small company, some number of vice presidents report to a president, each overseeing a different aspect of executing the company's strategy. A separate group of employees reports to each vice president. The organizational structure requires the president to delegate tasks to individual vice presidents, who in turn delegate tasks to their employees.

Suppose that the NNW Company has a goal to earn $100,000 in profit. Part of its strategy is to advertise in social media outlets to encourage more teenagers to buy its leading product, the MacGuffin. The company hopes the ads will lure more teens to MacGuffins, increasing the company's sales and net income.

To implement this strategy, NNW needs to prepare a master budget (which I discuss in Chapter 14) that provides a kind of a road map to outline how exactly the company plans to sell more MacGuffins and increase its profits. The budget breaks up the strategy into different tasks and objectives, assigning them to managers and departments throughout the company. For example, NNW's Advertising department takes responsibility for creating a social media campaign. Sales agents are responsible for identifying new distribution channels for MacGuffins (which in turn will increase sales and profitability). A factory worker's role is to produce MacGuffins (increasing sales and profitability). A maintenance worker's role is to keep the office in shipshape condition so that other employees can effectively work to increase MacGuffin sales while keeping costs down.

The management controls in Chapters 15, 17, and 18 help managers identify weaker and stronger areas within the organization and understand how performance in those areas affects the implementation of the overall strategy.

For example, suppose NNW senior managers budget $50,000 for the Advertising department to spend on the new MacGuffin social media campaign. When examining the advertising budget report, senior managers notice that the department only spent $30,000 on the campaign, a favorable variance of $20,000 (*favorable* because it increased income; refer to Chapter 15 for more on variances). Managers now need to ascertain why the Advertising department spent so little on its social media campaign even though the social media angle is such an important part of its growth strategy.

When delegating tasks, managers must give both authority and accountability to complete those tasks:

- ✔ **Authority:** The subordinate must receive authority to perform the task.

- ✔ **Accountability:** The subordinate must be accountable to the manager for performing the task.

For example, an NNW sales agent receives office space, samples, and computer software needed to serve customers, but she's also accountable for sales made to those customers. The factory worker receives a workstation and job responsibilities to produce goods and then is made accountable for the amount and quality of goods produced. The maintenance worker receives the supplies and equipment needed to keep the office clean. A supervisor checks to make sure that all cleaning procedures were followed. The following sections look at a couple of important points to consider about organization structure and accountability.

Decentralizing

Decentralization is the process of moving decision-making powers down the chain of command. In a highly decentralized organization, frontline managers and staff often make important decisions. On the other hand, in a highly *centralized* organization, senior managers at the top of the organization chart make the decisions.

Decentralization offers several benefits:

- ✔ Large corporations may need to oversee many diverse subsidiaries, making it impossible for a top-level manager to call all the shots.

- ✔ Frontline employees usually have closer access to the information needed to make decisions, enabling them to respond more quickly than senior managers can.

✔ Decentralization empowers employers to make more independent decisions with less red tape from senior managers, often improving employee morale.

✔ It facilitates speedy customer service because it doesn't require employees to wait for supervisor approvals.

As an example of decentralization, many discount stores train and empower service desk employees to decide which customer returns to accept and which to reject. After all, those folks should best know which returns appear reasonable, and anyway, the dollar value of each return is low. A more centralized organization would impose stricter requirements on which returns a service desk employee can or can't accept, leaving very little to the employee's own judgment.

That said, decentralization has some problems, so it isn't for every organization. Decentralized organizations often must devote duplicate assets and duplicate efforts to get things done. Furthermore, decentralization can make it difficult for senior managers to fully monitor and control a large number of frontline employees making decisions. As such, poor or self-interested decisions may lead to errors or even fraud.

For example, when issuing home mortgages, most banks require that a central department approve every mortgage applicant. Although this process delays the application process (and damages the perception of customer service), it also reduces the proportion of bad loans.

Distinguishing controllable costs from noncontrollable costs

Because authority and accountability go together, you can only hold individuals and units in an organization accountable for those things that they can control. If you don't give subordinates authority to do something, how can you hold them accountable for doing it?

Suppose Eve asked Alfred to walk her dog for a week. However, she refused to give Alfred the keys to her apartment, so he had no access to the dog. Because Eve didn't give Alfred the authority to do his job, Eve can't possibly hold him accountable for not walking the dog (or for the resulting mess in her apartment).

Given the organization's goals and strategies, every required task and decision should be under someone's watch. Responsibility accounting allows you to hold subordinates responsible for all tasks over which they have control.

In the realm of budgets and costs, therefore, the budget should carefully designate which departments have authority over and are responsible for which costs. If a department has authority and responsibility for certain costs, those costs are called *controllable costs*. The *noncontrollable costs* are those costs that a department doesn't have authority over and can't change.

Overhead allocations, described in Chapter 6, are usually inconsistent with the idea of controllable costs. Overhead allocations use allocation rates to assign overhead costs based on number of units, direct labor hours, or other cost drivers to individual departments. Each department must then include a portion of this overhead as a cost in its own budget, even though these departments usually have little or no say over how money is spent for this overhead. Even when one of these departments closes completely, its overhead costs often remain and get assigned to other departments. In this way, arbitrary overhead allocations often result, forcing departments to accept responsibility for overhead costs that they have little or no control over — noncontrollable costs.

Identifying Different Kinds of Centers

Responsibility centers are identifiable segments within a company for which individual managers have accepted authority and accountability. Responsibility centers define exactly what assets and activities each manager is responsible for.

Companies have four basic kinds of responsibility centers:

- ✔ Revenue centers
- ✔ Cost centers
- ✔ Profit centers
- ✔ Investment centers

How to classify any given department depends on which aspects of the business the department has authority over. The following sections cover each type of center in more detail.

Managers prepare a *responsibility report* to evaluate the performance of each responsibility center. This report compares the responsibility center's budgeted performance with its actual performance, measuring and interpreting individual variances. Responsibility reports should include only controllable costs so that managers are not held accountable for activities they have no control over. Using a flexible budget, which I cover in Chapter 15, is helpful for preparing a responsibility report.

Revenue centers

Revenue centers usually have authority over sales only and have very little control over costs. To evaluate a revenue center's performance, look only at its revenues and ignore everything else.

Think about an arena concession stand owned by BIG Concessions and run by a guy named Al. BIG Concessions' senior management sets the prices, and the purchasing department buys food products at the lowest possible cost. Therefore, Al, as the manager of the concession stand, can influence only one factor: how many hot dogs, hamburgers, and soft drinks he sells during a game. This setup means that the concession should be classified as a revenue center.

This season, BIG budgeted Al to sell 100,000 hot dogs for $5 each. At this price, he and his concession stand actually sell 105,000 hot dogs. Take a look at the responsibility report in Figure 16-1.

BIG Concessions
Stand No. 347 (run by Al)
Responsibility Report
For the Year Ended December 31, 2014

Sales	Budget	Actual	Favorable / Unfavorable
No. of units	100,000	105,000	
Price	$5.00	$5.00	
Total revenues	$500,000	$525,000	$25,000 Favorable

Figure 16-1: A revenue center's responsibility report.

Illustration by Wiley, Composition Services Graphics

Here, a $25,000 favorable variance makes Al look good.

Revenue centers have some drawbacks. Their evaluations are based entirely on sales, so revenue centers have no reason to control costs. This kind of free rein encourages Al the concession manager to hire extra employees or to find other costly ways to increase sales (giving away salty treats to increase drink purchases, perhaps).

Therefore, sales centers need to keep tight restrictions over costs. In this example, BIG probably institutes rules that the concession manager can't hire additional employees without approval from BIG managers.

Cost centers

Cost centers usually produce goods or provide services to other parts of the company. Because they only make goods or services, they have no control over sales prices and therefore can be evaluated based only on their total costs.

Suppose that the Farm department of fictional company Gray Gardens Florist grows flowers. To evaluate the Farm department, the managers' focus is strictly on its costs.

Such an approach may encourage the Farm Department to produce fewer goods. After all, one easy way to reduce costs is to make and do less. As I explain in Chapter 15, flexible budgets take into account how unexpected increases or decreases in volume affect total costs. Therefore, a flexible budget holds the department accountable for its costs at the actual volume level rather than at a hypothetical budgeted volume level.

Figure 16-2 provides a responsibility report for Gray Gardens' Farm department. This analysis includes only the costs that Judy, supervisor of the Farm department, can control. It doesn't include any noncontrollable overhead allocated from other departments.

Judy has a lot of explaining to do. For this level of production, the flexible budget predicts that the Farm department should have costs of $580,000. However, costs went up to $630,000, causing an unfavorable variance.

Gray Gardens
Farm Department
Responsibility Report (based on Flexible Budget)
For the Year Ended December 31, 2014

Controllable Cost	Flexible Budget	Actual	Favorable / Unfavorable
Units of production	300,000 flowers	300,000 flowers	
Direct materials	$200,000	$207,000	($7,000) Unfavorable
Direct labor	80,000	83,000	(3,000) Unfavorable
Overhead	300,000	340,000	(40,000) Unfavorable
Total costs	$580,000	$630,000	($50,000) Unfavorable

Figure 16-2: Responsibility report for a cost center.

Illustration by Wiley, Composition Services Graphics

One way for a cost center to reduce costs is to buy inferior materials, but doing so hurts the quality of finished goods. When dealing with cost centers, you must carefully monitor the quality of goods.

Profit centers

Profit centers are businesses within a larger business, such as the individual stores that make up a mall, whose managers enjoy control over their own revenues and expenses. They often select the merchandise to buy and sell, and they have the power to set their own prices. Profit centers are evaluated based on *controllable margin* — the difference between controllable revenues and controllable costs. Exclude all noncontrollable costs, such as allocated overhead or other indirect fixed costs, from the evaluation. The beautiful thing about running a profit center is that doing so gives managers an incentive to do exactly what the company wants: earn profits.

When a company both makes and sells a particular good, the manufacturing and retail departments aren't automatically classified as profit centers. Unless the company utilizes *transfer pricing* (which establishes the prices for goods bought and sold between departments of the same company; refer to

Chapter 13), the manufacturer is just a cost center, and the retailer is treated as a revenue center. You can see this setup in Figure 16-3a. However, a transfer price allows the manufacturing department to record sales to the retail department, transforming manufacturing from a cost center to a profit center. Similarly, the same transfer price sets a cost for the retail department, transforming retail's status from revenue center to profit center (as shown in Figure 16-3b).

Consider Blake, a company that makes and sells the Replicon fashion line. Blake's Manufacturing department makes Replicon swimsuits for the company's own retail department, so the company's responsibility centers can be classified a couple of different ways, as I describe earlier. For this example, assume that Blake's Retail department is a profit center (this is the profit center section, after all). Figure 16-4 provides a responsibility report for Blake's Retail department.

The Retail department had an excellent year, reporting a $109,000 favorable variance. Note that the responsibility report covers only controllable costs.

Without transfer price

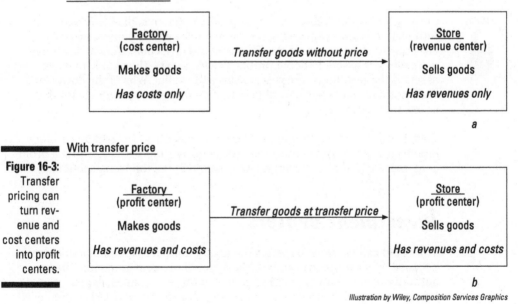

With transfer price

Figure 16-3:
Transfer
pricing can
turn rev-
enue and
cost centers
into profit
centers.

Illustration by Wiley, Composition Services Graphics

Blake-Runner, Inc.
Retail Department
Responsibility Report (based on Flexible Budget)
For the Year Ended December 31, 2014

	Flexible Budget	Actual	Favorable / Unfavorable
Sales	$1,000,000	$1,100,000	$100,000 Favorable
Controllable costs:			
Cost of goods sold	450,000	445,000	5,000 Favorable
Selling & administrative	100,000	96,000	4,000 Favorable
Total expenses	550,000	541,000	
Controllable margin	$450,000	$559,000	$109,000 Favorable

Figure 16-4: Responsibility report for a profit center.

Illustration by Wiley, Composition Services Graphics

Classifying responsibility centers as profit centers has disadvantages. Although they get evaluated based on revenues and expenses, no one pays attention to their use of assets. This scenario gives managers an incentive to use excessive assets to boost profits. For managers, the upside of using more assets is the resulting increases in sales and profits. What's the downside? Well, nothing; managers of profit centers aren't held accountable for the assets that they use.

This flaw in the evaluation of profit centers can be addressed by carefully monitoring how profit centers use assets or by simply reclassifying a profit center as an investment center, as explained in the following section.

Investment centers

You could call *investment centers* the luxury cars of responsibility centers because they feature everything. Managers of investment centers have authority over — and are held responsible for — revenues, expenses, and investments made in their centers. *Return on investment* (ROI) is often used to evaluate their performance:

$$\text{Return on investment} = \frac{\text{Controllable margin}}{\text{Average operating assets}}$$

In this formula, controllable margin equals the difference between controllable revenues and controllable costs. To improve return on investment, the manager can either increase controllable margin (profits) or decrease average operating assets (improve productivity).

Suppose that Blake's Retail department is budgeted to have $2,000,000 in average operating assets. Its budgeted controllable margin is $450,000, as shown in Figure 16-4. Compute the department's budgeted ROI:

$$\text{Budgeted ROI} = \frac{\text{Controllable margin}}{\text{Average operating assets}}$$
$$= \frac{450,000}{2,000,000}$$
$$= 22.5\%$$

Suppose that the company dramatically increases its inventory and other operating assets, driving up average operating assets all the way to $3 million. Actual controllable margin is $559,000 (from Figure 16-4). Calculate the department's actual ROI:

$$\text{Actual ROI} = \frac{\text{Controllable margin}}{\text{Average operating assets}}$$
$$= \frac{559,000}{3,000,000}$$
$$= 18.6\%$$

Even though the Retail department's controllable margin had a very favorable variance (see Figure 16-4), its actual ROI fell below the budget to just 18.6 percent because of excessive investments in operating assets. In future periods, the Retail department will need to either increase its controllable margin to justify the increase in operating assets or decrease its operating assets to become more productive.

Using return on investment to evaluate investment centers addresses many of the drawbacks involved in evaluating revenue centers, costs centers, and profit centers. However, classification as an investment center can encourage managers to emphasize productivity over profitability — to work harder to reduce assets (which increases ROI) rather than to increase overall profitability.

Chapter 17

Variance Analysis: To Tell the Truth

*W*hen things don't go according to plan, inevitably you're left asking "Why?" To find the answer, examine the factors under your control. For example, I don't like to diet. As an accountant, I should enjoy counting calories. But I don't. I don't like exercise either. That said, checking my weight often leaves me asking "Why?" Inevitably, I thought I was so careful this week. Why did I gain three pounds? It all comes down to three factors under my control:

✔ What I eat and drink

✔ How much I eat and drink

✔ How much I exercise

Examining each of these factors in more detail helps me change my routine so that I can diet more successfully in the future.

Variance analysis plays a similar role for business. When things go wrong, or even when they go more right than expected, variance analysis explains why. What caused higher-than-expected profits? What about unexpected losses? You can use all this information to improve future operations.

Setting Up Standard Costs

You can't measure variances without first setting *standard costs* or *standards* — predetermined unit costs of materials, labor, and overhead. Standards are really the building blocks of budgets; budgets predict total costs (as I explain in Chapter 14), but standards predict the cost of each unit of direct materials, direct labor, and overhead.

Standard costs provide a number of important benefits for managers:

- ✔ They help managers budget for the future.
- ✔ They help all employees focus on keeping costs down.
- ✔ They help set sales prices.
- ✔ They give managers a benchmark for measuring variances and identifying related problems.
- ✔ They simplify collecting and managing the cost of inventory.
- ✔ They provide useful information for variance analysis (which I explain in this chapter).

Implementing standards often forces managers to face a critical dilemma: Should standards be aspirational or realistic?

- ✔ **Ideal or aspirational standards** can encourage employees to work hard to achieve rigorous goals. However, overly aggressive standards can unduly pressure employees, causing them to report false information or to just give up on the standards out of frustration, deeming them unattainable.

- ✔ **Realistic standards** provide more-accurate cost information and are less likely to lead to the kind of unfavorable variances that result in lower-than-expected income. However, realistic standards don't always encourage employees to "go the extra mile" to improve cost control and productivity.

Therefore, the first step in variance analysis is to set up expectations: your standards. These standards must include both the cost and the quantity needed of direct materials and direct labor, as well as the amount of overhead required.

After you establish standards, you can use them to compute variances, which help explain why actual performance strayed from expectations.

Establishing direct materials standards

Direct materials are raw materials traceable to the manufactured product, such as the amount of flour used to make a cake.

To compute the direct materials standard price (SP), consider all the costs that go into a single unit of direct materials. Because several different kinds of direct materials are often necessary for any given product, you need to establish separate direct materials standard prices and quantities for every kind of direct materials needed.

Suppose that the Band Book Company usually pays $10 per pound for paper. It typically pays $0.25 per pound for freight and another $0.10 per pound for receiving and handling. Therefore, as shown in Figure 17-1, total cost per pound equals $10.35.

Figure 17-1:
Adding up direct materials standard price (SP).

Cost	Per Pound
Purchase price	$10.00
Freight-in	0.25
Receiving and handling	0.10
Direct materials standard price (SP)	$10.35

Illustration by Wiley, Composition Services Graphics

Another standard to consider is the *direct materials standard quantity* (SQ) per unit. This number is the amount of direct materials needed to make a single unit of finished product. It includes not only the direct materials actually used but also any direct materials likely to get scrapped or spoiled in the production process.

Variance costing involves juggling many different figures and terms. To simplify matters, use abbreviations like SP (for direct materials standard price) and SQ (for direct materials standard quantity). Doing so makes remembering how to calculate variances easier later in this chapter.

For example, assume that Band Book Company needs 25 pounds of paper to make a case of books. For every case, three pounds of paper are deemed unusable because of waste and spoilage. Therefore, the direct materials standard quantity per unit equals 28 pounds, as shown in Figure 17-2.

Figure 17-2:
Computing direct materials standard quantity (SQ) per unit.

Cost	Quantity (Pounds)
Required materials per unit	25
Waste and spoilage	3
Direct materials standard quantity (SQ)	28

Illustration by Wiley, Composition Services Graphics

Determining direct labor standards

Direct labor is the cost of paying your employees to make products. Proper planning requires setting standards with respect to two factors:

✔ The direct labor standard rate

✔ The direct labor standard hours per unit

To compute the *direct labor standard rate* or SR (the cost of direct labor), consider all the costs required for a single hour of direct labor. For example, suppose Band Book usually pays employees $9 per hour. Furthermore, it pays an additional $1 per hour for payroll taxes and, on average, $2 per hour for fringe benefits. As shown in Figure 17-3, the direct labor standard rate equals $12 per hour.

Figure 17-3:
Computing the direct labor standard rate (SR).

Cost	Per Hour
Average hourly wage	$9.00
Payroll taxes	1.00
Fringe benefits	2.00
Direct labor standard rate (SR)	$12.00

Illustration by Wiley, Composition Services Graphics

You also need to estimate the amount of direct labor time needed to make a single unit, the *direct labor standard hours* (SH) per unit. This measurement estimates how long employees take on average to produce a single unit. Include in this rate the time needed for employee breaks, cleanups, and setups.

For example, employees at Band Book Company need three hours to produce a single case of books, plus an average of 30 minutes of setup time and 30 minutes of break time. Therefore, the direct materials standard quantity equals four hours, as shown in Figure 17-4.

Figure 17-4:
Computing
direct labor
standard
hours (SH).

Cost	Hours
Average production time	3.00
Break time	0.50
Setup time	0.50
Direct labor standard hours (SH)	4.00

Illustration by Wiley, Composition Services Graphics

Determining the overhead rate

Standard costs also need to account for *overhead* (the miscellaneous costs of running a business; refer to Chapter 2) in addition to direct materials and direct labor. Overhead is much more difficult to measure than direct materials or direct labor standards because overhead consists of indirect materials, indirect labor, and other costs not easily traced to units produced. Therefore, measuring how much overhead should be applied to different units produced is very challenging. To assign overhead costs to individual units, you need to compute an overhead allocation rate, as explained in Chapter 6.

Remember that overhead allocation entails three steps:

1. **Add up total overhead.**

   Add up estimated indirect materials, indirect labor, and all other product costs not included in direct materials and direct labor. This amount includes both fixed and variable overhead.

   For example, assume that total overhead for Band Book Company is estimated to cost $100,000.

2. **Compute the overhead allocation rate.**

   Divide total overhead (calculated in Step 1) by the number of direct labor hours.

Assume that Band Book plans to utilize 4,000 direct labor hours:

$$\text{Overhead allocation rate} = \frac{\text{Total overhead}}{\text{Total direct labor hours}}$$
$$= \frac{\$100,000}{4,000 \text{ hours}}$$
$$= \$25.00$$

Therefore, for every hour of direct labor needed to make books, Band Book applies $25 worth of overhead to the product.

3. **Apply overhead.**

   Multiply the overhead allocation rate by the number of direct labor hours needed to make each product.

   Suppose a department at Band Book actually worked 20 hours on a product. Apply $500 worth of overhead to this product (20 hours × $25).

Adding up standard cost per unit

To find the standard cost, you first compute the cost of direct materials, direct labor, and overhead per unit, as I explain in the previous sections. Then you add these amounts up.

Figure 17-5 applies this approach to Band Book Company. To calculate the standard cost of direct materials, multiply the direct materials standard price of $10.35 by the direct materials standard quantity of 28 pounds per unit. The result is a direct materials standard cost of $289.80 per case. To compute direct labor standard cost per unit, multiply the direct labor standard rate of $12 per unit by the direct labor standard hours per unit of 4 hours. The standard cost per unit is $48 for direct labor. Now multiply the overhead allocation rate of $10 per hour by the direct labor standard hours of 4 hours per unit to come to a standard cost of overhead per unit of $40.

Add together direct materials, direct labor, and overhead to arrive at the standard cost per unit of $377.80. Making a single case of books costs Band Book $377.80.

Figure 17-5:	Type of Cost	Price or Rate	X	Quantity or Hours	=	Standard Cost
Summing	Direct materials	$10.35	X	28 lbs.	=	$289.80
up standard	Direct labor	$12.00	X	4 hours	=	48.00
cost per	Overhead	$10.00	X	4 hours	=	40.00
unit.						$377.80

Illustration by Wiley, Composition Services Graphics

Understanding Variances

A *variance* is the difference between the actual cost and the standard cost that you expected to pay. (I cover standard costs earlier in the chapter.) When actual cost exceeds the standard, then the resulting variance is considered *unfavorable* because it reduces net income. On the other hand, when actual costs come in under standard costs, then the resulting variance is considered *favorable* because it increases net income.

Variances can arise from direct materials, direct labor, and overhead. In fact, the variances arising from each of these three areas, when added together, should equal the total variance:

$$\text{Total} = \text{Direct materials} + \text{Direct labor} + \text{Overhead}$$
$$\text{variance} \quad \text{variance} \quad \text{variance} \quad \text{variance}$$

In turn, you can further break down direct materials and direct labor variances into additional price and quantity variances to understand how changes in materials prices, materials quantities used, direct labor rates, and direct labor hours affect overall profitability.

Computing direct materials variances

A direct materials variance results from one of two things: differences in the prices paid for materials or discrepancies in the quantities used in production. To find these variances, you can use formulas or a simple diagram approach.

Using formulas to calculate direct materials variances

The total direct materials variance is comprised of two components: the direct materials price variance and the direct materials quantity variance.

To compute the direct materials price variance, take the difference between the standard price and the actual price, and then multiply that result by the actual quantity:

$$\text{Direct materials price variance} = (SP - AP) \times AQ$$

To get the direct materials quantity variance, multiply the standard price by the difference between the standard quantity and the actual quantity:

$$\text{Direct materials quantity variance} = SP \times (SQ - AQ)$$

The total direct materials variance equals the difference between total actual cost of materials ($SP \times SQ$) and the budgeted cost of materials, based on standard costs ($AP \times AQ$):

$$\text{Total direct materials variance} = (SP \times SQ) - (AP \times AQ)$$

Consider the Band Book Company example I describe in "Setting Up Standard Costs" earlier in the chapter. Band Book's standard price is $10.35 per pound. The standard quantity per unit is 28 pounds of paper per case. This year, Band Book made 1,000 cases of books, so the company should have used 28,000 pounds of paper, the total standard quantity (1,000 cases × 28 pounds per case). However, the company purchased 30,000 pounds of paper (the actual quantity), paying $9.90 per case (the actual price).

Based on the given formula, the direct materials price variance comes to a positive $13,500, a favorable variance:

$$\begin{aligned}
\text{Direct materials price variance} &= (SP - AP) \times AQ \\
&= (\$10.35 - \$9.90) \times 30,000 \\
&= \$13,500 \text{ favorable}
\end{aligned}$$

This variance means that savings in direct materials prices cut the company's costs by $13,500.

The direct materials quantity variance focuses on the difference between the standard quantity and the actual quantity, arriving at a negative $20,700, an unfavorable variance:

$$\text{Direct materials quantity variance} = SP \times (SQ - AQ)$$
$$= \$10.35 \times (28{,}000 - 30{,}000)$$
$$= -\$20{,}700 \text{ unfavorable}$$

This result means that the 2,000 additional pounds of paper used by the company increased total costs $20,700. Now, you can plug both parts in to find the total direct materials variance. (You could just plug in the final results, but I show you the longer math here.) Compute the total direct materials variance as follows:

$$\text{Total direct materials variance} = (SP \times SQ) - (AP \times AQ)$$
$$= (\$10.35 \times 28{,}000) - (\$9.90 \times 30{,}000)$$
$$= \$289{,}800 - \$297{,}000$$
$$= -\$7{,}200 \text{ unfavorable}$$

Diagramming direct materials variances

Figure 17-6 provides an easier way to compute price and quantity variances. To use this diagram approach, just compute the totals in the third row: actual cost, actual quantity at standard price, and the standard cost. The actual cost less the actual quantity at standard price equals the direct materials price variance. The difference between the actual quantity at standard price and the standard cost is the direct materials quantity variance. The total of both variances equals the total direct materials variance.

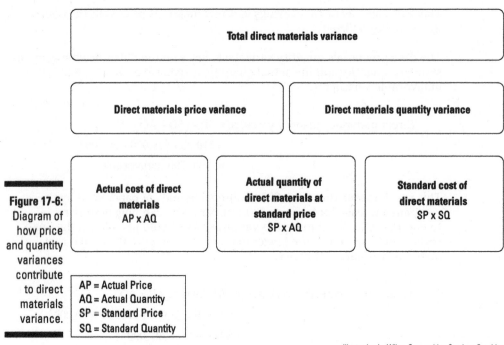

Figure 17-6:
Diagram of
how price
and quantity
variances
contribute
to direct
materials
variance.

To apply this method to the Band Book example, take a look at Figure 17-7.

Start at the bottom. Direct materials actually cost $297,000, even though the standard cost of the direct materials is only $289,800. The actual quantity of direct materials at standard price equals $310,500.

To compute the direct materials price variance, subtract the actual cost of direct materials ($297,000) from the actual quantity of direct materials at standard price ($310,500). This difference comes to a $13,500 favorable variance, meaning that the company saved $13,500 because it bought direct materials for $9.90 rather than the original standard price of $10.35.

To compute the direct materials quantity variance, subtract the actual quantity of direct materials at standard price ($310,500) from the standard cost of direct materials ($289,800), resulting in an unfavorable direct materials quantity variance of $20,700. Because the company used 30,000 pounds of paper rather than the 28,000-pound standard, it lost an additional $20,700.

This setup explains the unfavorable total direct materials variance of $7,200 — the company gained $13,500 by paying less for direct materials, but lost $20,700 because it used up more direct materials.

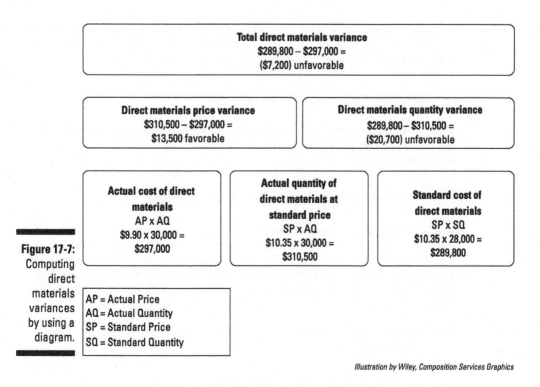

Figure 17-7: Computing direct materials variances by using a diagram.

Illustration by Wiley, Composition Services Graphics

Calculating direct labor variances

A direct labor variance is caused by differences in either wage rates or hours worked. As with direct materials variances, you can use either formulas or a diagram to compute direct labor variances.

Utilizing formulas to figure out direct labor variances

To estimate how the combination of wages and hours affect total costs, compute the total direct labor variance.

As with direct materials, the price and quantity variances add up to the total direct labor variance. To compute the direct labor price variance (also known as the *direct labor rate variance*), take the difference between the standard rate (SR) and the actual rate (AR), and then multiply the result by the actual hours worked (AH):

$$\text{Direct labor price variance} = (SR - AR) \times AH$$

To get the direct labor quantity variance (also known as the *direct labor efficiency variance*), multiply the standard rate (SR) by the difference between total standard hours (SH) and the actual hours worked (AH):

Direct labor quantity variance $= SR \times (SH - AH)$

The direct materials variance equals the difference between the total budgeted cost of labor (SR × SH) and the actual cost of labor, based on actual hours worked (AR × AH):

Total direct labor variance $= (SR \times SH) - (AR \times AH)$

Now you can plug in the numbers for the Band Book Company example earlier in the chapter. Band Book's direct labor standard rate (SR) is $12 per hour. The standard hours (SH) come to 4 hours per case. Because Band made 1,000 cases of books this year, employees should have worked 4,000 hours (1,000 cases × 4 hours per case). However, employees actually worked 3,600 hours, for which they were paid an average of $13 per hour.

With these numbers in hand, you can apply the formula to compute the direct labor price variance:

$$\text{Direct labor price variance} = (SR - AR) \times AH$$
$$= (\$12.00 - \$13.00) \times 3,600$$
$$= -\$3,600 \text{ unfavorable}$$

According to the direct labor price variance, the increase in average wages from $12 to $13 caused costs to increase by $3,600.

Now plug the numbers into the formula for the direct labor quantity variance:

$$\text{Direct labor quantity variance} = SR \times (SH - AH)$$
$$= \$12.00 \times (4,000 - 3,600)$$
$$= \$4,800 \text{ favorable}$$

Employees worked fewer hours than expected to produce the same amount of output. This change saved the company $4,800 — a favorable variance.

To compute the total direct labor variance, use the following formula:

$$\text{Total direct labor variance} = (SR \times SH) - (AR \times AH)$$
$$= (\$12.00 \times 4,000) - (\$13.00 \times 3,600)$$
$$= \$48,000 - \$46,800$$
$$= \$1,200 \text{ favorable}$$

According to the total direct labor variance, direct labor costs were $1,200 lower than expected, a favorable variance.

Employing diagrams to work out direct labor variances

Figure 17-8 shows you how to use a diagram to compute price and quantity variances quickly and easily.

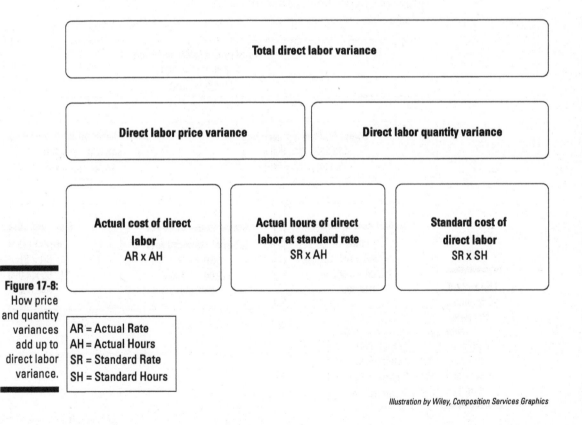

Figure 17-8:
How price and quantity variances add up to direct labor variance.

AR = Actual Rate
AH = Actual Hours
SR = Standard Rate
SH = Standard Hours

Illustration by Wiley, Composition Services Graphics

First, compute the totals in the third row: actual cost, actual hours at standard rate, and the standard cost. To get the direct labor price variance, subtract the actual cost from the actual hours at standard. The difference between the standard cost of direct labor and the actual hours of direct labor at standard rate equals the direct labor quantity variance. The total of both variances equals the total direct labor variance.

Take a look at Figure 17-9 to see this diagram in action for Band Book: Starting from the bottom, the actual cost of direct labor amounts to $46,800. The actual hours of direct labor at standard rate equals $43,200. The standard cost of direct labors comes to $48,000.

To compute the direct labor price variance, subtract the actual hours of direct labor at standard rate ($43,200) from the actual cost of direct labor ($46,800) to get a $3,600 unfavorable variance. This result means the company incurred an additional $3,600 in expense because it paid employees an average of $13 per hour rather than $12.

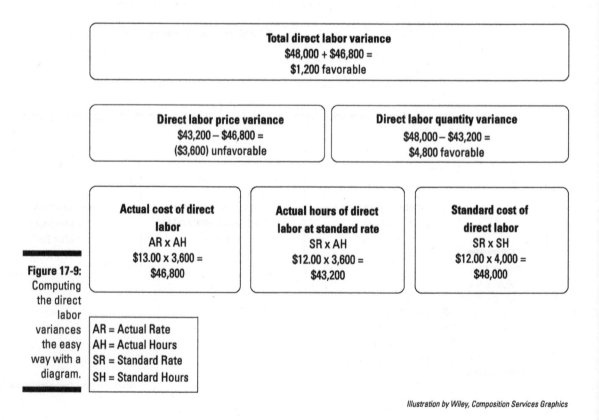

Figure 17-9:
Computing the direct labor variances the easy way with a diagram.

Total direct labor variance
$48,000 + $46,800 =
$1,200 favorable

Direct labor price variance
$43,200 – $46,800 =
($3,600) unfavorable

Direct labor quantity variance
$48,000 – $43,200 =
$4,800 favorable

Actual cost of direct labor
AR x AH
$13.00 x 3,600 =
$46,800

Actual hours of direct labor at standard rate
SR x AH
$12.00 x 3,600 =
$43,200

Standard cost of direct labor
SR x SH
$12.00 x 4,000 =
$48,000

AR = Actual Rate
AH = Actual Hours
SR = Standard Rate
SH = Standard Hours

To compute the direct labor quantity variance, subtract the standard cost of direct labor ($48,000) from the actual hours of direct labor at standard rate ($43,200). This math results in a favorable variance of $4,800, indicating that the company saved $4,800 in expenses because its employees worked 400 fewer hours than expected.

In summary, the $1,200 favorable variance arose because of two factors: the company saved $4,800 from fewer hours worked but incurred an additional $3,600 expense because it paid employees more money. This scenario begs the question "Are higher-paid workers more productive?", but I'll leave that discussion to the human resources experts.

Overhead any good variances lately?

Whenever you see direct labor and direct materials, overhead can't be far behind. To compute overhead applied, multiply the overhead application rate by the standard number of hours allowed:

Overhead applied = Overhead application rate × SH

So you can determine overhead variance by subtracting actual overhead from applied overhead:

Overhead variance = Overhead applied − Actual overhead

Band Book Company incurs actual overhead costs of $95,000. The company's overhead application rate is $25 per hour. (You can find the math for that calculation in the earlier section "Determining the overhead rate.") Furthermore, in order for Band Book's workers to produce 1,000 cases, you can expect them to work standard hours of 4 direct labor hours per case.

SH equals 1,000 cases produced × 4 direct labor hours per case, or 4,000 direct labor hours. This amount results in overhead applied of $100,000:

$$\text{Overhead applied} = \text{Overhead application rate} \times \text{SH}$$
$$= \$25.00 \times 4,000$$
$$= \$100,000$$

To compute the variance, subtract actual overhead from the overhead applied:

$$\text{Overhead variance} = \text{Overhead applied} - \text{Actual overhead}$$
$$= \$100,000 - \$95,000$$
$$= \$5,000 \text{ favorable}$$

Looking past the favorable/unfavorable label

Unfavorable variances reduce net income, while favorable variances increase net income. This terminology defines variances in terms of how they affect income only; it doesn't necessarily mean that favorable variances are always good and unfavorable variances are always bad. For example, a favorable variance may result because a company purchases cheaper direct materials of poorer quality. These materials lower costs, but they also hurt the quality of finished goods, damaging the company's reputation with customers. This kind of favorable variance can work against a company. On the other hand, an unfavorable variance may occur because a department chooses to scrap poor-quality goods. In the long run, the company benefits from incurring a short-term unfavorable variance to provide better-quality goods to its customers.

Overhead variances are often caused by spending too much or too little on overhead. They can also be caused by using overhead inefficiently.

Like direct labor and direct materials, overhead, too, can have price and quantity variables. However, fixed and variable cost behaviors considerably complicate the calculation of overhead variances. Therefore, this topic is usually covered in more-advanced cost accounting courses that are outside the scope of this book.

Teasing Out Variances

In your business, variance analysis helps you identify problem areas that require attention, such as

- ✔ Poor productivity
- ✔ Poor quality
- ✔ Excessive costs
- ✔ Excessive spoilage or waste of materials

Identifying and working on these problems helps managers improve production flow and profitability. Managers and managerial accountants often talk about *management by exception* — using variance analysis to identify *exceptions,* or problems, where actual results significantly vary from standards. By paying careful attention to these exceptions, managers can root out and rectify manufacturing problems and inefficiencies, thereby improving productivity, efficiency, and quality.

Interpreting variances in action

The previous sections in this chapter lay out what happened to the costs of the example firm Band Book Company over the course of a year. Figure 17-10 summarizes Band Book's variances.

A complete analysis of Band Book's variances provides an interesting story to explain why the company had a $1,000 unfavorable variance. The following events transpired:

✔ The company paid less than expected for direct materials, leading to a favorable $13,500 direct materials price variance.

✔ Perhaps because of the cheaper, lower-quality direct materials, the company used an excessive amount of direct materials. This overage resulted in a $20,700 unfavorable direct materials quantity variance.

✔ The company paid its employees a higher wage rate, resulting in an unfavorable direct labor price variance of $3,600.

✔ The company saved money because employees worked fewer hours than expected, perhaps because they were more productive, higher-paid workers. The favorable direct labor quantity variance was $4,800.

✔ The company saved $5,000 in reduced overhead costs.

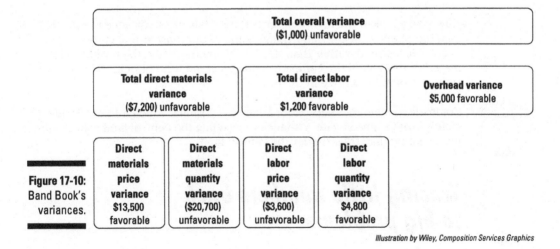

Figure 17-10:
Band Book's
variances.

Illustration by Wiley, Composition Services Graphics

Focusing on the big numbers

Management by exception directs managers to closely investigate the largest variances. For example, the two largest variances in Figure 17-10 are the direct materials quantity variance ($20,700 unfavorable) and the direct materials price variance ($13,500 favorable). Band Book's managers should focus on how the company buys and uses its direct materials.

Here, the direct materials quantity variance resulted because the company should have used 18,000 pounds of paper but actually used 20,000 pounds of paper. Why? Here are a few possibilities:

✔ The paper was poor quality, and much of it needed to be scrapped.

✔ The company underestimated the amount of paper needed (the standard quantity needs to be changed).

✔ Someone miscounted the amount of paper used; 2,000 pounds of paper are sitting in the back of the warehouse (oops).

✔ A new employee misused the machine, shredding several thousand pounds of paper.

Management by exception directs managers to where the problem may have occurred so that they can investigate what happened and take corrective action.

Now take a look at the favorable direct materials price variance of $13,500. How did the purchasing department come to purchase direct materials for only $9.90 a pound, rather than the $10.35 standard? Did the purchased materials meet all of the company's quality standards? Should the company reduce its standard price in the future?

Companies sometimes set *control limits* to determine which items are sufficiently large to investigate. Variances exceeding the control limit require more investigation than those under the control limit.

Tracing little numbers back to big problems

Be careful! Don't focus exclusively on the big numbers and ignore the little numbers. Big problems can also hide in the small numbers. For example, although many frauds (such as stealing raw materials) may trigger large variances, a well-planned fraud may be designed to manipulate variances so that they stay low, below the radar, where managers won't notice them.

For example, knowing the standard price of a raw material is $100 per unit, a crooked purchasing manager may arrange to purchase the units for exactly that price — $100 per unit — while receiving $10 per unit as a kick-back gratuity from the supplier. This scheme results in a direct materials price variance of zero, but it doesn't reflect what should be the company's actual cost of doing business. A more scrupulous purchasing manager would have arranged a purchase price of $90, resulting in a large positive direct materials price variance.

To avoid these problems, managers should still investigate all variances, even while focusing most of their time on the largest figures.

Placing blame for variances where it's due

When assigning responsibility for issues that arise, take care to hold subordinates accountable for decisions and events within their control. When suppliers increase their prices, don't go blaming your employees for the resulting unfavorable direct materials price variances; your employees had no control over these prices. Such misplaced blame may lead employees to make short-sighted decisions in the future. A purchasing manager who thinks that she'll be held responsible for suppliers' prices is liable to cut costs by purchasing poor-quality direct materials. Employees in positions of responsibility should know and understand that they aren't responsible for events beyond their control. (On the other hand, when an employee ruins an entire production batch because he didn't set up the machine properly, a little responsibility assignment may be in order.)

Chapter 18

The Balanced Scorecard: Reviewing Your Business's Report Card

. . . .

In This Chapter

▶ Looking at the benefits of the balanced scorecard

▶ Juggling the four perspectives of a business

▶ Measuring a business's qualitative performance

▶ Using the balanced scorecard to implement strategy

. . . .

*A*s much as I like numbers and accounting, sometimes I have to admit that they don't tell the whole story. Take profitability. I sure like to know a company's net income — the difference between revenues and expenses. To me, this figure is accounting's be-all and end-all, the ultimate and final buck-stops-here measure of performance.

And yet net income doesn't say much about a company's future prospects. A company may be profitable this year but unprofitable for the next five years. Furthermore, net income can come from good actions (like selling products with a nice markup) or bad actions (like selling off successful parts of a business).

For this reason, many companies evaluate their own performance by using a tool called the *balanced scorecard.* The balanced scorecard uses several different measures, some of which accountants and managers are used to seeing (such as sales and net income), and others of which help predict future success (such as research and development spending, the number of new customers, or employee satisfaction).

In this chapter, I explain and explore the balanced scorecard and how it gives a nuanced, predictive view of a company's or organization's performance.

Strategizing for Success: Introducing the Balanced Scorecard

Got big dreams? That's nice, but you're not likely to get anywhere without a plan. You have to know how you're going to reach your business goal. What's your strategy? How are you going to exploit emerging possibilities and gain an advantage over the competition?

Don't confuse strategy with budgeting. A master budget (see Chapter 14) is also a plan, but it simply specifies the details of how much you're going to make, when, for how much, where the money is going to come from, and how you're going to spend it so that you end the year with a profit and a sound balance sheet. Strategy is much bigger than that. It defines how you're going to get your customers to pay good money for your products.

The balanced scorecard is a report card for your company that indicates not only how profitable you were last year but also how well you're implementing your strategy in order to stay profitable for many years into the future.

The balanced scorecard concept was developed and introduced by Robert Kaplan and David Norton to help management accountants provide more information about companies' success in implementing strategies. Following the balanced scorecard, management accountants do much more than predict profits (as part of budgets) or provide information for decisions about pricing products or buying new equipment; they also provide information to help managers and investors assess how closely a company is moving toward meeting a broad range of goals and objectives.

Kaplan and Norton argue that a successful strategy must include four perspectives, which I cover in the following sections:

- **Financial:** Incorporates traditional measures of performance, such as net income and revenues
- **Customer:** Considers customer satisfaction and how well the company stacks up against its competitors
- **Internal business:** Considers how well the company develops, makes, delivers, and services products
- **Learning and growth:** Evaluates employees' ability to change and improve

Making money: The financial perspective

Like it or not, most businesses are in it for the money — net income, profits, and maximizing shareholder value. This fact means that no balanced score-card would be complete without considering shareholder profitability.

Or maybe not? What about not-for-profit organizations and governmental entities, which are explicitly set up with goals that reach beyond net income? For example, a child welfare agency may be set up to ensure that every child has a home. A political organization may be set up to win elections. A local fire department may be set up to put out fires. These organizations shouldn't have to worry about profits or finances, right?

Not quite. You can't eradicate homelessness, win elections, or put out fires without money. Even if these organizations don't try to buy and sell products at a profit, they still need funding in order to accomplish their noble goals. The financial perspective applies to every organization whether the entity is set up to earn a profit or not.

That said, different entities must look at the financial perspective in different ways. Not-for-profit organizations should look to increase donations or the number or amount of project grants. For-profit corporations usually want to earn profits to maximize shareholder value, but they may develop this profit-ability in different ways. Some companies, such as Tesla Motors or Tiffany & Co., rely on a market differentiation strategy that allows them to charge high prices while selling a fairly low volume of merchandise. Other companies, such as Kia Motors or Dollar General, use a competitive price strategy with low profit margins but very high sales volume. Although market differentia-tors may try to focus on increasing sales prices and gross profit (that's sales less cost of goods sold), competitive pricers focus on selling more goods: increasing the total number of units sold, number of sales outlets, or sales per outlet.

Here are some examples of performance measures from a financial perspec-tive for different kinds of companies and organizations:

- ✔ Return on investment
- ✔ Return on sales
- ✔ Return on assets
- ✔ Net income

- ✓ Net sales
- ✓ Credit rating
- ✓ Donations received
- ✓ Subscription income
- ✓ Share price
- ✓ Profit per employee
- ✓ Same-store sales

Managers and stakeholders need to carefully think about their company's priorities in order to identify which performance measures most closely align with the strategies and goals of the company. For example, a company focusing on growth will probably home in on net sales as one of the factors to add to its balanced scorecard. If it's a retail chain, it may also include same store sales. To round things out, managers may want to use a measure of profitability like return on assets. This approach focuses the company on growing net sales, same store sales, and return on assets.

A company trying to boost profitability of existing sales may select return on sales as one of its financial measures. This figure measures how much profit the company can squeeze out of its sales. A big-box retailer may focus on profit per employee, reflecting a goal of earning as much profit as possible from the existing workforce.

Some balanced-scorecard measures may be appropriate considerations for more than one perspective. For example, profitability per employee can probably fit into any one of the four perspectives depending on the business and its strategy.

Ensuring your clients are happy: The customer perspective

Because customers are the stakeholders who actually give you sales revenue, the balanced scorecard considers the customer perspective to be a critical aspect of strategy. After all, customers who like your business keep buying things; they're your key to future sales revenue. Unhappy customers patronize your competitors, so the balanced scorecard forces you to keep tabs on your customers as carefully as you keep tabs on your profits.

Some typical measures of performance from the customer perspective include the following:

- ✔ Results of customer surveys
- ✔ Number of new customers
- ✔ Response time to customer inquiry
- ✔ Market surveys of brand recognition
- ✔ Tracking customer complaints
- ✔ Market share
- ✔ Product returns as a percentage of sales
- ✔ Percentage of repeat customers
- ✔ Same-store sales

As with all measures on the balanced scorecard, customer perspective measures ought to reflect the company's strategy toward customer satisfaction. Big-box retailers usually try to satisfy customers with wide selection and low prices. These retailers may survey customers to make sure that they've found what they're looking for in the store and then include the results on their balanced scorecard. To measure how competitive their prices are, some retailers compare the cost of buying a sample shopping list in their store with key competitors. More-tony retailers, trying to attract wealthy clientele, may choose to focus on consumer profiles, such as the average family income of customers.

Keeping the clock ticking: The internal business perspective

Companies rely on an operating cycle, whereby they continuously work through the following steps:

1. Buy raw materials.
2. Pay for raw materials.
3. Put raw materials into production (work-in-process — flip to Chapter 4).
4. Complete work-in process (becomes finished goods inventory).
5. Sell finished goods inventory.

6. Deliver sales to customers.

7. Collect payment from customers.

This process is continuous. As the company collects cash payments, it purchases more inventory. As it purchases more inventory, it puts it into production to complete it and sell it to customers, who give the company more cash payments.

A company typically has other important processes, too, such as new product cycles and customer service. The internal business perspective considers how well the company works its way through these processes. Managers need to identify those processes most critical to its success and find ways to measure how successfully it works through these processes. For example, here are some typical measures of the internal business perspective:

- Raw materials inventory as a percentage of sales
- Work-in-process inventory as a percentage of sales
- Inventory turnover
- Cost of quality control
- Amount of inventory spoilage
- Setup time
- Number or percentage of product defects
- Number of *stockouts,* which occur when your business runs out of inventory to sell
- Variance analyses (refer to Chapter 17)
- Development time needed for new products
- Customer satisfaction with service calls
- Time to settle customer claims

To choose measures of performance in the internal business perspective, managers must think and strategize about which aspects of their operations are most critical to their success. For example, a fast food restaurant will probably focus on how quickly it can make and sell different food products or on minimizing spoilage. A more expensive restaurant, on the other hand, may focus on the number of stars it earns from the local newspaper. As always, the measures should reflect the strategy.

Can your workforce handle it? The learning and growth perspective

People who sit around and philosophize about how to make money instead of actually making it (like business professors) have theorized that a business is nothing more than a *nexus of contracts,* a huge bundle of relationships between different stakeholders. Employers work for their salaries and wages. Suppliers deliver merchandise and raw materials in exchange for payments. Customers buy finished goods and pay the company for them. Stockholders invest in the company and expect dividends. Any company or organization is actually a huge set of different people working together to make things happen for themselves and for each other.

These relationships need to function like clockwork. However, this complex bundle of relationships needs to be flexible enough to change along with the external business environment. Therefore, employees' ability to learn, to grow, to anticipate change, and to react to the external environment is absolutely critical to a company's success.

Suppose your convenience store sells soft drinks. The trend in soft drinks right now is toward offering consumers a wide variety of different products to choose from — fizzy sodas, energy drinks, protein shakes, drinks infused with vitamins, sugary drinks, sugar-free drinks, and even drinks imported from Mexico. Customers want to choose between high-caffeine, caffeine-free, and even stress-reducing drinks. They can even choose among different sizes of bottles and cans. In short, customers now expect to be able to walk into a convenience store and select from a multitude of different beverages.

Is your store aware of this trend? Is it ready?

Motivated and well-trained employees know what's going on and anticipate changes like these. They find ways to squeeze more varieties of soft drinks into their refrigerated display cases and think about creative new offerings that may appeal to customer niches. Without these motivated, well-trained, proactive employees, the entire nexus of contracts falls apart. A poor selection of products turns customers off, so sales drop, suppliers focus on your competitors, profits drop, and before you know it, stockholders start missing out on dividends.

Here are some measures that a business can use to better understand the learning and growth perspective:

✔ Average hours of training per employee

✔ Number of employees with college or advanced degrees

✔ Number of employees with professional certification

✔ Employee turnover

✔ Average employee earnings per year

✔ Percentage of employees who own stock in the company

The learning and growth perspective requires managers to carefully consider which employee skills most benefit the organization. An elementary school, where learning and growth are key to the success of the organization, may want to measure the percentage of teachers with certifications or advanced degrees. They may also count the number of in-service days, when teachers become the students and students get to stay home.

Measuring the immeasurable

Although some attributes, such as sales, are fairly easy to measure, other attributes — such as customer satisfaction — are tougher nuts to crack. These nonquantitative measures require special attention. How can you capture this information so that you can present it in a meaningful way?

For example, you can use market surveys or the percentage of customer returns to measure customer satisfaction. Or get creative. One fast-food chain knows that customers demand a speedy drive-through experience. Therefore, the chain electronically times how long each car takes to get its food and whiz out the drive-through.

Demonstrating the Balanced Scorecard

Management accountants (and the other 21 chapters in this book) focus almost exclusively on costs and profits. Part of the beauty of the balanced scorecard is how it considers a variety of different perspectives as critical parts of the company's strategy. To be successful, your company must be profitable, *liquid* (have enough money in the bank to pay bills due soon), and *solvent* (be able to pay its debts in the long term). It also needs to have happy customers who will continue to buy from it in the future. Its internals must function well — the company knows how to make, sell, and deliver products and services productively and at a profit. And it must be ready to adapt to future circumstances; employees should be quick to learn new things and ready for change. If all these perspectives are in shape and working properly, the company should thrive. However, if any of these perspectives falls short, the company must prepare for challenges ahead.

After you've developed your balanced scorecard, collect the necessary information and update it regularly. Then use the balanced scorecard much like you use the dashboard in your car — to see how fast you're going, how much gas is in the tank, and to estimate when you're going to reach your destination.

In my imaginary convenience store, I've discovered that customers expect to find an increasing variety of beverage choices in addition to the sandwiches, sundry snacks, newspapers, and magazines that I've always offered.

Up until now, I've been managing my convenience store like any well-meaning accountant. I watch sales and profits. I prepare a master budget before each month, projecting future profits and cash flows (Chapter 14). I compare these budgets to actual results, flexing when necessary (Chapter 15). I carefully designate standard costs of sandwiches and coffee made in my shop (Chapter 17) and use this information to set prices (Chapter 12). I even prepare a capital budgeting spreadsheet before buying so much as a new coffee pot (Chapter 10). However, I've identified a few problems:

1. My employees hate working here and don't like me.

2. Customers often have to wait several minutes to get a sandwich.

3. Customers don't seem to like my coffee or the bland, generic-brand beverages I sell.

4. Low profits and weak cash flow threaten to close the business.

The following sections detail how I can implement the balanced scorecard to address these issues.

Sketching a strategy that incorporates all four perspectives

First of all, I have to set a goal. My goal is to make money: good cash flow, plain and simple.

Next, I come up with a strategy to meet that goal. My strategy is to have happy and friendly employees (learning and growth perspective) who think about, understand, and meet customer needs (customer perspective).

Satisfied customers become regular customers, who pay premium prices for the wide selection of quality merchandise that they're looking for (internal business perspective). If everything goes right, I'll soon have healthy profits and cash flow (financial perspective).

As Figure 18-1 shows, my strategy considers all the key perspectives and how they relate to each other.

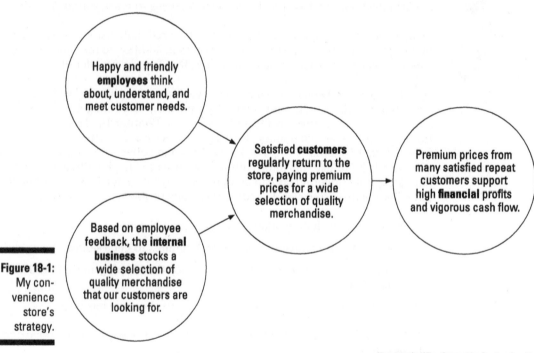

Figure 18-1: My convenience store's strategy.

Happy and friendly **employees** think about, understand, and meet customer needs.

Based on employee feedback, the **internal business** stocks a wide selection of quality merchandise that our customers are looking for.

Satisfied **customers** regularly return to the store, paying premium prices for a wide selection of quality merchandise.

Premium prices from many satisfied repeat customers support high **financial** profits and vigorous cash flow.

Illustration by Wiley, Composition Services Graphics

Identifying measures for the balanced scorecard

Now I have to figure out how to quantify progress for each perspective, using a combination of historic measures (that look back at the past) and predictive measures (that drive future results).

Unfortunately, most accounting information is historic — it looks at what happened in the past. This rear view is inevitable because the only way you can measure sales or net income is if they've happened already. The balanced scorecard, by its very nature, must include some of this retrospective information. However, the balanced scorecard should also include predictive and forward-looking information, information that decision-makers can use to predict future events. Items like the number of new customers or advertising expense all drive future sales and profits. Make sure your balanced scorecard includes a healthy dose of these predictive measures.

Making money

First of all, a convenience store is no charity. I need to keep an eye on the bottom line: net income. To evaluate financial performance, I use some of the measures in Chapter 16 and add others that focus on my strategy:

- **Net income:** Calculated as revenues less expenses. Alternatively, I can try controllable margin (revenues less controllable expenses).

- **Return on investment (ROI):** As explained in Chapter 16, to measure ROI, divide controllable margin by average operating assets:

$$\text{Return on investment} = \frac{\text{Controllable margin}}{\text{Average operating assets}}$$

  Accountants use a range of different formulas to measure return on investment. Rather than controllable margin, you can use operating income or net income. Rather than average operating assets, you can use stockholders' equity.

- **Dividends:** How much profit are you taking home?

- **Hours worked by owner:** As owner of the convenience store, perhaps part of my strategy is to stop working on my business 24/7. Therefore, the actual number of hours that I work may be a useful measure of the financial success of my strategy.

Satisfying customers

In order to make money, I've got to keep the customers satisfied. My strategy in Figure 18-1 says that customers like happy, friendly employees who are eager to meet their needs. They also like a broad selection of merchandise and hot, fresh coffee. But how can I know that customers are truly satisfied with their experience in my store — that I'm covering all my bases and they'll keep coming back for more?

Why, I can think about these measures:

- **Survey customers and would-be customers.** I offer my customers a hot, fresh cup of coffee if they complete a survey. Better yet, I mail a survey out to likely customers in the neighborhood to find out whether they visit my store (and if not, why).

- **Ask for customer suggestions and complaints.** If something is bothering a customer, I need to find out exactly what it is, and quickly. Slow service? Warm cola? A stomach-turning smell coming from the back room? Whatever it is, placing suggestion and complaint forms where customers can find them, fill them out, and drop them in a box gives me feedback I can act on.

- **Track the average purchase per walk-in.** Satisfied customers buy things. Therefore, I invest in a gadget that counts the number of customers who come in and out of the store. I then divide total sales each day by the number of walk-ins.

- **Compute gross profit margin.** *Gross profit* is the difference between sales revenues and cost of goods sold. This figure measures your markup — how much you make, on average, from each product you sell. To compute the gross profit margin, just divide gross profit by sales revenue:

$$\text{Gross profit margin} = \frac{\text{Net sales} - \text{Cost of goods sold}}{\text{Net sales}}$$

For example, suppose my store buys a bag of potato chips for $0.40, which I sell for $0.99:

$$\text{Gross profit margin} = \frac{\$0.99 - \$0.40}{\$0.99}$$
$$= 59.6\%$$

For these potato chips, 59.6 percent of each sale goes to profits. You can also calculate gross profit margin for all of the products you sell in total.

 TIP

Because the strategy requires customers to pay premium prices, keeping an eye on gross profit margin is a good idea; it indicates whether customers are willing to put up with my high markups.

Stocking merchandise that customers want

The internal business strategy dictates that the store must stock the wide selection of quality merchandise that our selective customers are looking for. Therefore, I need a few measures to see how well I'm implementing that strategy. Consider the following:

✔ **Total number of products stocked:** If customers are looking for a wide selection, then counting the actual number of different products in stock makes sense. The more variety the better.

✔ **Number of days' inventory:** The *number of days' inventory,* calculated as follows, measures how many days' worth of inventory I have in stock:

$$\text{Number of days' inventory} = \frac{365}{\left(\dfrac{\text{Cost of goods sold}}{\text{Average inventory}} \right)}$$

I use this number to determine whether I have the right amount of inventory. Having too much inventory can require exorbitant financing (increasing my interest payments) and can also lead to unnecessary spoilage and breakage. On the other hand, having too little inventory can cause me to run out of the goods my customers want, resulting in lost sales and, worse yet for my strategy, dissatisfied customers.

According to this balanced scorecard plan, the number of days' inventory needs to be just right, so the company may want to set a standard benchmark or target for this measure based on previous experience. This way, a measure that's too high above the company's benchmark indicates that the inventory may be getting old and may spoil. On the other hand, a measure that's too low indicates that the company may not be stocking enough inventory to satisfy customer demand.

✔ **Number of new products stocked because of customer requests:** I want to make sure I'm listening to customers, so I keep track of their feedback and actually count the number of new products I add to my inventory based on their requests. If the number of new products is too low, I need to find new ways to get customers to tell me what they want.

✔ **Average coffee life:** Customers want their coffee hot and fresh; nothing tastes worse than two-hour-old, lukewarm coffee. To ensure I'm providing the freshest coffee possible, I set up a timer to measure and keep track of the average time between when coffee is brewed and when it's served to customers.

✔ **Percentage of off-brand products:** Some customers insist on buying off-brand or generic products. However, anecdotal feedback and consumer surveys indicate that most customers are turned off by these products. They say that it makes the store seem cheesy. Therefore, I make a strategic decision to only keep between 6 and 10 percent of the total product items in the store as off-brand.

Producing happy and friendly employees

This whole grand scheme can't possibly work without an employee team that thinks about, understands, and meets customer needs. The following measures operationalize this strategy:

- ✔ **Average employment period:** On average, how long have my employees worked here? To understand and meet customer needs, employees should have a lot of experience working in my store. Plus, happy employees are less likely to quit.

- ✔ **Amount of employee training:** Training helps employees to know how to present a friendly face to customers and understand and meet their needs. Therefore, I measure how many hours of training each employee receives.

- ✔ **Surveys of employees:** Are my employees happy? Why not use an anonymous survey to ask them? While I'm at it, I ask them questions to see how well they understand customer needs. I survey them on which products customers typically ask for, focusing on the items that we don't sell . . . yet.

- ✔ **Employee compensation:** I figure good wages and benefits make my employees happy and keep them from leaving, so I measure the average employee compensation per hour to confirm that I'm keeping my workers satisfied on this front.

Chapter 19

Using the Theory of Constraints to Squeeze Out of a Tight Spot

In This Chapter

▶ Identifying constraints that choke up a system

▶ Following the five steps of managing and reducing constraints

Creeping to work every morning on the Garden State Parkway gives me an awful lot of time to think about constraints. On a typical day, I encounter at least one bottleneck along the way where everybody slows down. Sometimes it's because police are ticketing a speeder, or construction is blocking the road, or everyone's rubbernecking at a very intriguing accident. And then sometimes, I guess, people just feel like slowing down for no apparent reason.

The problem with a bottleneck is that it slows down all the traffic behind it. After all, if one car moves at 2 miles per hour through a bottleneck, then every single car behind it must also slow down to that speed (or else). A truly theatrical accident can back traffic up for miles in both directions. To get traffic moving again, officers need to exploit the constraint — to open up the bottleneck so that traffic can move again.

Manufacturing — and even services — often work a lot like the Garden State Parkway. To improve production, you need to focus on and then break the bottleneck or constraint.

Understanding Constraints

Constraints are anything that limits a system from achieving higher performance. On the highway, accidents that prevent you from driving 65 miles per hour to work in the morning are constraints. Constraints can occur in any process, whether in manufacturing or service industries.

Manufacturing constraints

In a manufacturing plant, constraints slow down assembly line production, gumming up the works so that you can't produce as many units as you need.

For example, consider the pork-processing plant at Pam's Canned Hams. (Try saying *that* five times fast.) Figure 19-1 illustrates Pam's production process.

Figure 19-1:
Pam's
production
process.

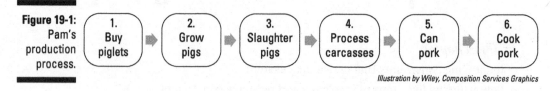

Illustration by Wiley, Composition Services Graphics

Department 1 buys piglets, the direct materials. Department 2 feeds and grows the piglets over a 12-month period. Department 3 slaughters the pigs. Department 4 processes the carcasses. Department 5 then cans the buttocks to make ham. Finally, Department 6 cooks the canned ham, resulting in finished goods inventory.

Figure 19-2 enumerates how many units of production each department can process during a single day.

Figure 19-2:
Each
depart-
ment's
maximum
daily output.

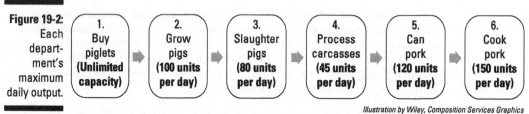

Illustration by Wiley, Composition Services Graphics

Pam's constraint is in Department 4, which can only handle 45 units per day. This constraint limits Pam's entire production capacity to just 45 units per day. All the additional capacity in the other departments is completely wasted as a result; the fact that Department 2 has enough employees, space, and equipment to grow 100 units a day or that Department 5 is capable of canning 120 units of pork per day doesn't matter. Department 4 slows every department down to just 45 units per day.

Service constraints

The constraint phenomenon isn't limited to manufacturers — it can also occur in service businesses. For example, consider a surgeon's office, where every patient must go through certain steps before and after surgery, as illustrated in Figure 19-3.

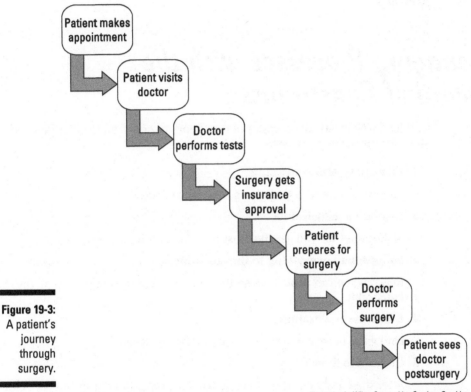

Figure 19-3:
A patient's journey through surgery.

Illustration by Wiley, Composition Services Graphics

In order to maximize the chance of a successful surgical procedure, each patient needs to go through a series of steps. The process starts when the patient makes his first appointment with the doctor. After this visit, the doctor orders a series of tests, reviewing the results. If the doctor deems surgery necessary, her office seeks the approval of the patient's insurance company. Next, the patient is prepared for surgery. Following the surgery, each patient needs a post-op visit.

Here, constraints can actually risk the health of patients. For example, if the doctor can only handle a limited number of patient visits per week, then every step that requires the doctor's involvement is slowed down, or constrained. Delays in obtaining insurance company approval have a similar effect.

In order to meet patient needs, managers in the doctor's office need to carefully manage these steps. Other service companies have similar processes to manage.

Managing Processes with the Theory of Constraints

Dr. Eliyahu Goldratt, the founder of the theory of constraints, identified five steps for managing processes:

1. **Identify system constraints.**

   Find the bottleneck that slows down the process.

2. **Exploit the constraints.**

   Make sure that you get the most out of constrained resources.

3. **Subordinate everything to the constraints.**

   Rearrange other processes so that they work at the same pace as the constraint.

4. **Break the constraints.**

   Find ways to increase the capacity of the constraint.

5. **Go back to Step 1.**

   After the constraint is broken, go back to Step 1 to identify another constraint to work on.

Step 1: Identifying system constraints

Inevitably, in any process, something slows everything else down; there's always a weakest link. When I hike with my kids, it's usually my youngest child, who has the shortest legs. In a production process, it's usually the department with the slowest output.

A number of factors can cause constraints. They can include

✔ Poorly trained people who lack the skills to do their jobs

✔ Inefficient equipment that has insufficient capacity to meet production needs

✔ Company policies (written, or unwritten) that prevent people or equipment from accomplishing more

According to the theory of constraints, every system has at least one constraint. But what if every step in the process operates below capacity? In that case, the constraint is customer demand.

Goldratt calls the constraint the *drum,* because it sets the tempo that the entire production process will need to follow.

Suppose that the fictional Axiamm Corp. manufactures Tex's Hot Sauce. Production requires five production steps, as shown in Figure 19-4.

Figure 19-4:
Steps in
making
Tex's Hot
Sauce.

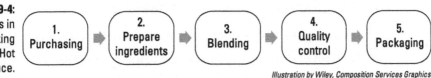

1. Purchasing ➡ 2. Prepare ingredients ➡ 3. Blending ➡ 4. Quality control ➡ 5. Packaging

Illustration by Wiley, Composition Services Graphics

Axiamm starts by buying the freshest and spiciest raw materials. These ingredients need to be prepared in various ways; some need to be pureed and/or cooked. Next, the Blending department measures the ingredients into a giant blender so that each batch can be mixed together. Then every batch needs to be tasted by a quality control inspector. Finally, each batch is bottled and packed into cases.

Alice, the plant manager, is concerned about the Quality Control department, which always seems backlogged. On any given day, six or even seven batches of hot sauce are waiting for inspection. This backlog then stops up the Blending department, forcing it to pause production while Quality Control catches up.

Alice identifies the Quality Control department as a constraint, primarily because of the lack of taste experts. The company has always had difficulty hiring well-qualified tasters who can verify that each product tastes right.

Step 2: Exploiting the constraint

After you identify the process that slows down the system, carefully consider how you can optimize the use of this constraint.

In parkway traffic, go to the bottleneck and try to get the automobiles to drive through it as quickly as possible. When hiking with small children, offer the youngest one incentives to move more quickly (snacks ahead, bears behind).

In a production process, you may be able to save time by setting up a *buffer* before the constraint. This buffer is a stockpile of inputs, ready and waiting for the constrained step in the process so that your constraint never needs to stop working in order to wait for more inputs.

You also may be able to exploit the constraint by maximizing contribution margin per unit of constrained resource, as explained in Chapter 11. For example, consider how Axiamm Corp. can use this technique. When making hot sauce, the Quality Control department already has a buffer waiting to get tested — the backlog of batches that stretch all the way back to the Blending department. Suppose that Tex's Hot Sauce comes in three different flavors, each of which provides a different contribution margin:

- ✔ Tex's Very Hot Sauce: Contribution margin of $1,000 per vat
- ✔ Tex's Super Hot Sauce: Contribution margin of $700 per vat
- ✔ Tex's Atomic Hot Sauce: Contribution margin of $500 per vat

To exploit this constraint, Alice should first have Quality Control test the Very Hot Sauce; this strategy will bring in the most contribution margin: $1,000 per vat. After the tasters get through the Very Hot Sauce, they should move on to the Super Hot Sauce, which has lower contribution, just $700 per vat. Finally, if they have any time left, they should test the Atomic Hot Sauce, which provides only $500 of contribution margin.

By exploiting the constraint based on contribution margin, the tasters are sure to test the most-profitable product before they work on less-profitable products.

Step 3: Subordinating everything to the constraint

In Step 3, you rework your entire production schedule so that it moves at the same pace as the drum. Any processes going faster than the drum produce unnecessary units. Goldratt calls this pacing of processes the *rope,* such that goods move through production like a single rope — all at the drum's pace.

In traffic, subordinating everything to the constraint means getting all the cars to drive at the same speed — the maximum speed that they can drive through the bottleneck. When hiking with small children, it means getting the older kids to slow down. For Axiamm Corp., it means purchasing, preparing, and blending the raw materials to make as much Very Hot Sauce as can be sold because this product has the highest contribution margin.

Step 4: Breaking the constraint

Breaking the constraint means creatively thinking about alternative ways around the constraint. In traffic, you can get off the parkway and take side streets. In hiking, maybe the little one can keep up by taking a shortcut.

At Axiamm Corp., Alice and her colleagues are thinking about how to increase capacity in Quality Control. They've tried recruiting more workers, to no avail. They've also tried forcing the tasters to test more vats of hot sauce each day. That didn't turn out well, either.

Then Alice had a great idea. The Blending department usually blends 50 gallons of hot sauce at a time and then sends them to Quality Control in 50-gallon vats. However, the blenders have capacity to handle 100-gallon loads. Therefore, why not blend 100 gallons at a time and replace the 50-gallon vats with 100-gallon vats? This increase can cut the required number of quality control tests in half.

Problem solved. Now the Quality Control department can handle a full production load.

Step 5: Returning to Step 1

After you break the constraint in Step 4, start over again. Take a look at the production process to identify new constraints, exploit them, subordinate everything to them, and then break them.

Part VI
The Part of Tens

The 5th Wave — By Rich Tennant

"I assume you'll appreciate the entreprenurial spirit behind our accounting methods."

In this part . . .

1 provide a quick reference to key formulas used in managerial accounting. I also lay out career options open to management accountants and name some of the people who have had a major impact on the profession.

Chapter 20

Ten Key Managerial Accounting Formulas

*M*anagerial accountants compute and provide information within a company. Like newspapers, their reports describe for managers the latest happenings inside their companies. However, unlike newspapers, which provide written articles, managerial accounting information is numeric, calculated using certain formulas. This chapter summarizes some of the most important formulas in managerial accounting.

The Accounting Equation

The accounting equation equates assets with liabilities and owners' equity:

Assets = Liabilities + Owners' equity

Assets are things owned by the company — such as cash, inventory, and equipment — that will provide some future benefit. *Liabilities* entail future sacrifices that the company must make, such as paying bills or other kinds of debts. *Owners' equity* represents the portion of the company that actually belongs to the owner.

To understand the accounting equation, it helps to see it with numbers. Suppose that Jasobo Co., owned by Jason Bone, has $1,000,000 in assets and owes $200,000 in debt. Jason's share of the company is worth $800,000:

$$\text{Assets} = \text{Liabilities} + \text{Owners' equity}$$
$$\$1,000,000 = \$200,000 + \text{Owners' equity}$$
$$\$800,000 = \text{Owners' equity}$$

A basic rule of accounting is that the accounting equation must always balance. If assets exceed the sum of liabilities and owners' equity, then the company holds things that don't belong to anyone. If the sum of liabilities and owners' equity exceeds assets, then owners and creditors lay claim to things that don't exist.

Net Income

Net income is called the *bottom line* because in many ways it's the sum total of accountants' work. To calculate net income, subtract expenses from revenues:

$$\text{Revenues} - \text{Expenses} = \text{Net income}$$

Revenues are inflows and other kinds of sales to customers. *Expenses* are costs associated with making sales. Accountants also sometimes need to add gains or subtract losses in net income; these gains and losses come from miscellaneous events that affect stockholder value, such as selling equipment at a gain or getting your factory destroyed by a mutated prehistoric survivor of the dinosaurs.

Suppose that the fictional *Daily Planet* newspaper had $100,000 in revenues, $80,000 in expenses, $5,000 in gains, and $4,000 in losses. What was *Daily Planet*'s net income?

$$\$100,000 - \$80,000 + \$5,000 - \$4,000 = \$21,000 \text{ Net income}$$

Investors love net income because it provides a simple measure of a company's performance that's easy to understand.

Cost of Goods Sold

For manufacturers and retailers, *cost of goods sold* measures how much the company paid — or will need to pay — for inventory items sold.

To compute a retailer's cost of goods sold, use the following formula:

$$\text{Beginning} + \text{Inputs} - \text{Ending} = \text{Outputs}$$

Cost of beginning inventory + Cost of purchases − Cost of ending inventory = Cost of goods sold

Here, a retailer's inputs are the cost of the purchases it makes. The outputs are the goods that were sold (recorded at cost, of course).

Suppose that Jersey Shore Surf Shop started the season with $100,000 worth of inventory. The company purchased an additional $200,000 worth of inventory. At the end of the season, Jersey Shore had $50,000 worth of inventory. What was the cost of goods sold?

$$\text{Cost of beginning inventory} + \text{Cost of purchases} - \text{Cost of ending inventory} = \text{Cost of goods sold}$$

$$\$100,000 + \$200,000 - \$50,000 = \text{Cost of goods sold}$$

$$\$250,000 = \text{Cost of goods sold}$$

You can adapt this formula to different scenarios. For example, suppose that your company makes, rather than purchases, the goods that it sells. To compute cost of goods sold, replace the cost of purchases with the cost of goods manufactured:

Cost of beginning inventory of finished goods + Cost of goods manufactured − Cost of ending inventory of finished goods = Cost of goods sold

Contribution Margin

Contribution margin measures how selling one item, or a group of items, increases net income. To calculate contribution margin, subtract variable costs from sales:

$$\text{Total sales} - \text{Total variable cost} = \text{Total contribution margin}$$

Contribution margin helps managers by explaining how decisions will impact income. Should you prepare a special order with a contribution margin of $100,000? Yes, because it will increase net income by $100,000. Should you prepare another special order with a contribution margin of *negative* $50,000? No, because it will decrease net income.

To compute contribution margin per unit, divide the total contribution margin by the number of units sold. Alternatively, you can calculate sales price less variable cost per unit:

$$\text{Sales price} - \text{Variable cost per unit} = \text{Contribution margin per unit}$$

For example, if a given product sells for $12 and has a variable cost per unit of $9, then its contribution margin per unit equals $3. Translation: Every unit of this product sold increases net income by $3.

To compute contribution margin ratio, divide contribution margin by sales, either in total or per unit:

$$\text{Contribution margin ratio} = \frac{\text{Total contribution margin}}{\text{Total sales}}$$

or

$$\text{Contribution margin ratio} = \frac{\text{Contribution margin per unit}}{\text{Sales price per unit}}$$

For example, if a given product sells for $12 and has a contribution margin per unit equals $3, then its contribution margin ratio equals 25 percent ($3 ÷ $12). This result means that every dollar of sales increases net income by $.25.

Cost-Volume-Profit Analysis

Cost-volume-profit (CVP) analysis helps you understand how changes in volume affect costs and net income. If you know sales price, variable cost per unit, volume, and fixed costs, this formula will predict your net income:

$$\text{Net income} = (\text{Sales price} - \text{Variable cost per unit})(\text{Volume}) - \text{Fixed costs}$$

First, understand where this formula comes from. Consider how production volume affects total costs:

$$\text{Total cost} = (\text{Variable cost per unit} \times \text{Volume}) + \text{Fixed costs}$$

As I explain in Chapter 5, variable cost per unit is the additional cost of producing a single unit. Volume is the number of units produced. Fixed cost is the total fixed cost for the period. Net income is just the difference between total sales and total cost:

$$\text{Net income} = (\text{Sales price} \times \text{Volume}) - \text{Total cost}$$

Combining these two equations gives you the super-useful formula for understanding how volume affects profits:

$$\begin{aligned} \text{Net income} &= (\text{Sales price} \times \text{Volume}) - \text{Total cost} \\ &= (\text{Sales price} \times \text{Volume}) - \left[\begin{array}{l} (\text{Variable cost per unit} \times \text{Volume}) \\ + \text{Fixed costs} \end{array} \right] \\ &= (\text{Sales price} \times \text{Volume}) - (\text{Variable cost per unit} \times \text{Volume}) \\ &\quad - \text{Fixed costs} \end{aligned}$$

$$\text{Net income} = (\text{Sales price} - \text{Variable cost per unit})(\text{Volume}) - \text{Fixed costs}$$

Not coincidentally, a critical part of this formula equals contribution margin — remember that sales price less variable cost per unit equals contribution margin per unit:

$$\text{Sales price} - \text{Variable cost per unit} = \text{Contribution margin per unit}$$

This formula lets you further simplify the CVP formula:

$$\text{Net income} = (\text{Contribution margin} \times \text{Volume}) - \text{Fixed costs}$$

Suppose that the Ice Cream Corp. expects to sell 10,000 ice cream cones next year, each with a contribution margin of $1. Ice Cream Corp. expects to pay $4,000 for fixed costs next year. How much income will the company earn next year?

$$\begin{aligned} \text{Net income} &= (\$1.00 \times 10,000) - \$4,000 \\ &= \$6,000 \end{aligned}$$

CVP analysis reveals that Ice Cream Corp. will probably earn $6,000 next year.

Break-Even Analysis

Break-even analysis helps you determine how much you need to sell in order to break even — that is, to earn no net loss or profit. To figure out the break-even point, use this formula:

$$\text{Break-even volume} = \frac{\text{Fixed costs}}{\text{Sales price} - \text{Variable cost per unit}}$$

Perhaps you recognize contribution margin in the denominator (Sales price – Variable cost per unit), allowing you to further simplify this formula:

$$\text{Break-even volume} = \frac{\text{Fixed costs}}{\text{Contribution margin per unit}}$$

To figure out the number of units needed to break even, just divide total fixed costs by contribution margin per unit.

Pecan Pie Corp. pays $30,000 worth of fixed costs each year. Each pie sells for $11 and has variable costs of $5 to make. Contribution margin per pie equals $6 ($11 – $5):

$$\text{Break-even volume} = \frac{\$30,000}{\$6.00}$$
$$= 5,000$$

In order to break even — earn zero profit or loss — Pecan Pie Corp. needs to sell 5,000 pies.

Price Variance

Price variance tells you how an unexpected change in the cost of direct materials affects total cost. Use this formula to compute price variance:

$$\text{Price variance} = (\text{Standard price} - \text{Actual price}) \times \text{Actual quantity}$$

Standard price is the amount you originally expected to pay, per unit, of direct materials. *Actual price* is the real price you paid, per unit, for direct materials. The *actual quantity* is the number of units purchased and used in production.

Suppose the Pig's Head Tavern made and sold 2,000 pints of ale last month. It expected to pay 5 shillings per pint. Actual price, however, was 5.5 shillings per pint. Plug in these numbers to compute the price variance:

$$\text{Price variance} = (\text{Standard price} - \text{Actual price}) \times \text{Actual quantity}$$
$$= (5.00 \text{ shillings} - 5.50 \text{ shillings}) \times 1,000$$
$$= -500 \text{ shillings}$$

The unexpected price increase hurt Pig's Head profits by 500 shillings.

Although the price variance formula focuses on the direct materials variance, you can easily adapt it to figure out the direct labor variance. To do so, replace standard price with the standard cost (per hour) of direct labor. Replace actual price with the actual cost (per hour) of direct labor. Then replace the actual quantity with the actual number of hours worked.

Quantity Variance

The direct materials quantity variance measures how using too much or too little in direct materials affects total costs. Stinginess in using direct materials should decrease your costs. However, wasting direct materials should increase costs. Here's the formula:

$$\text{Quantity variance} = \text{Standard price} \times (\text{Standard quantity} - \text{Actual quantity})$$

Remember that standard price is how much you originally expected to pay, per unit, of direct materials. Standard quantity is the number of units of direct materials that you expected to use. Actual quantity is the number of units of direct materials that you actually used in production.

Future Value

Future value measures how much a present cash flow will be worth in the future. For example, if you put $1,000 into the bank today, earning 6-percent interest a year, how much will you have ten years from now?

To solve these problems, many students use tables printed in textbooks or financial calculators. You can also solve these problems using the time value of money formula:

$$\text{Future value} = -\text{Present value} \times (1 + \text{Interest rate})^{\text{Years}}$$

Present value measures how much money you receive or pay now. Make this figure positive if you're receiving the money and negative if you're paying the money out. Future value is how much you can expect to receive or pay in the future (again, positive for incoming cash, negative for outgoing cash). The interest rate should be put in as the *annual* interest rate (rather than daily, monthly, or quarterly). The number of years is for the period of time between the date of the present value and the date of the future value, in years.

Therefore, if present value equals –$1,000, the interest rate is 6 percent, and the number of years is ten years

$$\text{Future value} = -\left(-\$1,000\right) \times \left(1 + 0.06\right)^{10}$$
$$= \$1,000 \times \left(1.06\right)^{10}$$
$$= \$1,000 \times 1.791$$
$$= \$1,791$$

The future value indicates that, if you put $1,000 away now, earning 6 percent, you can expect to receive $1,791 at the end of ten years.

Present Value

Okay, I lied. Did I say ten key formulas? I meant *nine* key formulas, because present value uses the same formula as future value. If you're trying to memorize these formulas, I'm sure you won't mind trying to remember one fewer:

$$\text{Future value} = -\text{Present value} \times \left(1 + \text{Interest rate}\right)^{\text{Years}}$$

Here's an example of how you can use this formula to compute the present value of a cash flow. Suppose that, four years from now, you want to have $5,000 (that's the future value). How much should you put into the bank today, earning 5-percent interest?

$$\text{Future value} = -\text{Present value} \times \left(1 + \text{Interest rate}\right)^{\text{Years}}$$
$$\$5,000 = -\text{Present value} \times \left(1 + 0.05\right)^{4}$$
$$\$5,000 = -\text{Present value} \times 1.2155$$
$$-\frac{\$5,000}{1.2155} = \text{Present value}$$
$$-\$4,114 = \text{Present value}$$

So if you put $4,114 into the bank today, earning 5-percent interest, then in four years you should have $5,000 to take out.

Here's a version of the formula to more directly compute present value:

$$\text{Present value} = -\frac{\text{Future value}}{\left(1 + \text{Interest rate}\right)^{\text{Years}}}$$

Chapter 21

Ten Careers in Managerial Accounting

Most of my students choose accounting careers because of the consistently high hiring demand for accountants. In its Occupational Outlook Handbook, the U.S. Bureau of Labor Statistics projected 16-percent growth for accountants and auditors between 2010 and 2020.

The starting salaries aren't bad, either. Cost accountants' starting salaries with large companies are projected to range between $43,000 and $53,750 per year, according to the 2013 Salary Guide published by Robert Half (see www.rhi.com/salaryguides). According to the same study, cost accounting managers are projected to earn between $79,250 and $108,500 in 2013.

All the salaries I cite in this chapter are starting salaries of accountants working for large companies (sales in excess of $500 million) and come from the Robert Half salary guide. These salaries vary by location.

In case you're curious, St. Louis, Missouri, has a salary index of about 100. If you're looking to work in St. Louis, these salaries should be on target. New York City boasts the highest salary index, 141, so salaries there should be 41 percent higher. Chicago's salary index is 123, and Los Angeles' salary index is 125. On the other hand, El Paso, Texas, has a salary index of just 70 (meaning salaries there are about 30 percent lower).

Corporate Treasurer

The coveted position of *treasurer* is the career summit that management accountants aspire to. Treasurers take responsibility for all financial activities within a corporation, including managing liquidity risk, managing cash, issuing debt, hedging foreign exchange and interest rate risk, securitizing, overseeing pension investments, and managing capital structure.

The corporate treasurer typically sits on the corporation's board of directors and chairs its finance committee but is usually not involved in day-to-day operations. A treasurer of a large company can expect to earn between $278,000 and $422,000 per year in 2013.

Chief Financial Officer

The *chief financial officer,* or CFO, runs all corporate finance functions on a day-to-day basis. The CFO acts as steward of the company's assets, minimizing risk and making sure that the books and financial statements are correct. The CFO also needs to run an effective and efficient finance operation within the company. The CFO installs a financial mind-set throughout the organization so that all parts of the business perform better. A CFO of a large company can anticipate earning between $280,500 and $430,250 in 2013.

Corporate Controller

Corporate controllers collect and maintain information about all aspects of a company's finances. They prepare financial statements, budget reports, forecasts, cost-analysis reports, profit and loss statements, recommendations for spending or cost cuts, and SEC reports and supervise other accountants in the company. They work to ensure that internal controls are in place and working properly, that the financial statements are prepared accurately, and that all of the company's finances are properly documented. They also make sure that moneys owed to the company are collected and that bills for the company's expenses get paid.

In a large company, a typical corporate controller can expect to earn between $147,000 and $207,750 in 2013.

Accounting Manager

The *accounting manager* prepares fiscal and budget reports for internal management and financial statements and other reports to stockholders and other external stakeholders. He or she also oversees the development of master budgets and other projections in order to make recommendations to management. An accounting manager at a large company can expect to earn between $77,750 and $109,250 in 2013.

Financial Analyst

Financial analysts help to prepare budgets, monitor task performance, keep track of actual costs, analyze different kinds of variances, review contract completion reports, and assist other executives in preparing forecasts and projections. Starting salaries for recent college graduates beginning as financial analysts with large companies are expected to range between $43,750 and $56,250 in 2013. More-experienced financial analyst managers can anticipate earning between $86,750 and $119,750 in 2013.

Cost Accountant

Cost accountants accumulate accurate data about the cost of raw materials, work-in-process, finished goods, labor, overhead, and other related manufacturing costs. They also set cost standards, such as how many hours of direct labor or direct materials manufacturing a widget requires. As I note in the chapter introduction, new college graduates' starting salaries as cost accountants with large companies are projected to range between $43,000 and $53,750 in 2013. More-experienced cost accounting managers are projected to earn between $79,250 and $108,500 in 2013.

Budget Analyst

The *budget analyst* prepares and administrates the master budget and then compares master budget projections with actual performance. To prepare this information, the budget analyst needs to become intimately familiar with all the operations in the budget and work closely with both cost accountants and production managers working on the plant floor. Starting salaries for recent college graduates starting as budget analysts with large companies are projected to range between $42,500 and $55,250 in 2013. More-experienced financial analyst managers can expect to earn between $83,250 and $116,500 in 2013.

Internal Auditor

Internal auditors ensure that various procedures, such as controls over cash and other assets, are working as they should. Internal auditors are often called on to investigate budget variances and are typically the first to look for — and identify — poor work quality, waste materials, fraud, theft, and deliberate acts of industrial sabotage.

Unlike external auditors, the internal auditors work for the very company that they audit. Therefore, they typically report to executives at a very high level in the organization (such as the treasurer). Starting salaries for recent college graduates entering the workforce as internal auditors with large companies are expected to range between $47,500 and $60,250 in 2013. Internal audit managers with more experience can anticipate earning between $93,000 and $132,250 in 2013.

Fixed-Assets Accountant

A *fixed-assets* accountant is responsible for keeping records related to a company's property, plant, and equipment. These folks inspect the property, the plant, and the equipment to verify the accuracy of the books. Furthermore, they oversee the computation of depreciation, as reported in financial statements and tax filings. Salaries for fixed-asset accountants generally range in the same area as for financial analysts, which I cover earlier in this chapter.

Cash-Management Accountant

The *cash-management accountant* is responsible for cash-related financial operations, including making transfers between accounts, monitoring deposits and payments, reconciling cash balances, creating and following cash forecasts, and abiding by the company's system of internal controls. Salaries for cash-management accountants are generally in the same range as those I list for financial analysts earlier in the chapter.

Chapter 22

Ten Legends of Managerial Accounting

*B*elieve it or not, managerial accountants have a number of legends to admire. A few people have made great contributions to the profession and to business as a whole through ingenuity, persistence, and a willingness to stand up for the principles that they believe in. I'm talking creative individuals who found new and better ways to solve old problems, famous whistleblowers who reported financial wrongdoings, and congressmen who led the U.S. federal government's move to regulate the accounting profession.

Dan Bricklin

Few people have changed the lives of all kinds of accountants more than Dan Bricklin, who had the idea for the first electronic spreadsheet program. While a student at Harvard Business School, he noticed that the new Apple II computer could be programmed to simplify many accounting and finance calculations. With Bob Frankston, Bricklin wrote the very first spreadsheet program, VisiCalc, for the Apple II computer.

Interestingly, even though VisiCalc led to the creation of Microsoft Excel, transforming both accounting and finance and vastly increasing the usability of personal computers, Bricklin and Frankston never patented their revolutionary idea for the electronic spreadsheet.

Cynthia Cooper

Cynthia Cooper, vice president of internal audit at WorldCom, noticed evidence that the chief financial officer, Scott Sullivan, was cooking the books. Members of her internal audit team secretly hacked the company's records, took them home, and spent many late nights investigating. Eventually, they accumulated evidence of billions of dollars worth of fraudulent net income and reported it to the board's audit committee and external auditor.

In 2002, Cooper and Sherron Watkins represented *Time Magazine*'s Person of the Year, the Whistleblower. (I devote a section to Watkins later in this chapter.)

Sergio Cicero Zapata

After being involved in a series of bribes to public officials in Mexico, Wal-Mart employee Sergio Cicero Zapata decided to come clean. He reported his activity to Wal-Mart's general counsel, who then investigated the allegations in detail. The investigation indicated that Wal-Mart employees regularly bribed government officials in order to obtain permits to build new Wal-Mart locations, a violation of the Foreign Corrupt Practices Act. (Flip to the "Ernest Hauser" section later in this chapter for more on the establishment of this legislation.) When he was dissatisfied with the progress of Wal-Mart's internal investigation, Zapata went to *The New York Times* and other public outlets.

Eliyahu Goldratt

Israeli physicist Eliyahu Goldratt noticed many parallels between physics and a manufacturing production line. He developed mathematical models to measure and describe logistics and the flow of goods through a factory. He later expanded his models to improve and optimize the performance of service companies. (You can read about his theory of constraints in Chapter 19.)

No big fan of traditional managerial accounting, Dr. Goldratt wrote a novel, *The Goal*, to describe how to apply his theory of constraints models to a manufacturing process. It seems that managerial accounting is no big fan of Dr. Goldratt, either. Many claim that his theories are copied from others or that they have limited applicability.

Ernest Hauser

Ernest Hauser, a former lobbyist for defense contractor Lockheed, admitted to Senate investigators that Lockheed representatives had paid at least $10 million dollars to West German Minister of Defence Franz Josef Strauss and his party for that country's purchase of 900 F-104G Starfighters in 1961. This confession led to the discovery of additional bribes made by Lockheed to foreign governments (and certainly didn't improve the public image of defense contractors). As a result of the Lockheed scandal and others, the federal government passed the Foreign Corrupt Practices Act of 1977, requiring companies to keep internal controls to ensure that bribes are not paid to foreign governments or officials.

Robert Kaplan

Harvard Business School Professor Robert S. Kaplan developed the balanced scorecard, which I explain in Chapter 18. Kaplan's revolutionary contribution to the field of managerial accounting was the fundamental idea that managerial accountants need to look past net income and other profit-oriented figures, which describe past activities, and toward predictive and other nonfinancial measures that help managers to project what will happen in the future. Kaplan's fame — and vast consulting income — have inspired many of his fellow accounting professors.

Harry Markopoulos

Harry Markopolous was chief investment officer of Rampart Investment Management when he noticed that the results of another investment manager seemed very fishy. Somehow, this investment manager, Bernard Madoff, managed to steadily deliver monthly returns between 1 and 2 percent. When Markopolous investigated Madoff's investment strategies, he concluded that they couldn't possibly work — and that Madoff's organization was probably a huge fraud. Although Markopolous alerted the authorities several times, Madoff's fraud wasn't discovered until years later, when his investment funds started to run out of cash. Madoff's scheme resulted in at least $65 billion in losses for his thousands of investors, even forcing the Wilpon family to sell a minority stake in the New York Mets.

Paul Sarbanes and Michael Oxley

U.S. Senator Paul Sarbanes and U.S. Representative Michael Oxley championed the Sarbanes-Oxley Act of 2002, also known as the Public Company Accounting Reform and Investor Protection Act. This law created the Public Company Accounting Oversight Board. It also requires companies to have effective systems of internal controls in place, making executives criminally responsible for issuing fraudulent financial reports to investors.

The Sarbanes-Oxley Act has forced many companies to improve their internal controls. It has also boosted the demand for — and salaries of — managerial accountants.

David Stockman

David Stockman was director of the office of management and budget under President Ronald Reagan from 1980 until 1985. Essentially, this position is the chief accountant responsible for planning and reporting the federal government's own finances, and Stockman is probably its best-known occupant. He was known as an outspoken deficit-fighter who continually argued with both the White House and Congress to reduce federal budget spending. He also derided the federal government's budget bureaucracy, at one point admitting that "none of us really understands what's going on with all these numbers."

Sherron Watkins

In 2001, Sherron Watkins, Enron's vice president of corporate development, noticed some internal reports that didn't quite make sense to her. She investigated them thoroughly and brought them to the attention of senior managers. After the Enron fraud was revealed, she was a key expert in explaining the nature of Enron's bizarre off-balance-sheet transactions.

Some people argue that Watkins wasn't a real whistleblower because she chose to internally report the frauds she discovered rather than bring them to the attention of the authorities. Others maintain that she is a true whistleblower because she risked her job and career to try to stop a massive fraud. In 2002, *Time Magazine* named the Whistleblower its Person of the Year, singling out Watkins and Cynthia Cooper, who I profile earlier in this chapter.

Index

Notes

Notes

Notes

Notes

Apple & Mac

iPad 2 For Dummies,
3rd Edition
978-1-118-17679-5

iPhone 4S For Dummies,
5th Edition
978-1-118-03671-6

iPod touch For Dummies,
3rd Edition
978-1-118-12960-9

Mac OS X Lion
For Dummies
978-1-118-02205-4

Blogging & Social Media

CityVille For Dummies
978-1-118-08337-6

Facebook For Dummies,
4th Edition
978-1-118-09562-1

Mom Blogging
For Dummies
978-1-118-03843-7

Twitter For Dummies,
2nd Edition
978-0-470-76879-2

WordPress For Dummies,
4th Edition
978-1-118-07342-1

Business

Cash Flow For Dummies
978-1-118-01850-7

Investing For Dummies,
6th Edition
978-0-470-90545-6

Job Searching with Social
Media For Dummies
978-0-470-93072-4

QuickBooks 2012
For Dummies
978-1-118-09120-3

Resumes For Dummies,
6th Edition
978-0-470-87361-8

Starting an Etsy Business
For Dummies
978-0-470-93067-0

Cooking & Entertaining

Cooking Basics
For Dummies, 4th Edition
978-0-470-91388-8

Wine For Dummies,
4th Edition
978-0-470-04579-4

Diet & Nutrition

Kettlebells For Dummies
978-0-470-59929-7

Nutrition For Dummies,
5th Edition
978-0-470-93231-5

Restaurant Calorie Counter
For Dummies,
2nd Edition
978-0-470-64405-8

Digital Photography

Digital SLR Cameras &
Photography For Dummies,
4th Edition
978-1-118-14489-3

Digital SLR Settings
& Shortcuts
For Dummies
978-0-470-91763-3

Photoshop Elements 10
For Dummies
978-1-118-10742-3

Gardening

Gardening Basics
For Dummies
978-0-470-03749-2

Vegetable Gardening
For Dummies,
2nd Edition
978-0-470-49870-5

Green/Sustainable

Raising Chickens
For Dummies
978-0-470-46544-8

Green Cleaning
For Dummies
978-0-470-39106-8

Health

Diabetes For Dummies,
3rd Edition
978-0-470-27086-8

Food Allergies
For Dummies
978-0-470-09584-3

Living Gluten-Free
For Dummies,
2nd Edition
978-0-470-58589-4

Hobbies

Beekeeping
For Dummies,
2nd Edition
978-0-470-43065-1

Chess For Dummies,
3rd Edition
978-1-118-01695-4

Drawing For Dummies,
2nd Edition
978-0-470-61842-4

eBay For Dummies,
7th Edition
978-1-118-09806-6

Knitting For Dummies,
2nd Edition
978-0-470-28747-7

Language &
Foreign Language

English Grammar
For Dummies,
2nd Edition
978-0-470-54664-2

French For Dummies,
2nd Edition
978-1-118-00464-7

German For Dummies,
2nd Edition
978-0-470-90101-4

Spanish Essentials
For Dummies
978-0-470-63751-7

Spanish For Dummies,
2nd Edition
978-0-470-87855-2

Available wherever books are sold. For more information or to order direct: U.S. customers visit www.dummies.com or call 1-877-762-2974.
U.K. customers visit www.wileyeurope.com or call (0) 1243 843291. Canadian customers visit www.wiley.ca or call 1-800-567-4797.
Connect with us online at www.facebook.com/fordummies or @fordummies

Math & Science

**Algebra I For Dummies,
2nd Edition**
978-0-470-55964-2

**Biology For Dummies,
2nd Edition**
978-0-470-59875-7

**Chemistry For Dummies,
2nd Edition**
978-1-1180-0730-3

**Geometry For Dummies,
2nd Edition**
978-0-470-08946-0

**Pre-Algebra Essentials
For Dummies**
978-0-470-61838-7

Microsoft Office

Excel 2010 For Dummies
978-0-470-48953-6

**Office 2010 All-in-One
For Dummies**
978-0-470-49748-7

**Office 2011 for Mac
For Dummies**
978-0-470-87869-9

**Word 2010
For Dummies**
978-0-470-48772-3

Music

**Guitar For Dummies,
2nd Edition**
978-0-7645-9904-0

Clarinet For Dummies
978-0-470-58477-4

**iPod & iTunes
For Dummies,
9th Edition**
978-1-118-13060-5

Pets

**Cats For Dummies,
2nd Edition**
978-0-7645-5275-5

**Dogs All-in One
For Dummies**
978-0470-52978-2

**Saltwater Aquariums
For Dummies**
978-0-470-06805-2

Religion & Inspiration

The Bible For Dummies
978-0-7645-5296-0

**Catholicism For Dummies,
2nd Edition**
978-1-118-07778-8

**Spirituality For Dummies,
2nd Edition**
978-0-470-19142-2

Self-Help & Relationships

Happiness For Dummies
978-0-470-28171-0

**Overcoming Anxiety
For Dummies,
2nd Edition**
978-0-470-57441-6

Seniors

**Crosswords For Seniors
For Dummies**
978-0-470-49157-7

**iPad 2 For Seniors
For Dummies, 3rd Edition**
978-1-118-17678-8

**Laptops & Tablets
For Seniors For Dummies,
2nd Edition**
978-1-118-09596-6

Smartphones & Tablets

**BlackBerry For Dummies,
5th Edition**
978-1-118-10035-6

Droid X2 For Dummies
978-1-118-14864-8

**HTC ThunderBolt
For Dummies**
978-1-118-07601-9

**MOTOROLA XOOM
For Dummies**
978-1-118-08835-7

Sports

**Basketball For Dummies,
3rd Edition**
978-1-118-07374-2

**Football For Dummies,
2nd Edition**
978-1-118-01261-1

**Golf For Dummies,
4th Edition**
978-0-470-88279-5

Test Prep

**ACT For Dummies,
5th Edition**
978-1-118-01259-8

**ASVAB For Dummies,
3rd Edition**
978-0-470-63760-9

**The GRE Test For
Dummies, 7th Edition**
978-0-470-00919-2

**Police Officer Exam
For Dummies**
978-0-470-88724-0

**Series 7 Exam
For Dummies**
978-0-470-09932-2

Web Development

**HTML, CSS, & XHTML
For Dummies, 7th Edition**
978-0-470-91659-9

**Drupal For Dummies,
2nd Edition**
978-1-118-08348-2

Windows 7

**Windows 7
For Dummies**
978-0-470-49743-2

**Windows 7
For Dummies,
Book + DVD Bundle**
978-0-470-52398-8

**Windows 7 All-in-One
For Dummies**
978-0-470-48763-1

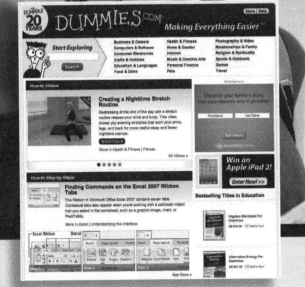